Vroom

by the

Sea

The sunny Parts of Italy on a Bright Orange Vespa

Peter Moore

VROOM BY THE SEA

This edition published in 2009 by Summersdale Publishers Ltd.

First published in Australia and New Zealand in 2007 by Bantam

Summersdale Publishers Ltd
46 West Street
Chichester
West Sussex
PO19 1RP
UK

www.summersdale.com

Printed and bound in Great Britain

ISBN: 978-1-84024-737-4

ABOUT THE AUTHOR

Peter Moore is an itinerant hobo who is lucky enough to be able to support his insatiable travel habit through writing. Author of the bestselling *No Shitting in the Toilet*, which grew from his award-winning website of the same name, as well as *The Wrong Way Home*, *The Full Montezuma*, *Swahili for the Broken-hearted* and *Vroom with a View*, Peter is the voice of independent travel in both Australia and the UK. A former advertising copywriter and website designer, he has visited ninety-eight countries on his travels. When he is not lugging his senselessly overweight backpack through Third World nations or zipping around Italy on a Vespa, Peter can be found at home in London playing devoted husband to his wife, Sally, and doting dad to his daughter, Daisy.

Also by Peter Moore:

No Shitting in the Toilet
The Wrong Way Home
The Full Montezuma
Swahili for the Broken-hearted
Vroom with a View

To Sally and Daisy

ACKNOWLEDGEMENTS

Filippo Lulli and Marco Quaretta, and their girlfriends (now wives), Valeriya Lulli and Lucilla Bertocchini – thanks to them, riding into Livorno feels like coming home.

Mario Zizi in Nuoro, Sergio Passalacqua in Palermo, Gianluca Grandi in Rome and Gioacchino Coco in Poggioreale for their hospitality and incredible local knowledge.

John Stillone, my accountant, not just for keeping the ATO off my back but for insisting I visit Poggioreale, his home town in Sicily. It was one of the highlights of my trip.

Cherry Brewer and Steve Dorrett for answering the question 'Insegnami a ballare il "Northern Soul"?'

Robert Viller for looking after the white PX200 I promised I'd sell.

Fiona Inglis for keeping my career on track.

Heather Curdie and Meredith Curnow at Random House for their patience and understanding. Anna Crago for her deft and superfast editing.

My nieces and nephews, Jessica Howard, Taylor Black, Amanda Howard, Harrison Black, James Howard, Kai Moore and Isaac Rosenberg, because they like to see their names in print.

Finally, Sally for her love and support. And Daisy, for giving me a really good reason for taking so long to write this book. Thanks, guys.

THE *VROOM BY THE SEA* SLIDE SHOW

Thanks to the Internet, a virtual tour of the sunny parts of Italy on a bright orange Vespa is only a few clicks away. Just point your browser towards www.petermoore.net and follow the links to the *Vroom by the Sea* slide show.

Before you know it, you'll be buzzing along narrow coastal roads, exploring ancient ruins and watching the sun set over gorgeous Italian beaches. If you're lucky, you'll get a ticking off from the *carabinieri* for not wearing a helmet. Indeed, it's all the fun of riding a Vespa around the islands of Italy without getting a speck of oil on your hands.

While you're there, check out the websites for Peter's other books, or subscribe to his online newsletter for up-to-date information and your chance to win an autographed copy of one of his books.

See you at www.petermoore.net. Ciao!

Peter Moore

CONTENTS

CONTENTS

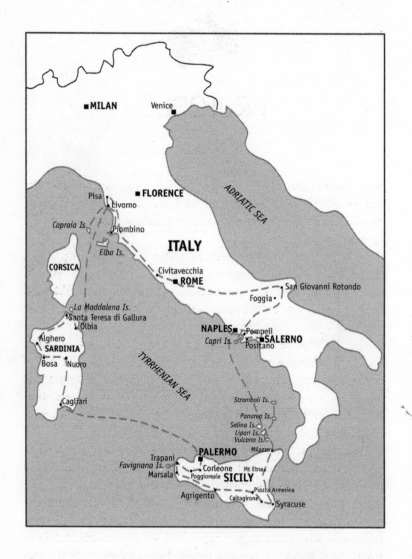

PROLOGUE

Two months after my first wedding anniversary and five months before the birth of my first child I found myself on a plane heading to Pisa and the embrace of a fading Italian beauty I'd met two years before.

We were going to spend one last summer together, enjoying a carefree jaunt through Sardinia and Sicily and along the Amalfi Coast. Then, with my skin tanned and my belly full, I'd head back to my wife in London and all the responsibilities that impending fatherhood brings.

The whole affair had my wife's blessing. Indeed it was Sally's idea in the first place. She said that it was better that I got it out of my system now rather than waiting until after our daughter was born. I guess it helped that the faded Italian beauty in question had been instrumental in getting us together in the first place. And that she was a 1961 Vespa called Sophia.

Those of you who have read *Vroom with a View* will know that I spent the summer of my fortieth birthday travelling from Milan to Rome on a coffee-coloured Vespa as old as I was. I rode past stone villas and fields of sunflowers, and the hook under the front of the seat was the perfect place for the breads, cheeses, hams and tomatoes that I bought fresh from markets in hilltop towns each morning. It was a magic three months with the sun on my skin and the smell of freshly cut hay in my nostrils.

Sally joined me for two weeks in Tuscany and then a weekend in Rome at the end. In Rome we pretended we were in *Roman Holiday*, scooting up cobbled streets past the Colosseum, right up to the Pantheon and to the tiny cafés and restaurants of Trastevere, ignoring police who tweeted at us with whistles. Sally made a good Audrey Hepburn. I was a decidedly low-rent Gregory Peck. Within a year we were married. A few months later Sally was pregnant. As I'm fond of telling anyone who will listen, inviting your girlfriend to ride around Italy on a Vespa can have serious consequences.

Still, a wild, two-stroke-powered fling around the sunny parts of Italy can hardly be considered a traditional way of preparing for fatherhood. A quick surf through the multitudes of parenting websites indicated that I should have been painting the nursery, assembling the cot and attending birthing classes. At the very least I should have been sorting out life insurance.

Sally was the first to spot that I was having problems coming to grips with the idea of fatherhood. Don't get me wrong. I was excited and elated about becoming a father. At forty-two years old I had long given up hope of doing my bit to help propagate the species. It was the prospect of added responsibilities – and the long-term nature of them – that I was having difficulty coming to grips with.

I'd spent my entire adult life living like a student. I lived in share households. I spent most of my money on CDs. And when I scraped up enough money I'd disappear and wander around the world a bit. I never went hungry but there were times I got close.

Even the first year of my marriage to Sally had a touch of transience about it. We'd spent the first five months of it travelling around Australia in an old car. And a few months into the pregnancy we decamped to London to start a new life there.

Now I was meant to be the responsible one. Another tiny human being was relying on me to provide food and shelter. I'd spent most of my life avoiding responsibility and now I had the biggest one of all on the way.

It didn't help that other fathers made fatherhood sound like a trial to be endured. One friend likened the arrival of a child to a bomb going off in your life. 'A good bomb,' he hurriedly corrected himself, but his scrambling only made it worse. A good bomb sounded like a euphemism for something really bad – like the term 'collateral damage' explaining away civilian deaths, or using 'extraordinary rendition' to describe being dragged off to Guantanamo Bay to have car batteries attached to your testicles.

So it was decided that I would spend the summer before my daughter was born with Sophia. Maybe Sally would join us for a week in July, around my birthday, somewhere on the Amalfi Coast. It would be the last week that she'd be able to fly.

I'd been dreaming of doing this trip since I'd finished the last one. I'd always imagined it as Sophia introducing me to the sunny parts of her country we hadn't got to the first time round. Now it would be a valediction to my old life and the last chance to savour heady moments of freedom before settling down to two-hourly feeds and, eventually, the less exotic school run.

On the surface it looked like it would be all glorious beaches, gourmet meals and Camparis at sunset. But the sheer number of kilometres I'd be covering meant that I'd also get the chance to get my head together. The thing about riding a scooter, especially an old one, is that you get plenty of time to think. I needed to forget about birth plans and nappies and get my head around what was about to happen to me, to us. If I didn't, no birth plan – no matter how detailed – was going to help.

I still felt guilty about going. Sally would be left to cope with her pregnancy on her own for a couple of months, and I'd miss the first few antenatal classes. Sally said she'd tell them that she was a single mum so when I turned up halfway through I'd be seen as some dashing chap, happy to get involved in the life of a child that wasn't his. She also said she was looking forward to getting the whole bed to herself.

And so it was, right in the middle of Sally's second trimester, in the twenty-fourth week of her pregnancy, that I boarded a Ryanair flight to Pisa. I felt like a sales rep going out on the road, leaving the wife and kids at home. Where your average sales rep has a snapshot of a loving family in his wallet, I had a twenty-two week scan. Sally told me not to start showing it to people – she thought that might be a little freaky. But she did suggest that I should pull it out occasionally and remind myself of the little baby on the way.

Sally and I said our farewells at Stansted airport, just outside WH Smith, and I put my hand on her belly before I walked towards security. I tried not to seem too excited about my trip. For all my rationalising and Sally being magnanimous, it wasn't really fair that I got this chance when Sally didn't. So I held it in, pretending for both our sakes that it was just another job.

But I *was* excited. Two years after our first summer together I was heading back to Italy and into the embrace of Sophia.

CHAPTER ONE

LIVORNO

PATRON SAINT: OUR MARY OF MONTENERO

Before I left for Italy, Sally and I made a list of all the things we needed to buy before our daughter was born. The list included a cot, a car seat, a changing table, sleep suits and nappies, a multitude of bottles and teats, a steriliser to sterilise them in, and an assortment of rattles, bells and mobiles to entertain her. It was an extensive and wide-ranging list that ran to 137 items and covered every conceivable contingency.

Exhaustive as it was, it did not include a 1972 Vespa Rally 200. The plan was to reunite with my beloved Sophia, the 1961 Vespa I'd left behind in Milan with her former owner, Gianni. Since then, Gianni's personal life had gotten complicated. His wife filed for divorce and he was afraid Sophia would get caught up in a messy custody battle. (She was still registered in his name.) So he de-registered her and sent her to my friend Marco in Livorno on the Tuscan coast.

Marco restores Vespas for a living so he had the space to keep her. He gave her pride of place in a line of other Vespas in his

15

workshop beside the Ligurian Sea. For the next 18 months Sophia convalesced in the invigorating sea air while I dithered about what I wanted to do with her.

Periodically Marco would email to ask if I had made a decision yet. It was usually when he had just finished a restoration project and had the time to organise for Sophia to be crated and put out to sea before he started the next one. I always fobbed him off. I said that Sally and I hadn't decided where we wanted to settle down yet. It could be England. It could be Australia. As soon as I knew I'd let him know. And wheels, pardon the pun, could be set in motion.

But now, unexpectedly, I had a temporary reprieve from impending fatherhood. I'd rung Marco to tell him I was coming, and I'd been in touch with Filippo, who I'd be staying with.

Along with Marco, Filippo had been the tour guide and social secretary on my first visit to Livorno. Together they had taken me to local bars and pine nut festivals, spirited me into Martini parties and organised crazy, pre-dawn, alcohol-fuelled boat tours of the city's ancient canals. It is thanks to those guys that Livorno remains my favourite place in Italy.

I was delighted to be back with my mates. And to see that they'd got themselves girlfriends. I was staying with Filippo and his girlfriend, Valeriya, in a villa in Cevoli, a small village in the heart of the Tuscan countryside. We'd been for a night out with Marco and his new girlfriend, Lucilla, to a restaurant down by the old canals where I was introduced to a local dish that dated from ancient times called *cacciucco*, a seafood stew served on a bed of garlic toast.

In fact, I'd been in Livorno for several days already and somehow I still hadn't clapped eyes on Sophia. I wasn't sure what was going on, but there was a whiff of evasion in the air. As much fun as I was having, I was itching to head to Sardinia.

In the car on the way back from the polling booth – it was local election time – I spotted a familiar street sign. I asked Filippo if we could call past Marco's workshop. I knew Livorno well enough to know we were very, very close by. If we cut down Viale Nazario Sauro and turned right just after the turnoff for the Armando Picchi football stadium, we'd be there.

'Didn't I tell you?' he hedged. 'Marco is cooking lunch for us at Lucilla's apartment. He's down the *mercato centrale* buying the ingredients now.'

Lucilla's apartment was back in the centre of Livorno, behind Piazza Micheli and the Hotel Gran Duca. Marco was back from the markets and greeted us at the door of Lucilla's apartment wearing an apron when we arrived. I was pleased to see that he went to the same lengths to keep his clothes immaculate as he did in his workshop.

While Marco put the finishing touches to the lunch – he was carefully placing slices of tomato around the edge of the plates when I poked my head into the kitchen – Lucilla gave me a quick tour of the apartment.

As befits a place so close to the sea, Lucilla had given her home a maritime theme. The shower curtain featured a seashell motif, and in the long room an old fishing net, complete with weathered plastic floats, hung from the ceiling, with photos of friends and family trapped in its web.

The sole concession to her new Vespa-loving boyfriend was a funky light-fitting made from two Vespa handlebars. Marco had made it himself, and it hung from the ceiling just above the dining table. When Lucilla flicked the light switch the headlights came on. Marco had given it to her – and installed it – for Valentine's Day. I was tempted to put in an order for a set myself but I didn't think Sally would be as enamoured with them as Lucilla clearly was.

Lunch was served on a table on the balcony that ran the length of Lucilla's top-floor apartment. We had a clear view over Medici harbour and the Fortezza Vecchia, to the modern harbour where ships heading for Sardinia and Corsica were docked.

After the first course – a delicious spaghetti with marinated scampi – I asked if that was where I would sail from when I finally set off on my journey.

'Which is the ship that goes to Sardinia?' I asked.

Filippo shifted uncomfortably and looked sheepishly at Marco. Marco shifted in his seat too before standing up quickly to clear away the dishes. Lucilla glared at them both before pointing to a large white cruise ship with Looney Tunes characters painted on the side of it.

'See the one with Sylvester and Tweetie?' she said. 'That's the one that goes to Sardinia.'

Marco brought the main course to the table and announced that it was '*tuna rost beef*'. It was a thumping great chunk of fish coated in olive oil, encrusted with sea salt and fresh rosemary, and seared so that it was still raw in the middle. It was so good that I didn't mention Sophia or Sardinia again until we were having coffee.

It is not the done thing to directly confront people in Italy. The concept of saving face is as strong there as it is in Asia. But with the birth of my daughter getting closer each day I needed to know when I could pick up Sophia and start my tour. I asked Marco and Filippo if there was a problem. Had Sophia been stolen? Was she damaged? Why hadn't they taken me to her?

'You'll see her tomorrow I promise,' Filippo said, unconvincingly.

The table fell silent. Valeriya glared at Filippo. Lucilla glared at Marco. Marco was the first to crack. He jumped up and got the keys to the Vespa GT200 he had parked outside.

'OK, come,' he said, tossing me a helmet. 'We'll go to the workshop now.'

Filippo followed in the car and we made our way along Viale Italia past Terrazza Mascagni as the sun was setting over the ocean. It was a balmy evening and the bars that lined the waterfront, new editions since my last visit, were already full of young Livornese arriving on motor scooters, desperately scouring text messages on their mobile phones to check that they were still in *the* place to be seen in Livorno that evening.

When we reached the workshop Marco unlocked the heavy metal door and flicked the light switch on. It gave a reassuringly industrial clunk and the bank of fluorescent lights flickered to life. I immediately spotted Sophia. She was at the back of the workshop, sitting on the rack Marco used to hold scooters while he was working on them. She looked as lovely as ever. Except for the gaping hole where her engine should have been.

Shit.

Before I had a chance to ask where the engine was, Marco silently pointed to a jumbled pile of parts on his workbench. The engine block had been stripped completely and was sitting in a vice. I stood there silently surveying the scene. I'm no expert, but it didn't look like I was going to be riding Sophia anywhere anytime soon.

Filippo spoke better English than Marco so it fell upon him to explain what had happened.

'Marco had misunderstood you when you called to say you were coming to Italy,' he said. 'He thought you were coming to arrange for Sophia to be shipped back to London.'

It was understandable I guess. I'd also told him that Sally was pregnant. When I spoke to him about a trip to Sardinia and Sicily he thought I'd been wistfully dreaming of what might have been. That didn't explain the state of the engine though.

Filippo explained that Marco had decided to recondition the engine for me. 'As a gift for your child,' he said. It had been Sophia's engine – the points in particular – that had given me the most grief on my first trip through Italy. Not only would the points be new and in better condition, the reconditioned engine would be tighter and more powerful. It would be like new, Filippo said. Better than new, interjected Marco.

OK. The engine was in parts. But Marco was one of the best Vespa mechanics in the country. Surely it wouldn't take him long to put it back together again. I asked Filippo when I could expect the engine to be fixed so I could set off on my journey. Marco shot him an uncomfortable look.

'There's a small problem,' said Marco, finding his voice. 'The engine needs a new flywheel and I'm having trouble finding one.' I asked how long he thought it would take to track down a new flywheel and he shrugged his shoulders.

Shit. Shit. Shit. And double shit.

My last blast of freedom was being doused before it even started. The release valve had been capped and I could feel the pressure of responsibility swelling in my chest. Filippo noticed my distress and tried to console me.

'It doesn't have to be a total disaster,' he said, putting his arm around my shoulder. 'There are other ways to do this trip.'

I shook my head. I couldn't do the trip by public transport. Sophia had opened so many doors for me on my first trip, charming the locals and showing me a side of Italy I wouldn't have otherwise seen. I suspected that all I'd see from a bus or a train were grimy factories and the forecourts of petrol stations.

Luckily, that wasn't what Filippo had in mind.

'You could always buy another Vespa,' he grinned.

The Vespa in question sat at the back of Marco's workshop. It was a 1972 Rally 200 in the same shade of orange as Donatella Versace with white, go-fast stripes down each side. It was bright and brash and made every other Vespa in the workshop look dull. Even sitting on its stand it had a swagger.

Marco was selling the Rally for a friend called Roberto. Roberto wanted €2000 (Euros) for the bike but Marco was sure I could get it for 1700. He wouldn't take a commission, passing the saving on to me instead. I think he was still feeling guilty about the misunderstanding that had left Sophia gutted and incomplete on the floor.

The Rally 200 was the hotrod of its day. It was loud and muscular and its beefy 200cc engine developed a chunky 12hp at 5700 rpm. Its top speed of 101 kilometres per hour was faster than any other scooter produced before it. The suspension had also been tuned to make it more comfortable for long-distance touring.

'It's *perfect* for what you want to do!' Filippo exclaimed. 'This thing will eat up the mountains in Sardinia and Sicily!'

The Rally was also a lot more reliable than the Vespas that had preceded it. The decrepit mechanical points system of earlier models had been replaced by an electronic ignition, bolted on the body of the Rally, just next to the engine.

The most important benefit of electronic ignition was that the Rally would start first time, every time. The journey I planned to undertake – through Sardinia and Sicily and then back up along the Amalfi Coast – was much more audacious than the trip from Milan to Rome I made on Sophia. For one thing it was longer. And it was a lot more mountainous. I would be travelling through some of the most sparsely populated regions of Italy so the friendly locals I had relied on to get me out of scrapes on my first trip would be few and far between.

Not that I needed much convincing to buy the Rally. It was one of the most desirable things I'd seen in my life. It was cool in a retro kind of way and its tangerine tones were suitably tutti-frutti enough for the Italian seaside. If my first trip on Sophia had been like the old black and white movies I'd seen as a teenager, then this trip, on this Vespa, was going to be in Technicolor.

I rang Sally to tell her the news. I wasn't sure how she would take it. The Rally would take my tally of Vespas to three. Sophia was one of them. There was also a nameless white PX in Sydney that I'd promised to sell when Sally got pregnant but never got around to doing. She grudgingly agreed that if I was going to do this trip I needed another Vespa. But I don't think my hastily arranged and ill-conceived argument that Sally, our unborn daughter and I would now have a Vespa each went down too well.

Marco rang Roberto, made him my offer, and relayed the information that it had been accepted. He would come by the workshop the next day to collect the money and hand over the paperwork. Filippo slapped me on the back. He was just as excited about the purchase as I was.

'What are you going to call it?' he asked.

'Something macho,' I said. A Vespa with so much testosterone pumping through its veins couldn't have a girl's name.

Both Marco and Filippo nodded in agreement. I tried to think of something but nothing sprang immediately to mind.

I thought, Italian. I thought, macho. But the best I could come up with was Rocky after Sylvester Stallone's character, Rocky Balboa.

'How about Marcello?' suggested Filippo. 'I seem to remember you are a big fan of Marcello Mastroianni.'

I smiled and nodded my head. Marco slapped my back with delight. '*Perfetto!*' he said.

That night back at the villa I consulted Filippo's library of scooter books and technical manuals to learn more about Rally 200s. According to the official Vespa *Technica Manual* (Vol. 3), Marcello was 1770 mm long, 670 mm wide and weighed 106 kg. He did 0–80 kph in 10.7 seconds and consumed fuel at a rate of 2.8 litres per 100 kilometres. The fuel tank held 8.5 litres, giving me a range of approximately 300 kilometres. In all, 41,275 Rally 200s had been made. And the shade of orange that Marcello carried with such panache went under the rather uninspired name of Max Meyer 12985875.

I also learned that the Rally 200 marked the moment when Piaggio abandoned Italian families and went after the burgeoning youth market instead.

It was a move driven by financial necessity. By the end of the 1960s Italy's standard of living was high enough for people to consider buying a car as the family vehicle rather than a Vespa. Indeed scooters became an unnecessary reminder of the tough times after the war. They were hidden in barns or shoved at the back of the garage, making way for the shiny new Fiat or Lancia.

The downturn in scooter sales killed off Piaggio's rivals, Innocenti. They stopped making Lambrettas in 1971.

Piaggio decided that the Vespa was the perfect vehicle for teenagers before they could afford a motorcycle or a car. Their research had identified that there were 16 million Italian teenagers itching to get mobile. Vespas were still a little too closely aligned to family values for your average rebellious teen, but that was nothing a funky new advertising campaign couldn't fix. Using the slogan 'He who Vespas eats the apple' Piaggio deftly re-aligned Vespas with the spirit of the times. Life, like an apple, was there to be eaten up.

It also helped that the new Vespas delivered on the promise. They were powerful, cool, and came in colours like fire-engine red, sunshine yellow, tangerine orange and electric blue – the kind of colours that gave the old grigi (grey-haired ones) heart palpitations. The revolution had begun. And the leader of the revolution, the Che Guevara if you will, was the Rally 200. On a Vespa like Marcello you weren't just getting an apple. You were getting the whole crate.

I found an English translation of the first 'Apple' ad in a book Filippo had called *The Cult of Vespa*. It was written by Gilberto Filippetti and rather more poetic than the ads we're used to today. It described how the 'apple' could be eaten alone or in company, at sunset, on the rocks or with your hair streaming in the wind. Just bite the apple, it said, rev up your Vespa and leave all those people devoid of imagination behind you.

I reread the ad and closed the book, convinced that buying Marcello was the right thing to do. Gilberto Filippetti's words summed up perfectly why I was doing this trip and captured exactly what it meant to me. I made a point of remembering it to quote to my daughter. There was bound to be some time during her rebellious teenage years when she confronted me about the time I left her and her mother to ride around Italy on a Vespa.

★

As a foreigner I couldn't register or insure Marcello in my own name. Italian law states that all motor vehicles registered in Italy must be registered to an Italian national residing in the country.

I'd had the same problem on my first trip with Sophia. I got around it by keeping the bike in the name of the guy I was buying it off. Gianni had called it an 'Italian solution' and it made sense to apply the same solution with Marcello. Only this time the name on the paperwork wouldn't be Gianni Giovanni of Milan, Lombardy. It would be a Mr Filippo Lulli of Cevoli, Tuscany.

'Luckily the paperwork is straightforward for this Vespa,' said Filippo. 'But we will still have to do everything by the book.'

Things hadn't been so straightforward with Sophia. Gianni had misplaced the registration papers and we had to go to a police station to report that they were lost. Then, the motor registry department said it would take six weeks for the papers to be reissued. It was only when Gianni promised to take the lady from the registry department out for lunch that they were issued immediately.

Filippo said such a 'solution' wouldn't be possible in this case. Before the paperwork could be transferred into his name, Marcello had to be issued with a certificate of roadworthiness.

'Things have tightened up since your last visit,' he said. 'The EU is insisting that everything is done to the letter of *their* laws!'

To illustrate his point Filippo told me about a bill that had just been introduced into parliament that would enable police to *confiscate* scooters from anyone travelling without a helmet or carrying too many passengers.

'Confiscate their scooters!' he reiterated, in a tone of disbelief. 'Over such a trifling matter!'

We took Marcello to a mechanic Filippo knew on a road leading out of town, just past the football stadium. The guy was a friend of Filippo's but the government crackdown meant that he still had to put Marcello through a battery of tests or risk losing his licence. He wheeled out a collection of machines that looked like they belonged in an ER ward, not the greasy forecourt of a garage, and hooked them up to Marcello.

'I prefer how they did it in the old days,' said Filippo as we watched the machines beep and ping. 'A guy would just walk around a Vespa and look at it.'

Half an hour later all the tests were complete and Filippo's friend printed out the results on an old dot matrix printer. It was the least hi-tech piece of his equipment. Marcello had passed with flying colours.

'The rear brakes were operating at 83 per cent and the front at 79 per cent,' said Filippo, authoritatively. I said I would have been happier with 100 per cent front and back, but Filippo assured me that it was a very good result for a Vespa that age.

Insurance was organised through another family friend, a gregarious middle-aged woman called Maria who had gone to school with Filippo's mother. Maria was also a duly authorised representative of the motor registry department. She took copies of all the test results and insurance certificates and issued the new registration papers in Filippo's name. Filippo joked that Marcello was now the most legal bike in the country.

'If the police pull you over they will think you are the most boring person in Italy,' he laughed.

Now that Marcello was legal, Filippo suggested a quick visit to Santuario di Montenero, a chapel that sits high in the hills above Livorno to the south of the city. Most people use a cable car to reach it and enjoy the panoramic views of the city, the port and the sea. But Filippo said that the steep, winding road that offered an alternative way there would give me a good idea of Marcello's capabilities for the trip ahead.

'After Sophia you'll be surprised by the difference,' said Filippo. 'The Rally 200 is a creamy ride!'

Santuario di Montenero housed one of the largest collections of ex-voto paintings in Italy. Votive paintings were given as a way of thanks, in this case to the Madonna for saving those that commissioned them from certain death. What made the paintings so special was that they depicted those near-death experiences. There was a baby falling from a balcony here, a horse kicking a man in the groin there. The paintings were done in a variety of styles, reflecting the fashionable art movements of the time, and in the top corner of every one was Our Lady of Grace, smiling enigmatically and looking rather pleased with herself that another life had been spared.

It wasn't just paintings that were left by way of thanks. In one corner of the chapel there was a pile of helmets that people who had survived motorcycle accidents were wearing at the time of their crashes. Like the paintings, they were from a variety of periods and reflected helmet design and fashion of the time. Some were quite old – and, according to Filippo, quite rare.

'I could get a *fortune* for that one on eBay,' hissed Filippo, pointing to a battered green helmet that looked like a painted soup bowl.

My favourite votive offering was a heavily embroidered vest. It was mounted and framed along with a pair of Arabian Nights shoes with curled up toes and had pride of place on a pillar at the front of the chapel. The clothes dated from the nineteenth century and had belonged to a local girl called Giovinetta who was kidnapped from Livorno by Turkish pirates. She was taken to Constantinople and sold into the Prince's harem. According to the plaque underneath the clothes she prayed every night to Mary of Montenero to be rescued. Her brother eventually went to Constantinople and rescued her, bringing her back to Livorno. The outfit on display was the one she was forced to wear in the harem.

Filippo hadn't brought me to Santuario di Montenero specifically to show me the harem outfit. Or the countless paintings of Vespa riders being knocked over by tractors, trucks and cars or wrapped around trees. He wanted to get me an 'Our Lady of Grace' fridge magnet from the gift shop to stick on the metal glove box for good luck.

'You have great responsibilities now,' he explained solemnly as he handed me the gaudy magnet. 'You need a great protector.'

This badge featured Our Mary of Montenero and a baby Jesus and was called a 'Holy Sticker' rather than the more secular sounding 'fridge magnet'. It came in a small packet with a backing card wrapped in cellophane. The back of the card featured a series of photos suggesting places to stick it. The dashboard of a car. Just below the speedometer of a motor scooter (where I planned to stick mine). A fridge door, of course. And, bizarrely, the bottom right-hand corner of a wide-screen TV. The blurb claimed it would also 'resist all atmospheric agents'.

Filippo had lectures at university that afternoon so he dropped me off at Marco's workshop. I always liked watching Marco work. He was dexterous and meticulous and each action, even the turning of a screw, was invested with importance. I always felt I was in the presence of a Great Master when I was in his workshop. Given Marco's reputation in the world of Vespa restoration, I guess I was.

Just after two Lucilla dropped in with delicious ham and cheese *panini* (sandwiches) for us for lunch. I was in Italy now so they weren't just any old ham and cheese sandwiches. The cheese was a local specialty made from goat's milk. And the ham was a thinly sliced *prosciutto* from the region just north of Florence. We sat outside in the warm afternoon sun devouring them in a blissful silence.

Lucilla had taken the afternoon off work to go swimming and after we finished the sandwiches asked me if I wanted to join her.

'I'll show you my favourite swimming spot in Livorno,' she said. 'It is like a jacuzzi.'

The swimming spot was south of the city, just at the point where the road that clung to the rocky coast started to climb steeply. Lucilla had said that the location was secret, but the gaggle of motor scooters parked at the top of the path suggested that at least a dozen other people knew about it. Lucilla parked on the roadside beside them and we clambered down the steep rocky path to the shore.

The swimming spot was not a beach or even a cove, but rather a picturesque collection of large flat rocks, just offshore. Lucilla pointed out that each rock was for a different kind of person and that it was important to sit on the right one.

'That rock is for people who wear Gucci,' she said, pointing to the one furthest from shore. 'And that one next to it is for those who prefer Prada.'

On one rock a woman sunbathed topless while working on a laptop computer. She appeared to be talking to herself but Lucilla pointed out the Bluetooth headset above her right ear.

'She is talking on her cell phone,' she said, as if it was the most natural thing in the world. I wondered if the person on

29

the other end of the line had any idea that they were chatting to a topless woman and whether I had inadvertently done so at any time in my past. As I'd never responded to a premium number ad in a risqué magazine – or conducted any business over the phone in Italy – I decided that it was pretty safe to say that I hadn't.

Lucilla and I clambered onto the rock for the people who didn't really have a style and didn't really care. 'The miscellaneous folk', as Lucilla called us. We laid out our towels and stripped down to our swimmers. It says a lot about Livorno that we were the only ones on the miscellaneous rock.

I pulled out my 30+ sunscreen and started lathering it on. Lucilla laughed.

'What *is* that stuff!' she said in mock disgust. 'Italians use nothing!'

I showed her the keratosis (sun spot) on my leg. She didn't understand the word in English, so I got out my Lonely Planet phrasebook to look for words that would help explain. The nearest I could find was melanoma. (It was the same word in Italian). It was a bit of a drastic simile but I got my point across.

'Ahhh, *melanoma*!' she said, making a mental note of the word in English.

She took my phrasebook and flicked through it. Like everyone, she turned to the 'Meeting People' section and, in particular, the section on lovemaking. She was a bit surprised at how forward and plain-speaking it was. Italians obviously invested foreplay with something more poetic than 'Hai un preservativo?' ('Do you have a condom?') Then she read a phrase that made her laugh until she cried.

'*Non mi si raddrizza. Mi dispiace*,' she choked. 'I can't get it up. I'm sorry!'

Our rock might have been bereft of style, but it was the best equipped on this part of the coast. There was a natural hollow in its lowest part and a shallow underwater ledge to sit on. Occasionally a wave would surge over the ledge making the water in the pool bubble and foam. This was the jacuzzi that Lucilla had spoken of and we spent a pleasant hour or so in it, basking in the sun and having our underarms tickled by the gentle sea.

I could have happily spent the entire afternoon there. The position of the pool meant that the other rocks and their inhabitants were out of my line of vision. I could look straight out across the glittering Ligurian Sea and pretend I was the only person in the world.

We finished the day with Marco at a small pizzeria further down the coast at Quercianella. It enjoyed uninterrupted views of the ocean through huge windows that were open to let in the cool late-afternoon breeze. We ordered pizzas and a bottle of wine and watched the sun sink below the horizon. We finished the meal with a round of Negronis – a typical Vespa drink, Marco said, made from Campari, gin and sweet vermouth. As we clinked our glasses to celebrate a rather pleasant day, Marco pushed a flyer across the table.

The flyer was for the sixth annual Scooter Rally Toscano on the island of Elba. It was on that coming weekend and its organisers, the Green Onion Scooter Club, claimed it was the 'Best Italian event'. There would be *vino e buffet* (wine and food), *birra a fiumi* (a river of beer), a scooter run, an *esposizione* (display) of scooters, a beach party and three Northern Soul all-nighters featuring international DJs and two bands, Kinky Faces and The Playboys. (They were big on the *scena scooteristica*, apparently.)

Marco and Lucilla were going and asked if I wanted to tag along. Marco felt that it would be a great opportunity for me to give Marcello a workout and fix any problems that might reveal themselves before I set off for Sardinia and Sicily.

VROOM BY THE SEA

Hmmm. A trip to one of the most beautiful islands in Italy and the chance to show off my new Vespa in front of a knowledgeable and appreciative crowd.

It might have been the Negronis speaking, but I said that it sounded like an excellent idea.

CHAPTER TWO

ELBA

PATRON SAINT: SAN MICHELE

Vespa riders are social creatures by nature and Piaggio was quick to realise the marketing potential of encouraging them to gather in large groups. In 1949, barely three years after the first Vespa was produced, the company hired Renato Tassinari, a journalist with *Corriere dello Sport*, to organise a mass gathering of 'Vespisti' at the Milan Fair.

Two thousand Vespa riders from all over the country responded to the call. Many of them were women, and each and every one of them was determined to have fun. Every major paper in Italy reported on the 'silver swarm of festivity' that had descended upon the city.

By 1952 there were 111 Vespa clubs in Italy. They operated under the umbrella of the Vespa Club d'Italia, the main governing body, of which Tassinari was president. Each club organised rallies and excursions, fancy-dress parades, races, treasure hunts, *concours d'élégances* and dances.

At the tenth Congress of the Vespa Club d'Italia Renato Tassinari described Vespa clubs as a movement that 'comes about, expresses itself and breeds to the beat of small engines and hearts serene and free in seeking far-off beautiful countryside and brotherly friendships'.

Tassinari's comments were a little too poetic perhaps. He had a reputation for a florid turn of phrase. But whenever a swarm of Vespisti passed through a town on their way to a rally no one who saw them was left in any doubt. Riding a Vespa was fun – and a great way of meeting people.

Marco and I set off for the rally in Elba just after ten. It was only 75 kilometres from Livorno to Piombino, the ugly steel town in southern Tuscany where the ferries left for Elba. But as with most of my Vespa trips in Italy with Marco it wasn't just a simple case of going from Point A to Point B. Along the way he wanted to take me to his favourite restaurant 'in the whole of Italy' then drop in on a friend who made olive oil and wine and lived close by.

I'd spent the previous afternoon washing and polishing Marcello until he shone like a medallion. Marco was on a brand new GT200 that he'd picked up that morning. Lucilla would be driving down in her car and joining us later in the day in Piombino. She still had a lot of work to catch up on after taking the afternoon off earlier in the week.

We avoided the state highway that ran a kilometre inland and stuck to the road that clung to the coastline instead. The scenery was varied and beautiful. At times the road was lined by a guard of oleanders, at others it wound its way through stands of thick, aromatic pines. Then, without warning, it would burst into dazzling sunshine and hurtle along the edge of sheer cliffs with massive villas tacked onto the side of them.

Our first pitstop was outside the villa that had once belonged to Marcello Mastroianni. Having just christened my Vespa Marcello it was an unexpected and welcome benefit of going to Elba this way.

The Mastroianni residence was a delicate salmon-coloured multistorey villa with a turret commanding spectacular views north along the rugged coastline. Marco insisted on taking my photo in front of it and risked his life by standing in the middle of a busy road to ensure that my Marcello, the villa and I were all in the shot.

The villa was just north of Castiglioncello and Marco told me that it was where the actor had spent his final days. Indeed, even towards the end of his life you could apparently see him hobbling down to the local café for a shot of espresso most days of the week.

Next stop was Marco's favourite restaurant in Italy. It was in Bolgheri, a small village 48 kilometres south of Livorno. Bolgheri sits 4 kilometres off the main road at the end of a long, straight avenue lined on both sides by majestic cypress pines over 25 metres tall. The Viale dei Cipressi ('Avenue of Pines') is mentioned in a poem called *Davanti a San Guido* by Giosue Carducci. The village is dominated by an ancient castle and surrounded by distinctive red brick walls that date from 800 AD and were embellished by Count Alberto Guido in 1895 when he added the distinctive crenellations and a tower. The only entrance is through a small arch in the walls and when we buzzed through I got the distinct feeling that I was stepping back in time.

We had arrived in Bolgheri right on 1 p.m. A table was waiting for us at Castagneto Carducci, Marco's favourite restaurant, and the waiter told us that we were just in time for the lunchtime special. Marco gave a look of astonishment as if this was a pleasant and totally unexpected surprise, but I knew that when it came to eating well Marco left nothing to chance. And with food as good as we ate at Castagneto Carducci that afternoon I can't say I blame him. My *gnocchi carducci*, sprinkled with pine nuts in honour of the great man's poem, was mind-blowingly delicious and the portions trouser-bustingly immense.

After lunch we tracked back through the arch in the castle wall and down the Viale dei Cipressi to a turnoff about halfway along. Marco's friend Simone had just started a small winery here, up the road from the Sassicaia vineyard, the first and only estate in Italy to have its own DOC category (quality wines produced in a specific region). Bolgheri is on the same latitude as the great Tuscan wine-producing towns of Montalcino and Montepulciano but has only recently started receiving recognition as a wine producer. Previously wine was only produced for home consumption but the creation of DOC Bolgheri Rosso and Rosso Superiore in 1994 has brought international recognition for the wines produced there.

We found Simone up a ladder trimming the branches of the mature olive trees at the back of his property. He was tall and gangly, with a scruffy beard and round John Lennon glasses perched on his nose. Until his wines gained more recognition he had to rely on the oil the olive trees produced to keep him afloat. He was only doing it half-heartedly, but such was the size of his enterprise that that was more than enough. A small Jack Russell terrier sat in the shade watching him.

On spotting Marco, Simone smiled broadly and clambered down the ladder. In Italy a visitor is a perfect excuse to stop working and he motioned for us to follow him to a rickety metal table set under a tree. He disappeared into the old stone farmhouse and returned with a couple of bottles of wine, crusty bread and some olive oil to drizzle on it. Both the wine and the oil were produce from his farm. Both were very good.

Simone told us that when he first took over the farm the trees had been neglected and weren't producing much fruit. He had to prune them quite aggressively. He attacked them with a chainsaw – a rustic Freddy Krueger – leaving only four branches that acted like compass points for the new growth. Some of the branches he lopped off were big enough to use as firewood for the next two years.

It took a while before the trees started producing fruit again. But it was worth it, he said. The yield was greater now. In fact the old owner had dropped by to see how he was doing and was surprised at the results.

One of the main reasons Simone's small farm produced so well was that it had a good pollinator. It was a different variety from his other trees. It was a maurino, which flower longer.

'The guy who planted these trees knew what he was doing,' said Simone. 'All the trees are within 30 metres of the pollinator.'

Simone sent most of his olives to be pressed at a local mill, but kept some for eating. Italy has one of the highest levels of organically grown crops in Europe, and, like most Italian farmers, Simone shied away from using chemicals. It wasn't just for environmental reasons. He was operating on a shoestring budget and chemicals were expensive.

'A lot of farmers cure the olives in lye (caustic soda),' he said. 'It leaches the bitterness from the fruit.' Simone preferred a more traditional and cost-effective manner. He immersed the green olives in cold water for ten days, changing the water each day. Then he made a brine solution, using enough salt so an egg could float in the water, and left the olives in it for three to four weeks.

I asked him what was done with all the leftover bits when the olives were pressed for oil. It had been my experience in small enterprises like this that nothing was left to waste. He pointed to a pile of briquettes under a tarpaulin beside the barn.

'It's called *sansa*,' he said. 'It's pressed into briquettes. The guys who operate the press give me a bag of the stuff when I pick up my oil. I use it for heating in winter.'

Simone tossed a gnarled pine cone towards the Jack Russell terrier. It attacked it like it was a rat.

'His name is Giosue,' said Simone. 'I named him after Giosue Carducci, the guy who wrote the poem about the cypress trees.'

Simone wore a hat that was shaped like a pork pie hat but was made from straw. I really liked it – I thought it looked cool and down home at the same time. I asked him where he had got it from and he said Sardinia. I told him that was where I was heading next and his eyes lit up.

'It is beautiful there,' he said dreamily. 'The sand on the beaches is white and the ocean is blue. You will think you are in the Caribbean.'

Marco looked at his watch and declared that it was time to leave. Lucilla would be in Piombino soon and he wanted to get to Elba before it got dark. As we stood at our Vespas saying our goodbyes to Simone, Giosue cocked his leg and pissed against Marcello's back tyre.

'You have been blessed!' laughed Simone.

Marco agreed. 'It is good luck for a dog to do this in Italy!' he said. All I could think of was the hour I'd wasted painting those tyres with tyre black so they'd look just right for the scooter *esposizione*.

We reached the outskirts of Piombino within the hour. It was as depressing as any other steel town I'd had the misfortune to pass through. It was grimy and smelly and the only splash of colour was the gaudy posters tacked on concrete pylons advertising a circus that was coming to town. Thankfully ferries left for Portoferraio on Elba every half an hour, so once we found Lucilla, bought our tickets, and wheeled our Vespas on board, we were on our way.

Elba is the third largest island in Italy after Sicily and Sardinia. It is a distant third – the island is only 28 kilometres long and 19 kilometres wide – but its mountainous, heavily wooded interior and stunning white sandy beaches make it one of the most beautiful. Roman legend has it that Venus, the goddess of love, was strolling through the Tyrrhenian Sea one day and accidentally lost a precious jewel from the necklace she was wearing. The stone fell into the water and became Elba. I first caught sight of the island twenty minutes into the one-hour ferry ride. After Piombino, it looked like a diamond.

Portoferraio was particularly lovely. It appeared on the horizon as a jumble of cobblestoned lanes and pastel villas with red terracotta tiled roofs. The highest point of the town was crowned by Villa dei Mulini, Napoleon's residence when he was exiled to Elba in 1814.

It is testament to just how far out of the political mainstream Elba was before Napoleon's arrival – and remained after he left – that his brief sojourn there remains the single thing that the island is best known for. Iron ore was mined here until the Second World War. And the Romans were partial to the wines that were produced there. But the regularity with which control of the island passed between Pisa and Genoa, then the

Medici, Spain, Turkey and France, seems to suggest that no one was really bothered if they kept it or not.

Napoleon only stayed on Elba for nine months but in that time he revamped the legal and education system, modernised the economy and built a network of roads. The flag that Napoleon designed to pass the time on his way over on the British frigate *Undaunted* still flies from the island's flagpoles. It features three golden bees, a nod towards the Medici dynasty that built the Portoferraio port. As Vespa is Italian for wasp, it seems highly appropriate that Italy's premier scooter rally is held here each year.

According to legend the first thing Napoleon noticed about Portoferraio was the stench. On Elba the locals still emptied their chamberpots straight onto the streets. One of Napoleon's first acts as sovereign of his new domain was to build latrines, employ refuse collectors and institute large fines for people who continued to soil the streets.

The first thing I noticed about Portoferraio was the smell of two-stroke engine fumes. There were at least two dozen other scooter riders on board and they sat revving their engines in the bowels of the ship as we waited for the ramp at the back of the ferry to lower onto the dock.

I didn't see much of Portoferraio, just the busy port to the left of the quaint old town. The headquarters for the Elba Rally was at Mandel 2, a small camping ground in Morcone in the south-east of the island. Marco suggested it would be a good idea to get there as soon as possible and register.

'The sooner we register, the sooner we can swim in the river of beer,' he grinned. It still amused him that it was the promise of a *birra a fiumi* on the flyer that had intrigued me most about the Elba Rally.

The road south to Morcone cut through farmland before climbing into the rugged mountains of the south-east. It soon became apparent that this part of Elba was caught in a parallel universe where every vehicle on the road was either a Vespa or a Lambretta. They sat getting gas at every bowser in every petrol station and formed neat lines outside every café and restaurant. Elsewhere they buzzed in swarms along the road that wound its way up a mountain and down the other side again. The two-stroke takeover was so complete that it almost felt like a scene from a horror movie. Except the air wasn't filled with the mumbled groan of decaying zombies; instead it reverberated with the high-pitched scream of two-stroke engines being caned.

On reaching Morcone, Marco, Lucilla and I made our way to the registration tent. It was pitched on a neat patch of grass by the beach and sat beside a larger marquee where a DJ absentmindedly spun discs in preparation for the beach party the next day. Volunteers from the Green Onion Scooter Club scribbled down our details and, in return for a crisp €20 note, gave us a plastic bag containing the official program, a map of the island, entrance passes for the three all-nighters, a voucher for the buffet and a commemorative patch to sew on the parka that they naturally assumed I had.

The area in front of the marquee that was usually a beachside car park had become an impromptu showroom for Vespas and Lambrettas of every marque and hue. They were parked in neat lines along the hedges that divided the area. Guys in parkas or dressed in full mod regalia wandered among the scooters, checking out the bikes – and each other. It was with great pride that I noted that Marcello got more than his fair share of admiring glances.

Lucilla watched the men with a smile on her face. There were two types of men who went to scooter rallies, she said. Short men with big beer bellies. And tall skinny men who smoked. I asked her which type I was – I didn't smoke so I feared the worst – and she laughed.

'There are exceptions, of course,' she said diplomatically.

As part of the registration process we were each given a laminated pass that we were supposed to wear at all times. It was this pass that would give us access to the vino and buffet, and, more importantly, the river of beer. I found the bar and grabbed three pints while Marco and Lucilla grabbed a table under one of the date palms that lined the beach.

It was a pretty spot. The beach was 500 metres long at most and sheltered at each end by a rocky headland covered in jojoba plants and *macchia*, the thick Mediterranean scrub that covers most of Elba.

Marco and Lucilla weren't camping at Morcone. They had rented an apartment in Capoliveri, the ancient town at the top of the hill. There was room for me to stay there too but I rather fancied the idea of camping beside the beach with the rest of the Vespisti. If things got rowdy, I wanted to be right in the middle of it.

I found a spot to pitch my tent under a stand of pine trees at the back of the camping ground. My neighbours were a noisy contingent from the Edinburgh Blues Scooter Club. They had only arrived that morning after a five-day trek across the Alps from Scotland but had made themselves at home by draping a huge flag featuring the Saint Andrew's cross between two poles. They were tucking into bottles of whisky that had made the long and treacherous journey from their homeland as well.

Their leader was a large bloke with a bald head called Sumo. He had tattoos up each arm and rode a red Rally 200 with a sidecar attached. It was the same model as Marcello so I was keen to hear how his Rally 200 had handled the 1500-kilometre journey. It hadn't missed a beat, he said.

Sumo's girlfriend, Daisy, had ridden in the sidecar. It was cramped and uncomfortable and she spent most of the trip gripping both sides of it in terror. The bike was registered in the UK so the sidecar was on the left-hand side. This was not a problem in Scotland where people drive on the left-hand side

of the road and she could gaze absentmindedly at the scenery. But in Europe, where people drive on the right, Daisy was left staring at oncoming traffic. And on the tiny winding roads across the Alps that oncoming traffic got a little too close for comfort.

'I thought I was going to die a number of times,' she said dryly. Sumo joked that he could have got her a cut-price funeral. He was an embalmer, you see.

I'd never met an embalmer before, so I used the opportunity to ask Sumo a number of direct and impertinent questions about his chosen career. Although I'm sure he'd been asked them a million times before, he answered with good grace and humour. It turned out that the worst part of being an embalmer wasn't sticking your hand up the orifices of a corpse as I had guessed. It was coming home smelling of embalming fluids.

Fifty years earlier Sumo could well have found himself featured in the Vespa Club d'Italia magazine. Each issue profiled a club member with an interesting profession, and journalists from the magazine prowled events throughout the country looking for suitable subjects. One issue featured a professional baker called Francesco Polga who attended rallies all over the country but always made sure he was back to open his shop at 3 a.m. Another profiled Aldo Ambrosetti, a one-armed war veteran who worked as an engineer for the Edison electrical company.

If a Vespa rider with an intriguing profession couldn't be found, the Vespa Club d'Italia journalist simply wrote a story about an interesting character that he had come across. My personal favourite was Giuseppe Palma from Milan, who was featured because he turned up at a rally in Torino clutching the ears of a hare he'd run over on the way. Sadly the profile didn't feature a picture of Giuseppe or the hare.

That night I met Marco and Lucilla in Capoliveri and we had dinner in a pizzeria on one of the cobbled streets that radiated off the main square. When our bellies were full we jumped on our Vespas and rode to Mandel Disco, a club that was three-quarters of the way down the hill to Morcone.

The club had been commandeered by the organisers of the rally as the venue for the Northern Soul allnighters. As the name suggests, the all-nighters went all through the night until dawn and gave scooterists the opportunity to listen to Northern Soul music and show off their dance moves.

The club sat alone and undistinguished, surrounded by scraggly farms in the barren hills. I'd ridden past it twice before and hadn't even noticed it. That night, however, you couldn't miss it. Both sides of the road, for hundreds of metres on either side of the club, were lined with Vespas and Lambrettas.

Marco, Lucilla and I flashed our laminated passes and were let through by the bouncers on the door. It was dark inside but once my eyes had adjusted to the low light from the stage I realised that every mod in Italy was there. They all wore Fred Perry shirts and Harrington jackets and handed their fishtail parkas over to the coat check beside the bar. A pack of Paul Weller look-alikes had commandeered the dance floor while their Mary Quant girlfriends stood to the side sipping cocktails and looking on. It was like we'd been transported back to the *Ready Steady Go!* studio circa 1964.

Mods and Vespas have always been inextricably linked. They both emerged from the ruins of the Second World War and were driven by the idea of the new. Piaggio used new technologies and concepts developed for aeronautical projects to produce a cheap means of transport for a country getting up off its knees. The mods, short for modernists, wanted anything that was new and exciting. And with a little help from a new thing called 'hire purchase', they wanted it now.

Vespas fitted the mod ethos perfectly. They were modern and sleek and, unlike motorcycles, you could ride them and keep your clothes clean. Most mods spent 80 per cent of their wages on clothes so it was an important consideration. Mud was the last thing you wanted on your John Stephens suit.

The Italians at the all-nighter that night had mimeographed the UK mod scene of that time perfectly, right down to the scooters they preferred. On the way in, Marco had pointed out that most of the Vespas parked out front were GS160s. They were the only Vespa any self-respecting mod would be seen dead on and were name-checked by The Who in *Quadrophenia*: *'I ride a GS scooter with my hair cut neat,'* snarled Roger Daltry. He also wore a parka to keep out the wind and sleet.

Along with the Small Faces, The Who were the big mod band in the sixties. But they wouldn't get a look-in that night in Morcone. It was a Northern Soul all-nighter so the English DJ stuck to the black American classics that were equally popular with mods. 'Moonlight, Music and You' by Laura Greene. '(I'm a) Roadrunner' by Jr Walker & the All Stars. 'The "In" Crowd' by Dobie Gray. 'The Champion' by Willie Mitchell. 'Stop Sign' by Mel Wynn & the Rhythm Aces – songs that were appreciated much more in the UK than they ever were in Australia.

The DJ wasn't very good. His call-outs were lame and he let records finish before starting the next one. But he had shaggy hair and he was English and as far as the Italian mods were concerned that made him authentic. They showed their appreciation by filling the dance floor.

For a scene that placed such importance on looking immaculate, its adherents seemed keen to work up a sweat. One chap wearing a Fred Perry tennis shirt and a pork pie hat was so serious about his dancing that he spent a solid fifteen minutes limbering up. First he shook each of his limbs loose, cricking his neck side to side. Then he commandeered one of the pylons in the club to perform a series of complicated stretching exercises. This was the first of two all-nighters and he had a long night ahead of him. He didn't want to pull a hamstring.

Like all good mod scenes, the all-nighter in the Mandel Disco had its Faces. The guy warming up wasn't a Face. He was trying too hard. Faces had an aura of cool about them and set the trends in fashion and hairstyles that everyone else followed. They certainly wouldn't start a trend that involved doing callisthenics against a pylon.

The Face that night was a tall skinny guy wearing an immaculately cut suit. He looked like a young Rod Stewart and as he made his way to the dance floor everyone else parted to form a path. His girlfriend was a stunning brunette with bobbed hair wearing a black and white checked A-line dress. She put down her drink and followed in his wake, taking up a position beside him and swaying from side to side as she watched him dance. She was an accessory every bit as important as the paisley cravat around his neck.

The Face performed a complex series of manoeuvres that I have since learned from back copies of NME was a dance called 'The Block'. It involved a considerable amount of twisting and shaking before culminating in the hand movement that gave the dance its name – raising arms to shoulder level with the left palm turned in and right palm turned out, and then finished with a clap. When poorly executed it looks like something an embarrassing uncle might do at a Christmas party. Done well – in the manner this guy did it – it looks very, very cool.

I've always envied people who can dance well. I'm either so self-conscious that I shuffle heavily like someone on horse tranquillisers. Or I have too much to drink and jerk about like I'm being electrocuted. Neither style has a place in mod dancing. I left just after midnight and returned to my tent ruing the fact that I didn't have the hairline, the physique or, it has to be said, the coordination to be a proper mod.

Just after lunch the next day everyone started gathering outside the marquee in Marcone for the ride-out. A ride-out is exactly what it says on the tin. Everyone gets on their motor scooters and goes for a ride along a predetermined course. It is the highlight of any motor scooter rally and the one event that everyone attends. It is a chance for everyone to get together – regardless of hairstyle, dancing techniques or type of scooter – and recreate that 'swarm of festivity' the world first saw in Milan in 1949.

The ride-out would take us up the hill to Capoliveri, down to Porto Azzurro and then along the north-east coast to Cavo, an old-fashioned resort town marked by a wooden pier. Right on 2 p.m. a rider from the Green Onion Scooter Club rode to the front of the pack and set off up the hill, beckoning through the fug of blue smoke for the rest of us to follow him.

We buzzed up the hill like a swarm of locusts that had just had their nest rattled. The cars that were coming down the hill sensibly pulled to the side rather than risk getting a Vespa squashed on the windscreen. As we swarmed through Capoliveri and then Porto Azzurro, tourists stopped and watched us pass. Their kids laughed and waved.

There is something about Vespas that makes people happy. If a similar number of motorbikes passed, people would cower or step away. With scooters, they smile. OK, they could have been laughing at us rather than with us. But either way, we'd made them happy.

After leaving Porto Azzurro, the road skirted along the bottom of low mountains that had once been mined for iron ore. The forest had grown back, making it one of the wildest parts of the island. At Rio nell'Elba the road turned back to the coast, following the rugged coastline that has remained empty and deserted since sea raiders destroyed the villages here during the sixteenth century.

At Cavo the rally organisers directed us to ride onto the wooden pier and park our scooters along it. I think they were going for a Brighton/*Quadrophenia* look but it didn't quite work. The beach was sandy. The water was blue. And the street behind it was lined with date palms, not Victorian terraces.

After strolling along the pier and checking out each other's scooters everyone retired to the Hemingway Irish Bar, a dark and dingy pub tucked away in the back streets of Cavo. I spotted the Face from the night before. He was wearing a brown suit today and his cravat wasn't paisley, but rather a solid orange in a shade not dissimilar to Marcello. For the first time I noticed that he was wearing ridiculously pointy shoes and wondered how he managed to work the rear brake of his Lambretta with them.

His girlfriend was still wearing the same black and white checked dress. Her bobbed hair was immaculate, without a single hair out of place. But she looked more haggard than I remembered her being the night before.

'Daylight is not kind to her,' noted Lucilla.

I'd been so impressed by the guy's dancing the night before that I went over and introduced myself. I discovered his name was Federico and he was from Rimini. He told me there was quite a big mod scene in Rimini. Every Easter they had a big meet there called The Italian Job. It was organised by the Smart Drivers Scooters Club, a group of mods living the mod lifestyle on the Adriatic Coast. It had become one of the big mod events on the international calendar. Federico ran the Lambretta Club there and listed some of the 'Faces'. He asked me if I knew them. I shook my head. He smiled weakly and turned back to his drink.

What happened next is positive proof that my testicles should be hooked up to a car battery and zapped every time I even attempt to speak a foreign language. Even though Federico spoke English perfectly, that afternoon in a dark corner of the Hemingway Bar I decided to tell him that he was a good dancer in Italian.

'*Balli benissimo* (you are a fantastic dancer),' I said slowly. I also enunciated it in a manner I thought an Italian would.

Federico said 'Pardon?' and I said it again.

He shifted uncomfortably in his chair, not sure what to say or where to look. His girlfriend overheard my second attempt and broke off a conversation she was having with another Mary Quant look-alike to pull Federico away from me. Marco and Lucilla laughed.

'Where did you get that line from?' asked Lucilla. 'Your phrasebook?'

I nodded and pointed to the line in question in my Lonely Planet phrasebook. It was in the *Frasi per rimorchiare* (pick-up lines) section but I thought it was innocuous enough to use in a non-amorous manner. I was wrong apparently.

'The poor man thought you were coming on to him,' laughed Lucilla. She kept laughing until tears ran down her cheeks.

Later that night I spotted Federico and his girlfriend at the all-nighter. I waved, hoping to get the chance to explain the misunderstanding, but before I got near them Federico grabbed his girlfriend and left, disappearing into the night. Lucilla laughed that I'd spoiled his night. It was the last all-nighter of the rally and his last chance to really strut his stuff. And some Aussie bloke with a thing for shaggy-haired mods had ruined it for him.

The rally ended the next day with an awards ceremony and final party that was held mid-morning. It was a public holiday but most people would be drifting off, back to their lives as bank clerks and shop assistants, where the idea of an all-nighter is reserved for the annual stocktake. A buffet of hams, salami, crusty bread and a huge barrel of red wine was laid out for participants, which I thought was a nice Italian touch.

I spotted the guys from Edinburgh tucking in. Sumo joked it was very different from the rallies they held.

'We always end up at the local chippie for a deep-fried Mars bar,' he joked.

A DJ called Elvis handed out the various prizes. A trophy for the 'Most Kilometres Travelled' went to the guys from Edinburgh.

'You're the fuckin' business!' said Elvis as he handed them the trophy.

After the awards were handed out Elvis cranked up the music and the tent was a seething mass of bald heads and feather cuts dancing to Madness songs. I cut a few moves before Marco flicked his head and said it was time to go.

Marcello had passed the test. He hadn't missed a beat.

It was time to set off on my big adventure.

CHAPTER THREE

SANTA TERESA DI GALLURA

PATRON SAINT: FRANCIS OF ASSISI

The ferry I caught to Olbia in Sardinia was called the *Moby Drea* and it was decorated with a mural of giant Looney Tunes characters three storeys high. Bugs Bunny, Tweety and Wile E Coyote surfed a wave on oversized surfboards on the side while Taz, the Tasmanian Devil, hung off the top deck like a gibbon. Sylvester stood tall in a pair of lurid board shorts on the funnel. It was not the most conventional livery I'd seen on an ocean-going cruise ship – most tend to go for your standard nautical white – but it laid down a marker for my trip. This journey was going to be bright, colourful and fun. But hopefully devoid of any Wile E Coyote style pratfalls off the edge of a cliff.

The cheerful note struck by the cartoon mural continued on board. Marcello was lashed to a bar running along the side of the car deck by a guy wearing overalls a brighter shade of orange than Marcello was. I was handed the key to my cabin by a female cruise director just as perky as Julie McCoy on *The Love Boat*. And each deck was packed with chirpy holiday-makers dressed in chic linen suits. They strolled along corridors looking for their cabins and chatting excitedly about their holidays ahead. It was all very buoyant and matched my mood perfectly. I was on my way to Sardinia at last. My great journey through the sunny parts of Italy was about to begin.

I had begun to suspect that I might never leave Livorno. When D.H. Lawrence set off for a one-week journey through Sardinia in 1921 he wrote: 'There comes over one an absolute necessity to move.' I knew exactly what he meant. I hadn't married my former professor's wife and then had that wife accused of being a German spy, but two weeks after arriving in Italy to start my wild pre-fatherhood two-stroke fling I was still in Livorno. My 'necessity to move' was more benign – a couple of inches added to my waistline from all the good food I'd eaten – but it was just as urgent.

Life was comfortable in Livorno. I ate well and cheaply. I had friends who took me to hidden bars and secluded swimming spots. And I spent my days riding along craggy coastlines and winding mountain roads on a Vespa that never failed to gain admiring glances. The biggest decision I had to make each morning was whether to have a *biscotti* or *bombolone* (donut) with my *macchiato*. Thanks to Marco and Filippo I was already living the *dolce vita* that I'd left London to go in search of.

The good life continued right up to the moment I boarded the ferry. Marco and Filippo organised a farewell dinner at Don Giovanni, a restaurant that overlooked the ancient market square in the centre of Livorno. It was a casual establishment that specialised in freshly prepared *panini* stuffed with fillings you pointed out behind a huge glass counter.

Marco insisted on finishing the meal with a *ponce*, a coffee and rum concoction originally devised to make the rough rum dumped on the city by English traders more palatable. On my last visit to Livorno every night out with Marco and Filippo had ended with a *ponce* at Bar Civili, a tiny and crowded bar with football pennants hanging from the low ceilings. It is the self-proclaimed 'Best *Ponce* Bar in the World' and over the course of my stay I acquired quite a taste for the stuff. Indeed Marco and Filippo had presented me with a genuine Livornese *ponce* kit as I left. It consisted of a bottle of Livornese rum, two *ponce* glasses and detailed instructions on how to prepare it.

Lucilla had told me that Marco only drank the stuff when I was around so I guessed he wanted to get a couple in before I disappeared for a few months. We raised our glasses and as I looked across the table at my beaming friends and their new girlfriends I thought of the line Al Pacino mutters in *The Godfather III*: 'Just when I thought that I was out they dragged me back in.' I didn't have to keep an unravelling crime family together but my task was no less challenging. I had to jump on Marcello, leave my friends and a ready-made social life behind and wobble off to the ferry terminal that was thankfully only a short ride away.

Lucilla's father was one of Livorno's longest established travel agents and had used his contacts to get me a single cabin on the upper deck for the price of a deck seat. If I'd made the same trip in winter, he said, he would have been able to get me the Moby Fantasy Suite that came with a king-size bed, colour TV, radio, phone, bar fridge and a complimentary breakfast of fresh fruit and pastries. As I threw down my bag I decided that would just have been gilding the lily. My standard single cabin with ensuite was already better than most hotels I'd stayed in.

The *Moby Drea* pulled away from the dock in the Stazione Marittima right on 10 p.m. and set off in a south-westerly direction towards Sardinia. I stood on the deck and watched Livorno recede. Its old forts and monuments were illuminated and still and the darkness hid its rough edges. It looked almost lovely.

VROOM BY THE SEA

I spent the first part of the journey in the Vegas-style show lounge watching two girls in sparkly outfits sing Italian pop songs. For a vessel that only ever sailed between Livorno and Olbia, the *Moby Drea* was surprisingly well-appointed. As well as the show lounge and attached casino it boasted an à la carte restaurant, self-service cafeteria, pizza point, *gelateria*, pub, pool, solarium, a lido bar where waiters brought you drinks as you swam, and a soft play area called Children's World that was also equipped with video games. It was kitted out like it was going on a 22-day trip through the Pacific, not a 12-hour, overnight journey to Sardinia.

At midnight the showgirls were replaced by a band of hairy leather-clad men who performed very poor cover versions of well-known power ballads. Despite the abundance of songs to cover in their chosen genre they had to play 'Wind of Change' by Scorpions twice to pad out their set. Most passengers used that as their cue to leave and have a late-night espresso in the fully appointed Italian-style café.

Things were livelier in Children's World. The sandwich board out front said that they would be showing *Finding Nemo* but the bank of televisions inside had been commandeered by a large group of male passengers intent on watching a football match between Portugal and Russia. They sprawled on various pieces of indoor playground equipment and gesticulated at the referee in a manner that suggested he was having a particularly poor game. When a mother complained loudly that they had made her son cry, one of the men told her that it was late and he should be in bed anyway.

Before I retired to my cabin for the night I did a lap of the deck outside. The wind coming off the sea was blustery and bracing and the only other people I saw were backpackers huddled in corners in their sleeping bags, passing around a bottle of vodka.

At dinner that night Filippo had reminisced about the trips to Sardinia he and his mates had made when they were teenagers. They slept on the deck too, passing around whisky and the occasional joint to help them get through the night.

I looked at the backpackers and felt a twinge of envy and regret. Not necessarily because of the drugs and the drinks. Rather the adventure of sleeping roughly in the open and waking up feeling seedy and groggy to the most amazing sunrise you have ever seen. I returned to my cabin and drifted off to sleep wondering if that was the sort of thing an expectant father should be envious of.

I woke the next morning to an announcement in four languages that we would be docking in an hour. I showered and packed and hurriedly joined a queue for a morning espresso and pastry. Just as I was about to be served there was an announcement over the loudspeakers.

'There is a short delay,' said a disembodied voice. 'It is not of our will.'

The Italian passengers did not react well to the news. The guy standing next to me slapped his hand on the counter and his wife let out a loud huff before abusing the guy making the coffee as if he was personally responsible. A cabin attendant who had inadvisedly chosen that moment to take a coffee break was surrounded by a pack of portly grandmothers who poked him in the chest and asked angrily when exactly we'd be docking. He turned and fled before things got really nasty and I wondered how the passengers would have reacted if the voice on the loudspeaker had admitted the delay *was* 'of their will'.

I left my fellow passengers to form vigilante groups and storm the bridge and ventured out onto the deck to catch my first sight of Sardinia. It lay ahead, emerging sleepily from an early morning mist and looking craggy, wild and empty. Elsewhere in Italy a stretch of coastline like this would be crammed with lidos, apartments, *gelateria* and pizzerias.

Here, on the north-east coast of the second-biggest island in the Mediterranean, there wasn't a single sign of human habitation.

Sardinia has always been a world apart. D.H. Lawrence described it as 'lost between Europe and Africa and belonging to nowhere'. The Phoenicians, Carthaginians, Romans, Pisans, Genoans, Spanish and Austrians all tried to get a foothold before abandoning the island to malaria and the fiercely independent locals who lived in the mountainous interior. It's been part of a unified Italy since 1861. Indeed Giuseppe Garibaldi used it as a base for his military campaigns. But it has steadfastly retained its own dialect, costumes, cuisine and tendency to resolve differences with the odd blood vendetta or two.

Olbia sat below low rocky hills at the end of a narrow bay in the western reaches of the Gulf of Olbia. The bay was filled with thousands of orange and blue plastic float balls, tied together and set out in neat rows. They marked the marshy shallows, and the only part of the bay that was clear of them was a passage as wide as a ship that led directly to the port. I remember thinking at the time that it was very considerate of the port authorities to mark the way so clearly. After a night in the gaming lounge with a showgirl on each arm a ferry captain needs all the help he can get.

Down on the car deck the Italian passengers turned their combustible impatience towards the deckhands responsible for unloading the vessel. The *Moby Drea* was still in the process of docking, shunting backwards and forwards, but the passengers yelled at the crew to start lowering the door so they could drive off the ship as soon it stopped. When it was finally lowered, they tore off the ship like each one of them had discovered a ticking bomb under their car. Italians, it seems, invest their holidays with the same manic energy that they do all other aspects of their lives.

The madness continued on the narrow cobbled streets of Olbia. The road that led from the port to the highway north was a mêlée of metal with cars jostling, crunching and scraping against each other and the buildings that overlooked them. When the Pisans completely rebuilt the town in 1198 they couldn't have known that every day around 10 a.m., 800 years later, the streets would be transformed into a smash-up derby track for a couple of hundred vehicles.

Fearing I might lose a limb, I rode Marcello onto the pavement and waited for the rest of the passengers to pass. I didn't wait long enough. As soon as I pulled out onto the road a Fiat station wagon screamed past with its horn blaring. It was driven by a harried-looking man trying to argue with his wife, chastise his children and break the land speed record at the same time.

I had seen the man's anxious countenance before. As the door was being lowered on the ferry he was desperately ushering one of his boys into the toilet. When the child didn't return within thirty seconds he went into the toilet to implore his son to go faster. I think he gave his son performance anxiety because it was another five minutes before they emerged. His attempt to make up for lost time proved just as fruitless. I passed him on the northern outskirts of Olbia, pulled over to the side of the road as the *carabinieri* issued him a ticket for not stopping at a stop sign.

I was heading to Porto Cervo, the town at the northernmost tip of Costa Smeralda (Emerald Coast), a 10-kilometre stretch of pristine coastline that is one of the most exclusive in the Mediterranean. Originally uncultivable farmland, the entire region was purchased in 1962 by a business consortium headed by the Aga Khan. Back then the local farmers were glad to sell. It was back-breaking work just to scratch an existence from it. Now it is home to some of the most expensive properties in Italy and the tiny bars in the hinterland are propped up by grizzled, bitter shepherds who claim they were duped out of their land.

The regional government wasn't so easily dazzled by the consortium's flashy plans. It imposed strict conditions on any development including an insistence on proper sewage disposal and treatment. Buildings could not exceed certain heights and had to be built using local materials. Multistorey hotels, fast-food restaurants and garish advertising hoardings were banned. In the sixties such restrictions were unheard of, especially in Italy. But it's why properties along the coast are in such demand today.

The sort of folk who hang out on the Costa Smeralda now include Silvio Berlusconi, the former Italian prime minister and richest man in Italy, who has a 27-room villa just outside Porto Rotundo. As I was passing through he was busily readying the 123-acre estate for a visit from then British prime minister Tony Blair and his wife, Cherie. They were only staying a couple of days but he was building a 400-seat amphitheatre especially for the occasion. It was to be inaugurated with a recital of Shakespearean texts and Silvio had told his gardeners to plant a dozen or so 100-year-old olive trees around it to remind the Blairs of their courtship in Tuscany. Each tree cost US$15,000.

The road to Porto Cervo hugged the coast, winding its way through craggy rocks and *macchia*, the olive-green scrub that grew profusely in this part of the Mediterranean. Marcello took to the dips and curves and inclines like he was born to it, effortlessly climbing up hills that would have left my first Vespa, Sophia, gasping for breath. The mid-morning sun was warm on my skin. I had the perfume of oleander and mimosa in my nostrils. And, thanks to the forward-thinking regional government, when I rounded a bend all I was greeted by was the sight of rolling hills covered in myrtle and the glittering sea, not a 24-sheet billboard suggesting I visit the local Hooters.

The only signs of human life were the white vans parked at panorama points selling local produce. They sold cheese and salami mainly, spread out on a table under the shade of huge umbrellas. My fellow passengers on the *Moby Drea* had passed long ago so the sellers were using the lull in business to take a nap in the back of their vans. They looked up lazily when they heard me approach and nodded in appreciation as Marcello passed by.

Porto Cervo is the 'capital' of Costa Smeralda and the place where the rich folk who holiday here go shopping. There were no cheap plastic thongs, bottles of gluggy sunscreen or crappy thermometers made out of seashells and coloured pipe cleaners to be seen. Everything came with a designer label. The men wore jaunty naval gear, the women wore flowing chiffon. Every whim of the very, very rich was catered for – caviar, champagne, truffles. I was sure if I looked hard enough I'd have found the shop selling $15,000 olive trees.

Normally I would feel self-conscious in such surroundings. My clothes have the kind of labels you'd cut off. And I don't change my sunglasses every season. I wait for them to fall apart. But Marcello gave me confidence. His garish orange tones, gaudy white stripes and sparkling chrome were so over the top that they could only be the height of fashion. And purely through association I was too. I wouldn't exactly say I fitted in with the lurid outfits, bling and oversized sunglasses. Let's just say that I didn't stand out, and in Porto Cervo that was saying something.

The marina in Porto Cervo is regarded as the best in Sardinia, with berths for 650 vessels. My guidebook also promised that it would be 'awash with the ostentatious baubles of the ultra-rich' so I made my way down past the tennis club and the new 'hobbit-themed' resort development to see how the other half lived.

Summer was still a month away so there was only one yacht in port. It was like a smaller, prettier sister of the *Moby Drea* –

without the Looney Tunes decals – but by the look of it, capable of making a pretty good fist of fitting in the 1800 passengers the *Drea* was capable of carrying.

According to the guard on the security boom gate it belonged to an American industrialist. I asked if I could take a photo of Marcello in front of it and he let me through. By rights only the owners of the yachts and their guests were allowed on the marina. But he had taken a shine to Marcello and let me pass.

The owner of the yacht was standing at the back of his boat sipping on a Scotch and ice and watched with interest as I set Marcello up for the photo. His wife, an older woman the same shade of orange as Marcello, was sunning herself on the deckchair and he called out to her to have a look. She looked up, gave an uninterested nod and returned to reading her book.

'Hey, nice scooter!' he called out to me. 'How much you want for it?'

I laughed and told him I'd only just started my trip. I still had the rest of Sardinia, Sicily and the Amalfi Coast to go. Marcello wasn't for sale.

'Too bad,' he said, with a grin. 'It would have been great for getting around on this boat.' His yacht was so big I wasn't sure if he was joking or not.

★

I didn't stay in Porto Cervo. The cheapest room in town was the €180 a night suite at the Cervo Hotel, a slick resort that was part of the Sheraton chain. The receptionist assured me that the same room cost €800 in the high season but I couldn't bring myself to take it. I've never been one for mindless extravagance in the first place, but with a baby daughter on the way I felt that each euro I paid over the odds was like taking food from her mouth.

Instead I continued on to Santa Teresa di Gallura, a more modest resort town that sits on Sardinia's northernmost point 50 kilometres away. I found a comfortable single in the modest Hotel Scano for a more reasonable €30 and a café that sold *panini* for €2 a pop just around the corner. The only downside was the Alsatian on the next street over that chased me and snapped at Marcello's back wheel whenever I rode past.

There have been settlements on the site of Santa Teresa di Gallura since Roman times but it wasn't officially founded as a town until an order came from King Vittorio Emanuele in 1808. He named the town after his Austrian wife, Maria Teresa, and the Spanish watchtower out on the point dates from this period. Indeed, it is the only relic from these times. The rest of the town takes its architectural cues from the development boom of the 1950s. Having said that, Santa Teresa di Gallura is not without its charms.

Life in Santa Teresa di Gallura is centred on the main square, Piazza Vittorio Emanuele. It was here that I found cafés, bars and restaurants, as well as souvenir shops selling all kinds of items made from shells, coral and pipe cleaners. The local businesses were getting ready for summer. Shops were getting a lick of paint. Temporary wooden pergolas were being thrown up outside bars to protect patrons from the summer sun. And the final touches were being put on improvements to the square itself, including a bandstand for the summer entertainment. I found a table outside the café that most appealed to me, Bar Conti, and ordered my first *caffè macchiatto* in Sardinia.

I based myself in Santa Teresa di Gallura for the next few days and started each one of them at Bar Conti. The routine was always the same. I'd park Marcello out front on the square and order a *caffè macchiatto* at the bar. At first I waited for the barista to make the coffee and then took it outside myself. In

Italy table service can double, even triple, the price of a cup of coffee. On the second day, the young barista – who was also the waiter – indicated for me to sit outside and he'd bring the coffee for me. I'd been caught out in similar circumstances on my first trip to Italy. A waiter in Pontremoli had indicated to me to sit outside too but only because he wanted to rip me off. The barista/waiter smiled at my reticence.

'Don't worry, I will charge you the same price,' he said. He took my money there and then so I could be sure.

A few minutes later he brought me my coffee. He introduced himself as Gianni and asked if he could sit down for a chat. It was early June so business was still slow.

'It will be crazy in August,' he said with a grin. 'I'm just taking it easy now.'

Gianni was studying sociology at the university in Pisa. He was born in Santa Teresa di Gallura and came home every summer to visit his family and work at Bar Conti. He pointed at Marcello and said he was the coolest Vespa he'd ever seen.

A pretty girl walked up and gave Gianni a hug. Her name was Cristina and she was his girlfriend. She looked at Marcello and asked who the cool Vespa belonged to. Gianni nodded at me and she said '*Bella moto!*'

Gianni told Cristina I was from Australia and she looked shocked. She had seen Marcello's Livorno number plates and naturally assumed that I was from there. She asked me if I'd visited the Maddalena Islands yet. I shook my head and she looked even more shocked.

'You must go!' she said. 'Many Italians go to the Caribbean but the Maddalena are more beautiful.'

Cristina grabbed a napkin and sketched a map for me. She listed all the places I should visit – Madonnetta, Cala Lunga and Caprera – and marked her particular favourites with not one but two exclamation marks. My mobile phone beeped and she looked up expectantly as if it was important.

'It's from my wife,' I explained. 'She's pregnant and texted to tell me that the baby just kicked.'

Gianni asked me when my baby was due and I said late September. Cristina clapped her hands with delight.

'She will be a virgin!' she said. 'Just like me!'

Now it was my turn to look shocked. It had been my experience that a) all children are born virgins and b) attractive girls you have just met don't blurt out their current status on the virginity front. Cristina compounded my embarrassment by proclaiming proudly that virgins were wonderful. Gianni noticed my incomprehension and explained.

'*Astrologica*,' he explained. 'Virg-o.'

Oh, *Virgo*! My daughter was going to be a Virgo. I felt much better.

I hadn't made up my mind about what I was going to do that day. I was tossing up between visiting the prehistoric nuraghic ruins at Arzachena or catching some rays at Spiaggia Rena Bianca, the pretty beach just north of the town. Cristina had made the Maddalena Islands sound so appealing that I declared that I would visit them instead. Cristina was impressed.

'It is typical of such a Vespa,' she said. 'To be, how you say, so *carefree*.'

The ferries for La Maddalena, the main island in the Maddalena Archipelago, left from Palau, a small port 25 kilometres east of Santa Teresa di Gallura. The ferries were operated by Enermar, left every hour, took twenty minutes to reach the island and cost twice as much for tourists as they did for locals. According to my guidebook the locals were also given priority in the high season when space was at a premium.

On my way to the Enermar ticket office I spotted a man selling straw hats like the one Marco's friend Simone in Bolgheri was wearing when we visited him. They sat in piles according to size and once I found one that would fit my head snugly I happily handed over €5. I considered it a bargain for a quality item of such distinction, even more so when I wore it into the ticket office and the Enermar clerk sold me a ticket to La Maddalena, the port and sole town on Isola della Maddalena, at the residents' rate.

I didn't stay long in La Maddalena. It was just another seaside town full of bars, restaurants and shops selling postcards and overpriced film. There were a few grand buildings and a waterfront avenue lined with date palms, but the island's charm lay in the little rocky coves that decorated the coastline, each with white sand beaches and turquoise waters so bright, so perfect, that they looked like they had been touched up using Photoshop.

Most of the beaches were empty. There was not a deckchair or an umbrella to be seen. Sometimes I spotted a car abandoned in a lay-by in the scrub and a few people sunning themselves on the sand, but only rarely. These were the beaches that the Italian Tourist Board described as 'treasures to discover and behold'.

I spent the day idling around the island, ticking off the beaches and beauty points that Cristina had awarded double exclamation points and discovering other places that I felt equally deserved such acclaim. I stopped occasionally to swim at a secluded cove or simply park on the side of the road to admire the view. The roads were empty so I hung my helmet on the hook under the seat and wore my new straw hat instead.

I caught a ferry back to the mainland as the sun set, putting my helmet back on once I disembarked, and rode back to Santa Teresa di Gallura pleased that I'd taken Cristina's advice. La Maddalena was one of the most beautiful places I had ever been to and I had seen the islands in the best way possible – on the back of Marcello and in June, before the hordes of summer arrived.

And so the days passed. I visited the ruins at Arzachena and marvelled at the *tombe dei giganti*, the 'giants' tombs' built in the

Bronze Age to serve as a collective burial chamber and a place of worship. The distinctive granite stele, over 4 metres tall, stood proudly in empty fields, grand and deserted, surrounded by wildflowers.

I worked on my tan on the sands of Rena Bianca, trying to match the nut-brown tones of the Italians around me but going an alarming shade of red instead. I'd have *panini* for lunch and then splash out on a delicious seafood dish like sardines or tuna, caught fresh that day, for dinner. I'd end the day with a quick lap of the town on Marcello, finishing, as always, with a quick drag up Via Liguria where my new friend, the Alsatian, lay in wait to ambush me.

On my last evening I rode out to Capo Testa, a rocky promontory surrounded by turquoise water 3 kilometres west of Santa Teresa di Gallura. I parked Marcello on the craggy rocks and took a photo of the sun setting in the west behind him. When it finally dipped below the horizon I rode back along the winding coast road with a cool breeze in my face and the smell of wild aniseed and the sea in my nostrils.

I had my final meal in Santa Teresa di Gallura in Bar Conti. Gianni wasn't working. A sad-looking guy who I'd never seen before was on duty instead. After I finished my meal of sardines lightly grilled in lemon he asked me if I wanted coffee or dessert and I decided a profiterole would go down nicely. Marco's friend Simone had told me that they were a local delicacy in Sardinia and that if I asked for them by their local name, *palle di ciuo*, donkey's balls, I'd get an extra-generous serving.

Despite my experience on Elba with the mod, I decided to ask in Italian. My Lonely Planet phrasebook didn't have the phrase in its entirety, so I cobbled the phrase together myself and asked the waiter, in Italian, if he had donkey's balls.

The waiter's reaction was not the one I had expected. In my mind's eye he'd say 'Certainly, sir!' and place the profiteroles before me with admiration. He might even reward me with an extra one for ordering in Italian and using a fruity idiom to boot. Instead he looked shocked, then angry, and then his lower lip quivered in a manner that suggested that he did indeed have donkey's balls and thought nobody else knew.

The manager came over to see what the problem was and the waiter told him what I had said. The manager informed me that Bar Conti was a café not an abattoir and that if I wanted that sort of thing I would have to go elsewhere. I was shocked by how heated he was and gingerly pointed at the profiteroles sitting on a plate in the display cabinet.

'*Profiteroles!*' said manager, giving me a look that said 'Why didn't you just say so?' Because some berk in Bolgheri thought it would be funny to have a laugh at a poor Aussie's expense, I thought.

It was my final evening in Santa Teresa so I wandered out along the *strada pedonale panoramica*, past the watchtower, to the viewpoint marked by a white impressionistic statue of Mary. A middle-aged couple and their teenage son were out there too, looking across the straits towards Corsica. They were Australian. They were staying at the Hotel Scano too – it was cheap, you see – and I'd heard their dulcet tones in the breakfast room and in the corridors. I said hi and the wife pointed to my Qantas bag and asked me if I'd been to Australia. I told her I was *from* Australia.

'Oh, you're an *Aussie!*' she said, surprised. 'When we saw you on your Vespa we thought you were Italian.'

I've never felt prouder in my life.

CHAPTER FOUR

BOSA

PATRON SAINT: SAN GAVINO

I started my last morning in Santa Teresa di Gallura like I always did – at Bar Conti. Gianni was working and asked me if I'd like donkey's balls with my coffee. I said it was a little early for something so substantial and he laughed. Word of my strange request the night before had spread quickly through the town and Gianni said that I'd gained a certain notoriety. I was already known as the guy on the orange Vespa so there was nowhere that I could hide.

I was sad to be leaving Santa Teresa di Gallura. I'd visited at just the right time. The weather was good and the tourist hordes that descended on the town in summer were still a month or so away. I'd made good friends in Gianni and Cristina. I'd even miss the Alsatian that snapped at Marcello's back wheel. On the way out of town I took a small detour down Via Liguria just so he could chase me one last time.

I rode west along the rocky coastline to Badesi Mare, a pretty beach that Gianni recommended I visit. It was fairly developed for Sardinia. A set of three concrete stairs ran the length of the beach. I sat on them, looking out at the sparkling sea and drinking juice out of a tiny blue bottle.

I'd quickly learnt in my travels that the primary purpose of Italian fruit juice is to look good. It comes in 150 ml bottles that are just the right size to assemble on counters in a pleasing manner but a little light on thirst-quenching capabilities. The ingredients are chosen based on what looks best on the beautifully designed labels. (I can't think of any other reason to combine carrot and parsnip.) The result is a package of rare beauty. But after an hour riding along the coast in the hot June sun, I could have done with twice as much in the bottle.

The umbrellas on Badesi Mare were arranged in lines along a neat grid and were the same orange as Marcello. They had white stripes too and I took this as a sign that here, in seaside Italy, Marcello had found his spiritual home. He was the Vespa equivalent of the hairy-chested man I watched prowling the beach in nothing but a tiny pair of Speedos and a porn-star moustache.

It certainly wasn't Sophia's scene. The Vespa from my first trip was a pale coffee colour that looked perfectly at home in the straw-coloured fields of Tuscany. Her muted tones were suited to the stone cities that topped the hills there. Here she would look like an unsophisticated bumpkin, her tan too pale, her curves a little too voluptuous. Not for the first time it struck me as *destino* that she was back in Marco's workshop and I was prowling the Sardinian coast on the metal incarnation of Colin Farrell.

The colours Vespas were produced in always matched the mood of the times. The MP6, the very first Vespa, was painted in an austere shade of aviation grey that Piaggio had left after the war. The muted sky blues and coffee hues of the late fifties reflected Italy's cautious economic recovery. The vibrant reds, yellows and electric blues of the late sixties and early seventies were spray-painted manifestation of the Age of Aquarius. The colour Piaggio decided to paint their Vespas each year was as accurate a barometer of Italy's current political and economic situation as the latest issue of *La Finanzia*.

Filippo had told me that Rally 200s like Marcello were the last to be painted such a bright colour. By 1973 Italy's economy was faltering, the lira was virtually worthless and terrorist groups like the Red Brigade were committing atrocities that impacted on the life of every Italian.

'*We called it anni di piombo*,' said Filippo. 'The years of lead.'

Italy was in the doldrums and, accordingly, the Vespas produced came in colours as dull, sombre and dark as the mood of the country itself.

I was only two weeks into my journey but Marcello already matched its disposition perfectly. My first trip had been rustic *trattorias* and stone hilltop towns. This one was white sand that burnt your feet when you went to the ice-cream stall. It was hotter and sunnier and I finished each day with my skin tingling with sunburn, sunscreen and salt. Just how different this trip was from the first was confirmed at Badesi Mare when an African guy selling fake Louis Vuitton bags saw Marcello and beamed '*Bella Vespa!*' He wouldn't have given Sophia a second look.

★

My plan had been to follow the coast road from Badesi Mare to Porto Torres before heading south to Alghero, an old Spanish fishing port on the north-west coast. But just after Castelsardo I got waylaid by a set of confusing road signs and found myself lost in Sardinia's northern interior.

I have always had problems with Italian road signs.

In Tuscany the challenge was to figure out which way they were pointing. A slight difference in angle meant that you

were supposed to go in a completely different direction. Here in northern Sardinia the difficulty was finding them. They appeared suddenly and then disappeared just as quickly.

There seemed to be no rhyme or reason as to where and when they popped up. At first I thought they only appeared when you needed to turn off. Until then you just continued to travel in the same direction. But that theory was quashed when I ended up at a lime factory a couple of kilometres after I should have made a turn. In the end I gave up and trusted my instincts, and treated the odd sign that did pop up as a kind of congratulations that I'd got it right.

And so it was that I found myself high in the hills above the Asinara Gulf riding through fields of freshly harvested hay and forests of cork trees and looking for a petrol station to fill Marcello's nearly empty tank. I finally found one in a tiny village that I think was called Bulzi. It was just after 2.30 p.m. so naturally the petrol station was closed for lunch.

On my first trip through Italy by Vespa I had noted with envy the easy working hours of the country's petrol attendants. For a while I entertained the idea of retraining to become one. (I only needed to develop two skills – eating and sleeping.) Instead I concentrated on figuring out how to use the automated bowsers, equipped with mini-Bankomats that accepted notes and dispensed the appropriate amount of petrol. That day in Bulzi, I didn't have a €5 note.

The village's small *alimentari* was open so I decided to break a €20 note there. The girl behind the counter looked like a young, bored Gina Lollobrigida and stopped chewing gum for a moment when I entered to tell me that I had a '*Bella moto*'.

I wandered through the aisles looking for tomatoes, ham and bread for a roadside picnic and the girl started chewing her gum again. She gazed at Marcello through the door with a wistful look on her face that suggested she wished it was her – not me – riding him out of town. She probably didn't know where to. When you're on a bright orange scooter with white stripes it doesn't really matter. Anywhere would be better than here. The metal shop sign swinging from the awning in the breeze was the liveliest thing in town.

Of course, she might not have been thinking that. She might have simply been remembering the mind-blowing sex she'd had with her boyfriend the night before. Nevertheless, I suddenly felt like an impostor. I was buying groceries. A person with such a dangerous-looking Vespa wouldn't buy groceries. I put the tomatoes and bread back and cancelled my order for six *fette* (slices) of parma ham. I picked up a pack of Mentos – the freshmakers – instead. The girl looked at me with disdain and I knew immediately I should have bought a pack of cigarettes.

My credibility was entirely shot so I got my map from Marcello's glove box and asked the girl to point out where I was. I *was* in Bulzi. And if I continued south towards Torralba I'd be able to stop briefly at Santissima Trinità di Saccargia, visit the prehistoric ruins at *Nuraghe* Santu Antine, and still reach Alghero by dark.

I'm not sure that the young girl from Bulzi would have agreed, but that sounded like one helluva wild ride to me.

★

Santissima Trinità di Saccargia is a stunning Pisan church that sits alone in a pretty valley 15 kilometres south-east of Sassari. Built in 1116, its zebra-striped façade and belltower are all the more striking for being set in such splendid isolation. Passengers on the Sassari–Chilivani train catch a glimpse of it as they pass along a distant hill. People driving along the SS597 to Olbia might spot it if they know where to look. But otherwise there is no indication that such a stunning building is even there.

When I arrived, the church was empty except for a bride and groom and their wedding photographer. They hadn't held the service there. Like most Italians they got married in a civil ceremony at the local town hall. The Santissima Trinità di Saccargia provided a more picturesque backdrop for the photos for their mantelpiece than the office where they paid their water rates.

The bride seemed to have very particular ideas about how she should look and as she got ready for the shots, the photographer asked me where I was from. I told him I was from Australia and he said he had a brother who lived in Melbourne.

I asked the photographer if he took many photos at Santissima Trinità di Saccargia. He said most of his clients insisted on it because of the '*heestory*'. Costantino I, the *giudice* (chief judge) of Torres, ordered the church built on the spot after an angel visited and told him that his wife was pregnant. (They were on their way to San Gavino's shrine in Porto Torres to pray for a child.)

'It is good luck for new couples to visit,' explained the photographer, 'especially if they are keen to start a family.'

After a dozen or so shots, each more elaborate than the last, the bride nodded her head towards Marcello and said something to the photographer. The photos with the groom looking up at her adoringly just weren't doing it for her, apparently. She wanted to know if she could have her photo taken sitting on Marcello. Naturally, I allowed it.

My first Vespa, Sophia, had appeared in wedding photos. Her original owner, Giorgio, had bought her especially to court his girlfriend, Valentina. He loaded Sophia with every accessory available to give Valentina's father the impression that he was a man of means. And because courtship was a long process, he installed a second saddle seat so that Valentina was inclined to say yes when he finally popped the question. Sophia was decked in white ribbons and used as the wedding vehicle.

It seemed only right that my second Vespa, Marcello, should continue the tradition.

I had expected that the groom would be in the photo too, assuming a suitably supplicant position, but when he headed towards Marcello the bride shooed him away. She was flying solo on this one and straddled the seat brusquely, a whitewash of meringue spilling either side. The photographer suggested she lean forward to give the impression of speed and trailed her veil behind her. It looked like the bride was making a getaway. And Marcello was the wanton Lothario facilitating it.

I know you shouldn't read too much into wedding photos. The one on the mantelpiece from our wedding day features me and Sally planting a coconut. (According to local Cook Island tradition the eight leaves that sprang from the nut meant that we were going to have eight children!) But the shot of the bride on Marcello was laden with so much subtext that I felt embarrassed for the groom. I stepped up to take a photo myself anyway – for all its subtext it was still a cool shot – but the groom gave me a look that suggested it wouldn't be a good idea. He'd only been married for an hour and his bride had already forgotten her vow about forsaking all others.

I left the newlyweds to squabble and make up and headed south along the SS131 to Torralba and *Nuraghe* Santu Antine. I was in the Valle dei Nuraghi now, a fertile valley of vineyards and wheat farms with a high concentration of ruins from the island's Nuraghic period. The Nuraghi were a society of builders, metallurgists, shepherds, farmers and fishermen and their culture was the predominant one in Sardinia from 1800 BC until the Phoenicians and Carthaginians started sniffing around in 900 BC.

Nuraghic settlements were always set around a *nuraghe*, a distinctive circular tower made from the square basalt blocks that gave the culture its name. The *nuraghe* at Santu Antine is considered the most technically perfect of all the *nuraghi* on Sardinia, set in a triangular bastion with smaller towers on each point. Archaeological finds suggest that it might have been a royal palace. It sits alone now, but in its heyday it would have been surrounded by the hundreds of homes, stables and workshops of a thriving community.

The car park at *Nuraghe* Santu Antine was open to the baking afternoon sun, so I parked Marcello beside a clump of bicycles under a grand ash tree opposite the ticket office. The woman at the counter refused to sell me a ticket until I moved Marcello.

'*Privato!*' she said, pointing her finger angrily at the sign attached to the rope that cordoned off the space. I pointed to the bicycles and argued that if they could park there so could I. She wagged her finger and said 'No!'

The woman was on the far side of her fifties and had a sour, wrinkled countenance that suggested she'd had a hard, unhappy life. Still, her attitude surprised me. Everywhere else on this trip people had cut me slack because of Marcello. At a café in Torralba just half an hour before, the manager had been so impressed with my Vespa that he gave me a free beer and a complimentary plate of salami. This woman was giving me a hard time.

I tried smooth-talking her. A Vespa would only take up a *little* more space, it wasn't that different from a bicycle. I had important things in the bag on the rack, I'd feel so much safer knowing that she was watching them. None of it worked. If anything, my schmoozing only made her more steadfast in her refusal.

I decided that she just didn't like my type. Well, the type she assumed I was. She'd spotted Marcello – aggressive, conspicuous and cocksure – and assumed I was like that too. I argued that while Marcello looked like he was always getting good girls pregnant it didn't necessarily follow that I was of the same disposition. It fell on deaf ears.

I told the woman that she was breaking my balls. (I think 'Che rottura di palle!' were the exact words I used.) It was a phrase that Marco and Filippo had assured me was in wide use in Sardinia and especially effective when combined with a series of low, suggestive hand movements. I had wanted to say 'Che rottura di palle di ciuo' – you're breaking my donkey balls – but in the heat of the moment the exact phrase escaped me. It didn't matter anyway. She still insisted I move Marcello before she sold me the €3 ticket. My outburst had only confirmed her initial assessment of me.

I moved Marcello to the main car park and left him exposed in the broiling late-afternoon sun. I told the ticket woman that if anything got stolen while I was wandering around the ruins I was holding her personally responsible. She gave me a look that suggested she couldn't care less.

It got worse when I reached the *nuraghe*. At 17 metres high and 15 metres in diameter it was impressive enough. But it was cordoned off by red tape, and a large blue crane was pulling it apart. I had hoped to clamber to the terrace on top where my guidebook said I'd be able see all the other major *nuraghi* in the valley. Nor would I be able to wander through the maze of passageways and confirm that, yes, *Nuraghe* Santu Antine was indeed one of the few 'corridor' and 'tholos' *nuraghi* ever made. (Corridor *nuraghi* lean on big rocks that become part of the building; tholos ones are cone-shaped with circular rooms.)

Naturally, I blamed the old bat at the ticket office. She could have warned me that the *nuraghe* was under (re)construction or at least given me a discount on the entrance price. Instead, as I left, she aped my hand signals from before to suggest that I was the one breaking her balls. I didn't doubt for a moment that she had them.

When Alghero was captured by the Spanish in 1353 they dispersed the local population to nearby Villanova and replaced them with Catalan settlers. The city walls were strengthened with ramparts and towers. Date palms were planted along the avenues. And new immigrants traded directly with Catalonia rather than other parts of the island. The Hispanicisation was so complete that Alghero became known as Barcelonetta – Little Barcelona. It retains much of that Catalan character today.

I approached Alghero from the hills in the east just as evening fell. I would suggest that there is no better time to catch first sight of the town. The western sky was streaked orange and pink and the thick walls surrounding the old part of town glowed golden as the lights that illuminated them came on for the night. The air was crisp and clean and I had the smell of the sea in my nostrils again. The only downside were the bugs that were more abundant this time of day and hit me with a greater velocity on Marcello than they ever did on Sophia.

I'd hoped to stay in the San Francesco, a former convent that is the only lodge in the walled city. But it was full and I had to stay in a multistorey hotel a couple of blocks away from the old part of town. It looked like something the Soviets might have thrown up and the young guy on the counter displayed all

the hallmarks of the Russian approach to customer service. He worked through the hordes of passengers that had just arrived on a Ryanair flight with a mixture of such boredom and disdain that I suspected he may have been related to the ticket seller at *Nuraghe* Santu Antine. I said I'd like a single room for the night and he tossed me a key for a room on the seventh floor.

'The lift is not working,' he said in a bored monotone. 'You'll have to take the stairs.'

I asked if there was anywhere I could park and he said there was a garage around the corner that cost €15 a day. He asked where my vehicle was now and I pointed to Marcello sitting outside on the pavement.

'Wow! What a Vespa!' he said with an enthusiasm I didn't think he was capable of. Then he shook my hand heartily and introduced himself as Cliff.

'I know, weird name for an Italian,' he said when I raised my eyebrows. 'My mum was a big Cliff Richard fan.' At least that explained the grumpiness.

Cliff closed the check-in counter and took me to the garage personally. He left behind a gaggle of Brits who had arrived late because Ryanair had lost their bags, but he was more interested in how fast Marcello was capable of going and how much he'd cost me.

After talking to the attendant on duty Cliff said I could keep Marcello there for free. He had a parking space there as part of his employment package and he wasn't using it. I asked him to let me pay him something but he wouldn't have it.

'A Vespa like this one demands special treatment,' he insisted.

Seemingly the owner of such a Vespa deserved special treatment too. When we got back to the hotel Cliff upgraded me to a double – he said he'd tell the manager there was a problem with the plumbing in my original single – and got the bellboy to carry my bag up to my room.

I ended up staying in Alghero for three days. I was particularly taken by the old town, a jumble of cobbled lanes, stone buildings and terracotta roofs. I'd wander down Via Carlo Alberto for a coffee and pastry in one of the cafés dotted among the tourist shops and bars. Then I'd duck down a lane that I'd chosen at random, deliberately getting lost and then stumbling upon a hidden church or piazza or a dog curled up asleep on a cobbled path.

The Spanish influence was never far away here. Piazzas were called *plaça*. Churches were *iglesia* not *chiesa*. And on most streets signs the word *carre* was used instead of *via*. One day I came upon a pair of old Catalan men with walking sticks and flat caps sitting on a step talking. They watched with curiosity as I passed.

I'd finish my days exploring the old town with a quick lap of the path between the city walls and the sea. It had just been upgraded by the city council. There were park benches and ornate gas lamp-posts dotted along it at regular intervals. It was a popular spot with locals for the evening *passeggiata* (promenade), especially as the sun was setting directly in front in the west. More often than not I'd end up in one of the bars that overlooked the port, sipping on an ice cold beer as lines of colourful fishing boats jostled against each other below.

Alghero also proved a perfect base for seeing sights slightly further afield. In quick succession I was able to tick off the imposing mountaintop town of Monteleone Rocca Doria; Sardinia's only natural lake, Lago di Baratz; and another *nuraghe*, this time at Palmavera. I even dropped by Fertilia, a land reclamation project initiated by Mussolini in the 1930s. He hoped the name would suggest agricultural abundance but the project quickly fell into a torpid decline. A few art deco monuments act as a reminder of the town's initial grand designs.

If Cliff was on duty when I stepped out for the day he would call me over and give me advice on the best things to do and see. When I told him I was planning to catch a boat out to Grotta di Nettuno, a series of marine caves set in the cliffs out on Capo Caccia, he suggested I ride Marcello instead.

'The boat will be full of package tourists,' he said. 'And the captain will rush you there and back. On your Vespa you can take your time. The bay at Porto Conte is one of the most beautiful places in Sardinia. On a boat you will hardly see it.'

I asked him which was the best beach in the area and he told me about a secret place near Capo Marargiu, just off the spectacular coast road that led south towards Bosa.

'It's in the reserve for griffon vultures,' he said. 'You're not supposed to go there but if you go down this track no one will know.' Apparently the track was made by Gladio, a secret, ultra-right-wing paramilitary group that used the peninsula as a training ground in the eighties.

Alghero is famous for its fish and seafood. And the Catalan influence has created a distinct *cucina algherese* – sea-urchin mousse anyone? But the abundance of tourists has created a lot of rather ordinary establishments with uninspiring set menus and rough and ready wine lists. Luckily Cliff's suggestions for dining out were as inspired as his recommended day trips.

'You should avoid any restaurants in the old city,' he told me one evening. 'They are for tourists. The prices are high and the quality is low.' He suggested a place without a name a block from the hotel where an old lady in a black shawl cooked the best seafood paella I have ever eaten.

On my final evening in Alghero I ate in a small café just outside the walls. Cliff hadn't recommended it. In fact it bore all the hallmarks of an establishment he'd suggest I avoid. My *fritto misto* tasted more like refried fish than simply fried fish and my beer cost three times the price of the one I'd enjoyed at the no-name restaurant. But I had a seat outside with a spectacular view of the sea and the sun as it set right in front of me.

On the way back to the hotel I passed a trendy baby clothes store. It was a sharp reminder that I was about to become a father. I contemplated buying the pretty cardigan with a daisy embroidered on it in the window to assuage my guilt but called Sally instead. She asked how my trip was going and I said OK. It didn't feel right to tell her the truth. That it was *fan-bloody-tastic*.

I left Alghero the next day along a wide road lined by date palms. It headed south towards Bosa, my next destination, but on the outskirts of town I reached a roundabout that offered up two different routes. I could turn right and go along the coast. Or turn left and go inland through the mountains. I'd already travelled three-quarters of the way along the coast route when I went to the beach in the vulture sanctuary, so I turned left and headed up into the mountains.

The road cut through a series of lemon orchards before winding its way up the face of the mountain in a series of tight switchbacks. Packs of motorcyclists dressed in heavy leathers gathered here, taking turns to race up the mountain, their bikes screaming like banshees. They leaned heavily into the corners, scraping their knee pads on the road, squeezing every ounce of power out of their bikes.

The next rider to set off saw me approach and indicated for me to go instead. I twisted the throttle as far as I could and tore up the hill, leaning into the corners as steeply as I could with a heavy motorcycle bag on the back. For a Vespa, Marcello made pretty good time. But it wasn't long before the motorcyclist who had waited for me was at the top of the hill beside me. I took heart from the fact that if I'd been on Sophia he'd still be waiting.

Once the motorcyclists got to the top of the mountain they turned around and raced back again. I had the road that ran along the plateau at the top of the mountain all to myself.

The road was so empty and deserted that the cow pats that decorated it were fully formed and free of tyre tracks. The fields here were awash with wildflowers and their heady scent hung in the air. I rode along through a cascade of colour with the sun on my back, as happy and content as I had ever been.

I'd been riding along the plateau for close to forty minutes when I heard a funny clanking noise. Not being mechanically minded I immediately suspected that something was wrong with Marcello. I pulled to the side of the road, convinced that the piston was shot or a wheel bearing had blown, but when I stopped and killed the engine the clanking continued. Bizarrely, it was louder than ever. I looked around, scratched my head in the manner of a character in a slapstick movie, and finally spotted a cow standing in a field with a bell around its neck.

I didn't set off again immediately. I sat on a low stone wall and soaked up the tranquillity. The mountains rose at my back, crowned in mist. The sea glittered in front of me. A breeze floated by carrying the scent of the wildflowers, the buzz of bees and the tweet of birds. And every now and then the cow bell added its syncopated charm to the tune. It was lovely.

The final stretch of road that wound down the mountain into Bosa was dotted with stone shepherds' huts, built centuries ago for shepherds who'd brought their sheep here to graze. They were still used. Occasionally I'd spot a young boy sitting in the shade of one, watching his flock nibble on grass nearby. They all had the same look on their faces when I passed on a bright orange Vespa. The look we'll all have on our faces when the Martians finally arrive.

Bosa sits 3 kilometres inland on the banks of the Temo River, Sardinia's only navigable river of any length. It is encircled by mountains and its tight, narrow streets press against a hill crowned by the atmospheric ruins of Malaspina Castle. Washing hangs from lines strung across the street. The shops sell useful things like lightbulbs and screwdrivers rather than tourist tat. And the wrought-iron balconies, iron coach lamps and art deco typefaces on illuminated signs give the town a distinctly 1920s feel. I decided immediately that I liked it.

I found a room in an *agriturismo* on a dirt road on the outskirts of town, out near San Pietro, an old cathedral built on the site of an early Christian necropolis. The *agriturismo* was set on an organic farm, in a low adobe building painted the same orange as Marcello.

I sat in the bright dining room looking out over the mountains through French doors while an old lady in a shawl checked me in. There were certificates of bio-ecological adherence on the wall, a coat of arms for the Bosa Commune 1589–1982, and a tapestry depicting a meeting of nobles at the castle in 1848. All the nobles had sideburns. The really important ones had moustaches too.

The old lady copied the details from my passport into a ledger so old and battered it could have been from the meeting of nobles. When she got to the last column she looked up and asked if I was alone.

'*Solo?*' she repeated, incredulously. She looked at the bike and then at me as if wanting to know how someone on such a nice bike could be alone.

My room had a veranda that looked directly across fields full of organically raised tomato vines and the rocky mountains beyond. I spent the afternoon there, soaking up the view and drinking cold water that the old lady brought to me periodically. Just after 4 p.m. a German couple with severe haircuts arrived driving a Golf and asked if they could have a room. They'd spotted Marcello – and the crash helmet beside me – and figured I was the manager because both the *agriturismo* and my Vespa were the same colour. I said that was a scary thought.

'It would have been scary if you had been orange too,' said the one with the moustache. Who says the Germans don't have a sense of humour?

That night I decided to leave Marcello at the *agriturismo* and walk the 2 kilometres into town. It was a balmy evening and the buildings and palm trees that lined the river looked particularly lovely. With twilight, a calm descended on the town and the only sounds I heard were the clunks and scrapes of the local fishermen tidying up their boats after a day's fishing.

I found a tiny restaurant in an alley up near the castle called Borgo Sant'Ignazio. It had yellow walls and yellow tablecloths and old black and white photos of Bosa on the wall. I was the only person there but it still took over an hour for them to serve me my meal. I passed the time taking photos of myself on my digital camera and trying to guess exactly what the loud clanking noises I could hear had to do with the preparation of my meal. Thankfully the suckling pig stew was worth the wait.

I finished the meal with *seadas*, a typical Sardinian dessert. It was a square flat pastry stuffed with cheese and smothered in honey. It wasn't until I bit into it that I realised with alarm that there was orange zest in the middle with the cheese. My first reaction was 'Wait a minute, there's something wrong here.' Then the cheese kicked in and then the honey and somehow it worked.

I walked back to the *agriturismo* satiated and content. I stopped beside a stone wall just past the river and listened to the sheep bells. It was a magical sound, made doubly so by the smells that assaulted me from the dark.

The smell of aniseed was particularly intense. It reminded me of my childhood growing up on the outskirts of Sydney. Whenever we drove into Liverpool we'd spot old women in black shawls and men in flat caps on the side of the road picking what we thought were weeds. Dad told us they were picking aniseed to use in cooking and for drinks. It finally struck me that they were probably Sardinian migrants.

My eyes adjusted to the dark and I spotted an old couple walking ahead of me. They were out for their evening constitutional. When I caught up with them they smiled and wished me a *buonanotte*, nodding at a man a further 200 metres down the road having an argument with a stone wall.

I figured the man was either mad or drunk. There aren't too many other reasons for arguing with an inanimate object. By the time I reached him, the wall's seeming indifference had made him incandescent with rage. He yelled. He spat. He cursed. And, in a final fit of pique, he whipped out his penis and pissed against the wall. When that didn't have the desired effect he slumped against the wall and let out a primal howl of defeat.

His howl made the dog across the road start barking. That in turn set off another dog up the road and then another. Soon the whole valley was echoing with the barking of dogs and the incoherent howling of a madman/drunk.

It struck me that I should get off the Vespa more often and just watch. Italy always puts on a good show.

CHAPTER FIVE

MONTE ORTOBENE

PATRON SAINT: CRISTO REDENTORE

Before I could leave Bosa for the mountains of Sardinia's rugged interior I had to get a key cut. It was the key that worked both the steering lock and glove box. I'd bent it trying to force open the glove box when the locking mechanism jammed on one of the holy fridge magnets I'd stuck on the inside of the lid. Now the serrated part of the key was bent at an awkward angle and a crack in the metal was working its way to the edge. It was the only key I had and it was in danger of breaking in two.

Vespas weren't built with glove boxes until 1963. It was one of the most welcome 'improvements' Marcello had over the more mature Sophia. With careful consideration I found I could fit in a 1-litre container of oil, the special cup for measuring the mix, a small toolkit comprising a spanner and a spark plug shifter, a rag to wipe up any oil I spilled, a plastic wallet holding all of Marcello's paperwork, a map, a guidebook and a 750 ml bottle of water. And up until now there had also been room on the inside of the lid for half a dozen magnetic holy folk. The

Madonna del Mare I'd picked up at Bosa's rococo cathedral was obviously a saint too far.

The old lady who ran the *agriturismo* told me that I could get a new key cut at a small hardware store in the centre of Bosa. It was on a corner towards the edge of town where the apartment blocks huddled up against the mountains. It was only 7.30 in the morning but the pavement outside the store was cluttered with baths and basins and a wheelbarrow loaded high with bags of cement. It could have been a building supplies shop anywhere in the world except there was a gaggle of three-wheeled *Apes* parked haphazardly outside instead of the customary white vans or utes.

Apes (pronounced *Ah*-peys) are small, three-wheeled commercial vehicles with a cabin up front and a cargo tray at the back. Based originally on Vespas, they are compact and versatile with low fuel consumption and an excellent carrying capacity. (The latest model can carry up to 900 kilos.) As Piaggio like to say, the '*Ape* is to Vespa as ox is to horse'.

Their size and manoeuvrability make them perfect for negotiating the tight cobbled streets of Italian towns. They can nip along lanes too narrow for normal vehicles and squeeze through passageways to areas usually reached only by foot. *Ape* means 'bee' in Italian and in any town on any day you'll see dozens of them buzzing around, busy as the proverbial.

The first *Ape* was produced by Piaggio in 1947. According to Corradino D'Ascanio, the man who designed the original Vespa and subsequently the *Ape*, it was an attempt to provide a 'means of post-war utilitarian locomotion'. It was an instant hit with businesses, from one-man outfits to large corporations. Every one of them had their business name spray-painted on the back, creating an animated series of mobile advertising hoardings.

Social commentators at the time claimed that *Apes* gave Italian industry 'dignity' and facilitated the 'flowering of small-scale entrepreneurship in towns and in the countryside'. Local councils were not unaware of the benefits *Apes* offered either. One of the most popular exhibits at the Vespa museum in Pontedera is a bright red *Ape* kitted out as a fire engine, complete with a rather short ladder on the back.

The local tradesmen of Bosa had stocked up on the supplies they needed for the day and were gathered around a beat-up espresso machine at the back of the store. They joked and gossiped and drank thick black coffee from chipped espresso cups stained with age and neglect. I asked which one was the manager and they pointed to the only man who wasn't wearing overalls splattered with paint or grime.

I'd spent the night before composing a complicated phrase in Italian explaining what had happened to the key and absolving myself of any blame. But when the moment came to deliver it I simply held out my right hand with the damaged key resting on it. The tradesmen let out a collective gasp as if I had just unveiled a holy relic.

The reverential silence only lasted a second. Soon each tradesman was giving me his opinion on how it should be fixed. The plumbers thought the key should be heated first with oxyacetylene to make it more pliable. The carpenters favoured the more brutal approach of just whacking it with a hammer. Each opinion was expressed at the same time, at the same volume (loudly), and accompanied by florid hand movements that suggested that if the key wasn't cut *exactly* the way they suggested then life on earth as we knew it was *over*!

The manager sided with the carpenters and proceeded to hammer the key flat with a mallet. The carpenters were still high-fiving each other when he placed it in the key-cutting machine. Their celebrations proved premature. The first key he cut didn't work. Neither did the second. When the third key cut failed, the debate on what should be done was re-ignited.

Now things got really heated. The plumbers cast doubt on the parentage of the carpenters' offspring. And the carpenters taunted the plumbers about jobs that they'd done that hadn't turned out quite right. Then one of the carpenters argued that it was the execution of the idea that was the problem, not the idea itself, and the manager threw down the keys in a huff. He stormed off to his office saying they were all *figli di puttana* (sons of whores) and if they thought they could do a better job they were welcome to do it themselves. I was the only one who hadn't said anything and it was my keys that were in danger of not getting cut.

One of the older plumbers, a guy with black hair greying at the temples, took my original key and beckoned for me to follow. He heated it with an oxyacetylene set in the back of his *Ape* and then tapped the key into shape from the top, rather than lying it on its side. Then he returned to the shop and fired up the key-cutting machine like he'd been cutting keys his whole life.

Once the machine had finished cutting the key the plumber took it from the machine, rasped it with a file and then handed it to me with a wink. I went outside and, with a posse of tradesmen as my witnesses, tried the key in the glove box. It worked first time. I was slapped on the back, called a lucky *figlio di puttana* and dragged back inside for a celebratory espresso.

*

The road east to Nuoro climbed steeply out of Bosa and I soon found myself riding along a high plateau of golden fields. The fields were dotted with mauve and pink wildflowers and stretched to a series of dark low hills in the distance. Even by Sardinian standards it felt lonely and still. The only sign of life was the odd crumbling villa, boarded up and empty, and the flocks of long-haired sheep that used them for shelter.

I stopped for petrol at Macomer. It was a nondescript agricultural town 30 kilometres east of Bosa. I would have pushed on for Nuoro immediately afterwards but as I was filling the tank a boisterous man wearing a bright pink shirt and a camouflage vest and riding a hybrid moped/bicycle called a Ciao pulled up beside me. He introduced himself as Marcello and declared that my Vespa was the most magnificent bike he had ever seen. When I told him that it was called Marcello too, his eyes lit up.

'No!' he said in disbelief. 'We must have a drink!' After I paid for the petrol he jumped back on his Ciao and wobbled off, beckoning for me to follow.

It was only just after 10 a.m. so I assumed that we were going to a café for an espresso. Marcello had other ideas. He parked his Ciao on the footpath outside a seedy-looking bar and indicated for me to do the same.

'Not so far to stumble,' he said.

As we entered the bar I asked him if they sold coffee and he gave me a look of mock disgust.

'Not café,' he said with a grin. *'Birra!'*

The bar was dark and dingy and I immediately recognised it as the kind of place where direct eye contact with fellow patrons should be avoided at all costs. The tables were scratched with graffiti, the felt on the pool table was worn and the jukebox wore an out-of-order sign after being kicked one too many times. Thankfully most of the patrons were already slumped on their tables so evading their line of vision was easier than it might otherwise have been.

Marcello, the human, was a lively companion. In between knocking back his beer in record time he told me he was the gardener at the local children's park, had three Italian 'wives' (one in Florence, one in Rimini and one in an unspecified location in Sardinia) and spent every winter 'working' in Egypt. He had a wife in Egypt too, he said, but it was hard to remain faithful to her because she kept offering him her cousins. I began to suspect that the word 'wife' meant something different to Marcello than it did to me.

The barman tried to follow our conversation in English but in the end asked Marcello in Italian who I was and what was I doing in Macomer. I heard the words *'Australiano'* and *'bella Vespa'* and saw Marcello point to my bike parked outside. The barman slid across two beers with an approving nod.

'To Marcello!' said Marcello with a grin.

'To Marcello!' I replied, not sure which Marcello – human or Vespa – I was toasting.

I should point out that drinking beer at 10 a.m. is not something I normally do. And it's probably not something that an expectant father should do, especially when that expectant father still has another 50 kilometres of treacherous mountain roads to negotiate. But Marcello was such an affable chap it seemed churlish to decline. He told me he really wasn't a heavy drinker anyway. If he'd been working that day he would have stopped after two. The trouble was I wasn't sure if he meant two drinks or 2 p.m.

Marcello had an 'appointment' at 11 with another 'girlfriend' so I was able to leave the bar relatively sober. Before he disappeared he insisted on showing me the way to a 'scenic' route to Nuoro that would take me past the Byzantine chapel of Santa Sabina and the small *nuraghe* beside it. He stopped when we reached the crossroad, pulled two small stones from his pocket, and asked me if I'd like to buy a genuine nuraghic souvenir.

'*Genuine*,' he said. 'Not imitation.'

Now I didn't know what the official line was in Sardinia on selling antiquities but I was sure it didn't sanction scruffy gardeners selling the island's heritage to equally scruffy Aussies on Vespas. I declined the offer and Marcello shrugged as if it was my loss. Then he cheerfully kick-started the Ciao and wobbled off back towards Macomer.

'Ciao, Marcello!' he called out over his shoulder. 'You are beautiful!'

Somehow he managed to stay in a relatively straight line and on the right side of the road. But only after narrowly avoiding an *Ape* coming in the opposite direction.

I arrived in Nuoro just in time for lunch. It was a small provincial town with neat buildings and people going about their business at a leisurely Sardinian pace. The old town was neat and compact and dotted with a few Fascist-era buildings that managed to complement the older buildings rather than overwhelm them. The newer part of town was clean and functional with buildings that were neither extraordinary nor offensive. The streets were lined with trees and sleepy cafés. Indeed the only thing that set Nuoro apart from any other Italian town of its size was its setting. Monte (Mount) Ortobene sits on its north-east corner, and beyond that the Sopramonte massif, a sheer wall of granite that looked positively otherworldly.

I'd wanted to visit Nuoro ever since I'd seen photos of the Sagra del Redentore. It is an annual procession held every August where people from all over the region dust off their traditional costumes and make their way to the huge bronze statue of Cristo Redentore (Christ the Redeemer) that tops Monte Ortobene. It is ostensibly a religious festival, but in reality is imbued with all kinds of pagan rites that date back to the times of Dionysus.

I was particularly taken by the photos of the *boes*, the evil-looking characters wearing shaggy sheepskin coats and wooden ram masks with long pointy horns. They came from the wild Barbagia region to the south and their blank, soulless expressions gave the impression that they were off to a Wicker Man-style human sacrifice. I wouldn't get to see the procession – it was still only June – but I figured that a town that hosted such an event just had to be interesting.

Other authors have not shared my enthusiasm. When D.H. Lawrence arrived in Nuoro he wrote that he felt as though he'd reached the end of the world. Local author Salvatore Satta wrote that Nuoro was 'nothing but a perch for the crows'. The only writer with a nice word to say about the place was the Nobel prizewinning author Grazia Deledda. She spent her life writing about the day-to-day life of Nuoro's 'simple folk' and was rewarded with literature's most sought-after prize in 1926.

I bought some bread, ham and tomatoes from a small *alimentari* near the railway station and made my way to Monte Ortobene.

It rose suddenly from behind the north-east corner of the town and my goal was to have a picnic beside Cristo Redentore. I raced towards it along a steep, winding road that snaked its way up through a forest of myrtle and pine, and within twenty minutes I was there. If I'd been on Sophia I wouldn't have made it to the top before sunset.

The 7-metre tall bronze statue was erected in 1901 by Vincenzo Jerace to act as a focal point for the Sagra del Redentore procession. It sits near the top of the mountain at 995 metres and boasts stunning views across a forest of trees and rocky outcrops to the terracotta roofs of Nuoro below.

The Cristo Redentore is popular with pilgrims throughout the year, not just during the Sagra del Redentore. When I arrived, an old lady in a black shawl was placing a trinket at the base of the statue. Then she rubbed Christ's left big toe. She wasn't the first. Christ's feet were covered with photos, beads and flowers and his toe had been rubbed into a golden sheen.

My guidebook was rather poetic in its description of the statue. It said that it 'stands poised in an attitude of swirling motion over the immense void'. When I stood below it I could kind of see what the writer meant. Christ's metallic robe did appear to be billowing in the breeze. But a less generous soul would say that Christ the Redeemer looked like he had tripped on a tree root and his hand was outstretched not in an inclusive gesture of forgiveness, but rather to break an undignified landing on the buildings of Nuoro nestled below.

I pondered the theological implications of deities having accidents as I rode back down the mountain to a B&B that I'd spotted on the way up. It was called Casa Solotti and sat perched among a stand of trees looking out across the Marreri Valley. I'd been surprised to see a family home on the mountain – I was under the impression that it was a designated national park – but the idea of staying here, in the wilderness, appealed to me immensely.

Casa Solotti was owned by Mario Zizi. He had dark foppish hair and movie-star good looks and he greeted me as I reached the end of his driveway. He was quite taken by Marcello and circled him in admiration.

'*Bella Vespa!*' he said with a smile. 'I saw you ride past before and hoped you would stop.'

Before I got the chance to ask Mario if he had any rooms available and how much they cost, he set off down a narrow path that ran between a flowering hedge and beckoned for me to follow. It led to the basement under the house and for one moment I feared that perhaps this would be my room for the night. Once my eyes had adjusted to the murky light I noticed a 1964 GS peeking out from underneath a tarpaulin. Mario was restoring it in his spare time. By the looks of it, he was close to finishing it.

'The president of Vespa Club Italy stayed here and told me it will be worth €4000,' Mario said proudly. 'He sent me a list of original parts to use.'

Quite by chance I had stumbled upon a Vespa-loving household. Mario asked me if someone had told me that he was a Vespa aficionado. Perhaps the president of Vespa Club Italy, who he assumed I knew by name. I shook my head and told him that my original plan was to stay in a hotel down in the town. He became convinced that it was *destino* – destiny – that I had found his home and saw quite clearly in this the handiwork of a higher being.

Mario also believed Vespas had human emotions.

'If it is raining my Vespa won't start,' he said by way of proof. 'If it is sunny it starts first time.'

It was something that had crossed my mind at times with both Sophia and Marcello. I remembered many a morning on my first trip when Sophia refused to start because it was too cold. And the way Marcello attacked mountain roads with gusto reminded me of an ageing Lothario trying to prove to the young bloods that he still had it. But I had kept those thoughts to myself, fearful that I might be locked up if I expressed them out loud.

As a fellow Vespa rider I was given the best room in the house, a grand room on the second floor with an attached bathroom and a balcony that afforded stunning views across a deep valley to the Sa Serra plateau and Monti di Alà in the distance. It had a stone floor and was decorated with rustic furniture. There were old lithographic prints of people wearing local traditional costumes on the walls and a rickety wooden rocking chair in the corner. As I threw myself on the huge soft bed it struck me that the tradesmen in Bosa were right. I *was* a lucky *figlio di puttana*.

After I'd freshened up I joined Mario for a glass of wine in the sitting room. I sat on one of the low wooden sofas while he got wine to celebrate destiny bringing me to his house. It was a *Nuraghe* Sella e Mosca – 'Typical of the region,' said Mario – and it was rather good.

The sitting room was decorated in an eclectic ethnic fashion. The cushions on the sofa were covered in batik from Indonesia. A wooden bust from Ethiopia sat on a side table with a mosaic top from Morocco. A rug from Turkey lay on a typically Italian floor of terracotta tiles. It was all held together by a simple red and black painting that hung over the fireplace. It was an impressionistic interpretation of a *boe*, one of the ram men I had been so taken with, and it had been painted by Mario's wife.

Mario also had an extensive collection of masks. They came from Japan, Africa and Sardinia. Some of the masks I assumed were African were in fact from Sardinia, a reminder that the island is as close to Africa as it is to Italy.

'Masks are a very important part of Sardinian life,' explained Mario. 'They allow the ordinary peasant to aspire to something more mystical and extraordinary than their dreary, everyday life.'

Mario was obviously a man of good taste and intellect. His bookcase groaned under heavy tomes on nuraghic history, Sardinian customs and corruption under the presidency of Berlusconi. Over one glass of wine he'd already given me a précis of the role of masks in Sardinian society and told me that Nuoro was known as the Sardinian Athens because of all the artists and writers that have lived there, including the authors Grazia Deledda and Salvatore Satta, the sculptor Francesco Ciusa, and the artists Antonio Ballero and Giovanni Nonnis.

I should have used my time in the company of such an intelligent and articulate host to discuss the issues that had been troubling me on this trip. Not just the theological dilemma over whether gods could fall over, but more typically Sardinian concerns – like what exactly was a *nuraghe*? And why did the name refer to both the buildings and the people?

Instead my eye was drawn to a photo on the mantelpiece. It featured a very young Mario in football gear standing next to another young player who looked a lot like Gianfranco Zola, the ex-Italy and Chelsea footballer. Mario saw me looking and confirmed that it was Zola.

'He was always short,' he said with a smile.

Zola was born in Oliena, a small town sprawled along the side of Monte Corrasi, 12 kilometres southeast of Nuoro. It is best known for its colourful Easter celebrations and its wine, a dark drink that turns lighter and stronger over the years. As teenagers, Mario and Zola played football together at Nuoro. Zola went on to fame and fortune. He was currently finishing his career in Cagliari, a promise he made in his final year at Chelsea. Even Roman Abramovich's millions couldn't change his mind, which tells you much about the kind of man he is.

I asked Mario if he had been a good footballer and he shrugged.

'At fourteen I was a promising player,' he said enigmatically.

I asked what went wrong. Was it an injury that cut his career short? Or was it wine, women and song? He just shrugged again, this time a little sadly. I think I must have touched a raw nerve because he put down his glass and went down to the basement to tinker with his Vespa. I went to my room to rest. I'd spent the day drinking – coffee with the tradesmen, beer with Marcello, now wine with Mario – and I needed a break.

That night I ate at Ciusa, a restaurant at the foot of Monte Ortobene named after the local sculptor Francesco Ciusa. Mario made a reservation for me especially. It was the best restaurant in Nuoro, he said, and the owner would appreciate such a *bella Vespa*.

I think Mario must have phoned them when I set off because I was met at the door by a guard of honour that included the manager, the maître d' and the chef. I was guided to the best table in the house – a setting for two just outside the door with stunning views back across the granite church (where Grazia Deledda lay in rest) to the brooding Monte Ortobene. A complimentary glass of Oliena wine and a plate of mixed antipasto were laid before me to enjoy while I chose what I wanted to eat.

Mario had given me strict instructions on what to order. He and his wife were regular visitors to Ciusa and had sampled nearly everything. He described each meal on the menu from memory before deciding on aut *delize di mare troffuette acca Ciusa* as a starter and *filetto al Cannonau* for main.

'If you order these things you will have a wonderful meal,' he said.

I noted a tone of envy in his voice and asked him if he wanted to join me. For a moment I thought he was going to accept but he didn't. His wife was visiting family in Cagliari and he was expecting a call from her that night. She would be upset if he went to their favourite restaurant without her.

When the waiter came, I showed him the suggestions that Mario had written down. He nodded and said I had made a very wise choice. The *filetto al Cannonau*, he said, was excellent.

Filetto al Cannonau was not on the menu. It was a house specialty that only regulars the chef liked knew about. Basically it was a fine fillet of beef braised in a Cannonau wine sauce and I swear Mario started drooling when he suggested it. I'd never ordered off the menu before. I'd never even considered it an option. It made me feel very sophisticated.

After the meal I sat looking back across Monte Ortobene and sipping an espresso, as content with life as I had ever been. I texted Sally a brief outline of my day – the key drama, meeting Marcello, the Vespa-loving B&B, the amazing meal I'd just devoured – and surprised myself with how much had happened to me. Sally replied that the baby was kicking, the thought of such rich food turned her stomach and that, generally speaking, she was FVB. (Feeling very bad.)

Two of the kitchen-hands came outside to have a cigarette, using their nicotine habit as an excuse to check out Marcello. They walked around him, peering at the leg shields and the side panels, trying to figure out what model he was. The Rally 200 badge above the tail-light was covered by the luggage rack I'd fitted so they were left scratching their heads. I told them it was a Rally *Duecento* (200) and they nodded an 'Of course!' They'd seen the stripes and thought it was a Rally. But their mate had put the same stripes on a 125 TS once so they couldn't be sure.

It was dark when I headed back up into the mountain, invigorated by the emptiness of the road and the slight chill in the air. As I swept around curves the headlight would momentarily illuminate a scene before me – a stand of trees, a small stream burbling over rocks, a startled rabbit scurrying off into the undergrowth. Occasionally a glint of reflection momentarily blinded me, bouncing off the windscreens of cars parked in little lay-bys just off the road, their windows all steamed up.

I spent the next three days venturing out from my mountain base on excursions suggested by Mario. A quick trip to Oliena. A little further afield to Bitti to see a museum dedicated to local farming and peasant culture. (It's called Museo della Civiltà Contadina e Pastorale – just in case you're thinking of adding it to your itinerary.) And I visited the cork groves around the pretty granite village of Alà Dei Sardi.

Mario was thrilled that I was doing it on a Vespa.

'It is the best way to see this country,' he said, waving his arms and filling his lungs with a deep breath. It was the best way to soak up the air, the smells, the atmosphere, he said. I could only agree.

Each day began in the same way. Mario and I would stand on the balcony at the back of the house and gaze out across the valley and mountains before us. Mario would make a suggestion, point to an indeterminate spot in the distance and then give me a potted history of the place. If he wasn't sure of a fact he scurried back inside and consulted one of the many history books on his shelf.

Mario prefaced all his suggestions with a quick 'in my opinion'. I soon learned that Mario's opinion was to be highly valued. Each day trip was as memorable as the next and the titbits of history helped flesh out what might have otherwise been a trip to another boring pile of stones. At Romanzesu, a nuraghic complex near Bitti, I could imagine the potters' huts just to the right of the *nuraghe* and spot the stables on the perimeter. Thanks to Mario I could almost smell the smoke of the prehistoric fires that had once been lit there.

The most evocative trip was my journey to Su Tempiesu, a sacred well hidden in the mountains behind Orune that dates from nuraghic times. It was tucked high in the folds of a wooded valley, a collection of simple stone slabs set over a water source that was believed to have healing and prophetic qualities. It was only rediscovered in 1953 when a farmer stumbled upon it. As I looked out across the isolated valley it wasn't hard to see why.

As idyllic as Su Tempiesu was, it was the journey back that I remember most vividly. As I bounced along a tiny mountain lane, with the sun on my back and the scent of wildflowers in my nostrils, I came upon a flock of sheep being herded by an old man wearing a flat cap and wielding a gnarled stick. I stopped to let them pass and for a minute I was swept up in a whirlpool of wool and bleating, the air thick with the smell of lanolin and sheep droppings. For a split second I felt like I was almost part of the flock. It was a magic moment that I got to experience simply because I was riding a Vespa.

Mario's sterling advice went beyond day trips and places to eat. I had promised Filippo I'd buy him a shepherd's knife. I had planned to get it from Pattada; its shepherd's knives were the most famous in Italy. Mario warned me that the knife makers there had become complacent. The quality had dropped and the prices had risen. Instead he pointed me towards Moledda Coltelli, a small knife maker on Via San Nicolò in the old part of Nuoro, whose knives were sought after by those in the know. Not only was I able to sit and watch Master Moledda at work – something the knife makers of Pattada never allow anymore – I was able to get Filippo a beautiful knife with a ram's-horn handle for a fraction of the cost of something of inferior quality in Pattada.

On my last night on the mountain Mario invited me to watch football with him. Italy were playing Bulgaria in a European Cup qualifier and the men who lived on the mountain were gathering in the small bar beside the statue of Cristo Redentore to watch it. The bar usually closed at sunset but the owner was keeping it open especially. He dragged the television out from the bar and hoisted it onto a bench so we could sit at the tables outside and enjoy the balmy evening.

Pizzas were supplied by Fratelli Sacchi, the hotel restaurant at the top of the mountain. The owner of the restaurant called the owner of the bar when the pizzas were ready and Mario and I went to collect them on Marcello. We'd barely had time to stop before a fat boy ran out excitedly wanting a ride on Marcello. His name was Giuseppe and Mario said he was the restaurant owner's son. To be honest, I'd already guessed. His physique kind of gave the game away.

Italians can get a scooter licence when they are fourteen and Giuseppe was turning fourteen that summer. By law he would only be able to ride a scooter with a maximum of 90cc. Marcello was over twice as powerful as that but Giuseppe was insistent that he could handle it. He was so buzzed by Marcello I didn't have the heart to turn him down. I told him he could ride Marcello as long as I sat on the back, with my hands on the controls at the same time.

I can say without reservation that I never want to be on the road when Giuseppe gets his licence. He loved the way Marcello's acceleration made his head snap back and twisted the throttle with reckless abandon. I spent the entire ride twisting the throttle back and pressing my right foot on the back brake. It was all I could do to prevent us from careering off the side of the mountain.

Giuseppe's father came outside with our pizzas and watched us ride around the car park. I thought he might be worried by his son's erratic driving but instead he beamed with pride.

'He is a good rider, no?' he grinned. I just smiled that crazy smile you get when you have looked death in the face and barely survived.

The rest of the evening was less stressful. I sat under the stars with the men of the mountain and drank beer, ate pizza and cheered Italy to a 2–1 win. A draw between Sweden and Denmark meant that Italy wouldn't be progressing any further, but the men drifted off down the mountain and back to their homes happy enough with the win and an evening out with their mates.

Mario and I rode back with our helmets off and the cool evening breeze in our hair. There were no police lurking on corners at this time of night. Nor was there any hurry. We meandered down the mountain, soaking up the smells and the sounds. Mario indicated for me to pull over at a viewpoint that looked out across a valley to the Sopramonte massif. The mountains were dark. Their outline was barely visible. The lights of the tiny settlements were twinkling like stars. Mario took in a deep breath and sighed.

'This mountain is like a mother to me,' he said.

I nodded. And for three days – and that night in particular – I felt like I had been taken into the bosom of the mountain family too.

If it hadn't been for Marcello and the mobility he gave me I would have stayed down in Nuoro in a soulless hotel. I probably would have only stayed a day, leaving Nuoro with an opinion of the place little better than the one formed by D.H. Lawrence 80-odd years before.

Instead, *destino* led me to Casa Solotti. And, like Mario, I was going to find it very difficult to leave.

CHAPTER SIX

CAGLIARI

PATRON SAINT: SANT'EFISIO

I headed south from Nuoro through the wild mountains of Barbagia. It wasn't the most direct route south to Cagliari. It would add a few days to my journey and take me through some of the most remote parts of the island. But I still had a week before I caught an overnight ferry from Cagliari to Sicily and I felt I couldn't leave Sardinia without getting at least a glimpse of its legendary 'dark heart'.

As I left Casa Solotti, Mario warned me that the mountains were isolated. In his poetic fashion he said that they were 'an island within an island'. They were the only region of Sardinia that had never been subdued by foreign conquerors. And the fiercely independent locals still liked to indulge in a bit of petty banditry and the odd blood vendetta. Indeed, the night we watched the football in the café on the top of Monte Ortobene Mario admitted that one of his uncles had been a bandit, shot dead by police.

'Not all bandits were bad,' he said enigmatically. 'Some had philosophies.'

He told me the story of the Italian publisher Giangiacomo Feltrinelli. He had been convinced that the bandits of Sardinia were just unreconstructed proletarian freedom fighters. He visited Cuba to secure the rights to Fidel Castro's memoirs and returned with a burning desire to turn Sardinia into the Mediterranean version of that socialist island. He changed his name to Osvaldo and arranged a meeting with bandit leaders in Orgosolo.

'He asked them what the structures of their organisations were and they said they were bandits not revolutionaries,' chuckled Mario. 'Then one of them said that if the meeting was over he knew where they could steal some sheep.'

In Orgosolo I'd come across some bandits of my own, two young boys I caught clambering on Marcello. I had stopped there to check out the left-wing murals the town is famous for. The boys said they were watching Marcello for me and cheekily requested €5 for their services. Even as the eldest held out his hand for the money the other was testing the handlebar to see if he could work loose the steering lock.

The rest of the time it was just me, Marcello and the wild mountains of the Barbagia. I chose a route that was deliberately perverse. When I came upon a crossroad I chose the option that looked less travelled. I was rewarded with twisting mountain roads that wound through wild groves of cork and oak trees and the odd incongruous vineyard. And views of jagged granite peaks that appeared hostile and unconquered. It was empty too. The only sign of life was the occasional wild pig scampering across the road, startled by Marcello's two-stroke growl.

Occasionally I would come upon a small village, often no bigger than a dozen or so simple houses and a tiny church. The novelist Salvatore Satta compared the isolated settlements stranded in the mountains here as 'minuscule, remote stars'. The sound of Marcello's engine drew people to their doorways where they stood and watched silently as I passed. The men wore breeches and flat caps. The women sported thick black shawls over long embroidered skirts. The looks on their faces suggested that in this part of Sardinia a bright orange Vespa was considered the work of the devil. I wondered what they would make of the bikini-clad girls lying on beaches less than an hour away.

South of Sorgono, right in the heart of Sardinia, the mountain roads were so bereft of traffic that I took to riding along without a helmet. I wore the straw hat that I'd bought on the way to Isla la Maddalena instead. I liked to think it gave me a rakish charm while keeping the warm Sardinian sun off my face at the same time.

Suddenly my journey had a soundtrack. I heard the crunch of the loose gravel and the gentle roar of the mountain streams. Sounds that had been muffled beyond recognition by my helmet were now sharp and audible. I rode along taking in deep breaths of the pure mountain air, laughing at the cries of the goshawk and sparrow-hawk above my head. I decided that I would ride as much of the way to Cagliari without a helmet as I could.

I got as far as Meana Sardo, a small village 14 kilometres south of Sorgono. The local *carabinieri* had set up a roadblock on the edge of town and I spotted the two policemen leaning against their car under a tree. The bigger one was a dead ringer for Carlos from *Desperate Housewives*. His offsider was a smaller, weedier type and had a touch of the Ed Nortons about him.

I considered doing a U-turn and high-tailing along one of the dirt tracks that led up into the mountains. Perhaps I'd find a shack there and a family with a long history of banditry willing to take in a fugitive. Instead I pulled over about 300 metres before I got to them, took off the cowl and began tinkering with the engine.

I put on quite a show. I removed the spark plug and cleaned it. I unscrewed the carburettor cover and put it back on again.

Ten minutes later I carefully wrapped the tools and placed them back into the glove box with a studied determination. Then I kick-started Marcello, put on my helmet – not my hat – and rode towards the police, trying hard not to catch their eye.

It didn't work. Just as I reached the tree the one who looked like Carlos whistled and waved me over. He had a look of weary disdain on his face that I hadn't seen on a policeman since my days as a P-plater in the western suburbs of Sydney.

My repair charade had failed so I immediately reverted to Plan B. It was a cunningly simple plan where I played a dumb tourist who didn't understand a word the police officer was saying. It was not without its risks. Both these guys wore Kevlar vests and had semi-automatic assault rifles slung over their shoulders. (Do the Sardinians have a pathological dislike of being pulled over for traffic infringements?)

It has been my experience with Italian officials that they'd rather let things slide than make work for themselves. On my first trip a policewoman let me ride along a restricted street in Rome when it became apparent that it would take more than her blowing her whistle to stop me. I asked Carlos in English if he spoke English – just to establish my bona fides as a particularly dense foreigner – and he shook his head.

I handed over Marcello's documents, my passport and my driver's licence and hoped for the best.

My passport took Carlos by surprise. Like most of the Italians I had encountered he'd seen the number plates and figured I was Livornese.

'*Australiano*?' he asked. I nodded and he said 'No!' Carlos, it seemed, had an uncle who lived in Griffith.

Carlos handed my documents to Ed Norton who went to the back of the car and copied the details from them. Carlos put his arm around my shoulder and led me back to the bike. He had a bit of friendly advice for me. The advice was in Italian but by now I had enough of a vocabulary in the language to get the gist of what he was saying. (It's when I try to speak the language I get myself in trouble.)

'I don't know how to say it in English,' he said, 'but you were riding without a helmet and that is illegal here.' He then said something about the *questura* (police headquarters), *multa* (fine) and my *moto* (scooter) being *confiscato* (confiscated) if I didn't pay them.

Ed returned with my documents and handed them to Carlos.

'It is good that your papers are in order,' said Carlos.

It meant that I hadn't put them in a situation where they *had* to do something. There wouldn't be a ticket after all. Instead Carlos handed me my documents and wished me a *buon viaggio*.

I was so thrilled at getting off I asked Carlos if I could take a photo of him and Ed standing next to Marcello. I wanted a souvenir of my encounter with the feared *carabinieri* of central Sardinia and they happily agreed. Carlos obliged by pointing to the helmet in an admonishing manner. Sadly the grin on his face lessened the impact of the safety message he was trying to promote.

★

And so I came to Cagliari. After my time deep in the mountains of Sardinia I arrived feeling distinctly out of my depth. I gawped at the traffic lights and tall modern buildings. I stared at people with tattoos and Africans selling pirated Louis Vuitton bags from blankets on the street. And when I spotted the shell of a burnt-out car in a lane just off Via Roma, I was convinced the same fate awaited Marcello. I almost turned around and headed back into the sanctuary of the mountains.

My state of mind had more to do with the remoteness of the mountains I had just passed through rather than any simmering menace exuded by Cagliari. In fact it was the sight of the bare midriffs of the pretty girls who walked the streets of Cagliari that affected me most. Compared to the heavy traditional clothes the women wore in the mountains, the glimpse of a feminine bellybutton was truly shocking.

Having said that, Cagliari is actually quite a pretty town. Not quite the 'new Jerusalem' that DH Lawrence once claimed, but lovely nonetheless. It is set on a wide sweep of a bay, backed by mountains, and flanked by lagoons dotted with migrating flamingos from Africa. And beyond that, a stunning coastline dotted with some of the most beautiful beaches in Sardinia.

Nor is Cagliari a particularly big city. The population hovers around a quarter of a million people and most are squeezed into four small neighbourhoods – Castello, Marina, Stampace and Villanova – perched on a hill that rises sharply from the waterfront. Each of the four districts bears a legacy of the different civilisations that have ruled over the city in its 2000-year history, including a couple of buildings thrown up by the charmingly named House of Savoy, the only civilisation that sounds like it built its economic base selling suits.

I had booked a room in A&R Bundes Jack, a cheap hotel in one of the charming pastel-coloured buildings on Via Roma that overlooked the harbour. My room had tall shuttered windows and overlooked a boulevard of palm trees, a line of yachts and, beyond that, the glittering sea.

It was also in the heart of the Marina district, an area my guidebook described as 'lively'. After a week in the mountains my interpretation of 'lively' was a restaurant that stayed open after eight. The *Rough Guide* obviously had a more cosmopolitan outlook. In this part of Cagliari 'lively' translated as a warren of narrow lanes lined with bars and populated by drunken sailors stumbling along with the support of girls wearing too much make-up and not enough clothes.

The entrance to the hotel sat at the back of an open-sided arcade and I had to run a gauntlet of crowded cafés, fake designer bag sellers and beggars to reach it. Beside the entrance a man had set up a box with a cat and three mice on it. I stopped and watched open-mouthed as the cat happily let the mice play in front of it. Like the locals who had watched me pass in the mountains, I wondered what kind of devilry was afoot.

Despite its 'lively' position, the A&R Bundes Jack was a sanctuary of calm. It was on the third floor of an old building and was painted a soothing shade of white. My room was basically furnished – I was reminded immediately of a monk's cell – but after my brusque reintroduction to city life it was exactly what I needed. I ventured out reluctantly to get some money from an ATM in the foyer of the railway station nearby and spotted a family from the provinces picnicking on the benches there. They nodded at me as I passed, recognising in an instant that I was feeling as overwhelmed as they were.

When night fell I was confronted with another dilemma. The hookers that worked the nearby bars started leaning on Marcello while they touted for business. I suspected their pitch was 'You think this Vespa looks racy, wait until you try me!' I chased away a few as I ate a hastily grabbed meal from one of the restaurants in the arcade, but like cats watching a bird in a cage they kept coming back.

The manager of the hotel suggested I park Marcello in a garage instead. She was a grandmotherly type and said that my Vespa was the kind that 'captures attention'.

'It is best to keep it out of sight,' she said. It was her way of telling me that if I left Marcello parked out front he wouldn't be there in the morning.

That was one of the problems I was having doing this trip on a bright orange Vespa. As lovely as Sophia was, her beauty was more discreet. She had blended in with the shadows. Marcello was the Vespa equivalent of a high-visibility safety vest.

The garage the manager suggested didn't exactly put my mind at rest. It was tucked up a dirty lane off Corso Vittorio Emanuele with an unsecured entrance and fluorescent lights that were either smashed or only flickered to life momentarily. I wandered among the cars parked there for five minutes before I found another living soul, a dark West African man sorting out fake Louis Vuitton bags on a tattered piece of cardboard on the concrete floor.

It turned out he was the 'after-hours' manager. He pointed to where I should park Marcello and told me to hang the keys on a board with all the others as I left. I could pay when I picked up my bike.

I'd never had the opportunity to talk to a fake bag seller before, so after I parked Marcello I squatted beside the man as he sorted his bags and asked him how it worked. He was surprised by my forthrightness, but after looking at me, and then at Marcello, he decided I could be trusted.

'I'm Ibrahima from Senegal,' he said, extending his hand and laughing that African laugh. I told him I was Peter from Australia.

According to Ibrahima, the bags were imported from China by a 'mysterious' investor and divided into packs of thirty or forty bags. Individual sellers then bought the packs for a set price and any profit they made selling them was theirs to keep.

Ibrahima said most of the bag sellers came from Senegal. I asked if there was a particular reason they came to Italy and he said no. They just knew someone from Senegal here already.

Ibrahima had moved up in the chain. He supplied bags to sellers who had just arrived and didn't have the capital to buy the bags themselves. In return he took a set fee on top of the normal selling price.

'At first I'd take a percentage of their profits,' he said. 'But some of the boys lied to me about the prices they got.'

I asked what happened if the bags got confiscated by the police.

He laughed. 'That would never happen!' The police made a show of chasing them away to keep their bosses happy. And if they did take the bags, Ibrahima simply bought them back 'at a very good price'.

As I left the garage Ibrahima offered me a bag from his Monogram Multicolore range. He held it up against Marcello to show me how well it matched. He said it was a Priscilla – a 'feminine city bag' according to the official LV website – and one of the new lines he'd just got in.

'Good price,' he said. 'No middle man.'

I thanked him for his kind offer but declined. While Marcello was more than macho enough to carry it off, I wasn't so certain that I was.

★

I spent the next day wandering around Cagliari on foot. I started the day with a *caffé macchiatto* and a *bombolone* in a café in Piazza Yenni, happily paying extra to sit at one of the tables outside and soak up the sun. My xenophobia had ebbed away to the point that I barely noticed a group of punks hanging out under the statue of King Carlo Felice, handing around an early morning joint.

King Carlo was the titular head of the House of Savoy and was King of Sardinia from 1821 to 1831. That morning his statue was wearing a cape in the Cagliari football club colours – blue and red – with the name Zola and the number 10 embroidered on the back. Cagliari had just won promotion to the Serie A. His outstretched arm pointed towards a plinth with a ball on top, seemingly rallying the troops into battle against AC Milan and Juventus and the other big boys of Italy's premier football league.

I started my sightseeing at the Church of Sant'Efisio. Sant'Efisio is the unofficial patron saint of Cagliari, a Roman soldier from Asia Minor who refused to give up his Christian beliefs and was beheaded for it. Over the centuries various miracles have been attributed to him. He rescued the city from a plague in 1652 and kept the French at bay when they tried to take the city in 1792. He is remembered every May by Sardinia's largest religious festival, the Festa di Sant'Efisio, a procession along the coast from the church to Nora, 40 kilometres away, where he lost his head.

I cut across Stampace to the ruins of the Roman amphitheatre, a 10,000-seater cut into the side of a hill. Along the way I dropped in on the garage to see if I still had a Vespa. I was pleased to see Marcello was where I'd left him. Ibrahima was not on duty; a pimply lad of seventeen or so seemed to be the day manager. I was equally pleased that he challenged me when he caught me looking at Marcello. I finished my morning's sightseeing with a set-price *turistico* menu in a small café overlooking Piazza

Costituzione and the imposing marble stairway to Bastione San Remy.

With a delicious *risotto alla pescatora* under my belt and my head light from the complimentary carafe of red wine, I slowly made my way up the triumphant staircase to the terrace at the top of it. Here Bastione San Remy felt like a veranda suspended high above the city. A football pitch-sized veranda, dotted with palm trees and enjoying uninterrupted views over the city below to the stunningly blue sea beyond. Looking south towards the ocean I felt like I was standing in one of those infinity-edge pools, the edge of the city walls seemingly part of the horizon.

I was startled from my reverie by a commotion behind me on the eastern wall. A woman was sitting on the very edge with her legs dangling over the side threatening to jump. Two *carabinieri* were trying to talk her down – a young guy whose uniform still bore the creases from when he took it out of the packet and an older guy who puffed on a cigarette the way Marcello Mastroianni used to. A gallery of locals watched from the balconies and windows of their homes overlooking the square. This being Italy, each one of them had an opinion on what should be done and weren't afraid of expressing it. Half of them implored the *carabinieri* to do something. The other half yelled for the woman to go ahead and jump already.

The woman was in her mid-thirties or so. She appeared drunk and wore a clingy dress that did her chubby figure no favours. Her dated beehive hairstyle reminded me of showgirls in *La Dolce Vita* and, as is my way, I immediately created a back story. She'd been replaced at the saucy revue by a younger girl. A cad had taken advantage of her – probably some bastard on an orange Vespa. And now she'd been kicked out of her home because she couldn't pay the rent. I managed to catch a slurred insult against the Banco di Sardegna so I could well have been right about the last bit.

The younger *carabinieri* didn't know what to do. He rushed from the police car to the wall and back again, before getting on the radio to tell headquarters what was happening, his eyes wide with terror. The older cop, however, had seen it all before. He sat on the wall a couple of metres from the woman and lit up a cigarette. After a couple of insolent drags he offered it to the woman. When she reached out to take it he grabbed her and bundled her off the wall and onto the terrace.

It was over in a second, but in the process the woman's dress went over her head to reveal a pair of Bridget Jones-style big pants. (Like many of us watching I had been fearful that she'd be wearing something more minuscule.) She struggled to her feet and took a swing at the older cop, who batted her arm away. She wasn't angry that he'd stopped her from jumping. I think that was the plan. She was pissed off that he'd done it in such an undignified manner.

The police car drove away and the gawpers drifted back into their living rooms. I wandered through the cobbled lanes of the Castello district to the Cittadella dei Musei and its famous wax anatomical models, the Mostra di Cere Anatomiche. As I looked upon the perfect wax replicas of internal organs and anatomical cutaways (including one displaying a foetus inside a womb) – all lovingly crafted by Clemente Susini in the eighteenth century – I couldn't help thinking that but for the quick actions of a seasoned old *carabinieri*, the people of Cagliari could have been looking at the real thing on the pavement below the city walls.

Soon it was my last day in Cagliari. I was catching an overnight ferry to Palermo so it was my last day on Sardinia too. I was heading to Sicily and an altogether different type of Italy – one redolent of crushed lemons and *mafiosa* intrigue.

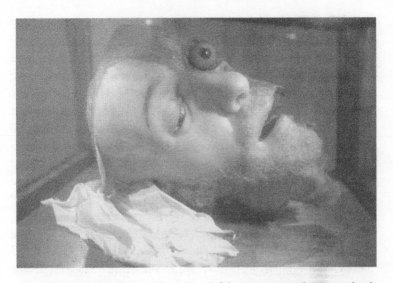

I would miss Sardinia. The island felt remote and untouched, something I hadn't encountered in Italy before. And the contrast between the sophistication of the coast and the insularity of the mountains gave it an intriguingly split personality. There was something about the place that got under my skin – and not just the bugs that splattered against me as I rode through vast plateaus swathed in wildflowers.

The ferry to Sicily didn't leave until 7 p.m. I had to check out of the A&R Bundes Jack by 11 a.m. I found myself at a loose end so I gave the president of the Sardinian Vespa Club a call.

I'm not in the habit of telephoning Vespa club officials out of the blue. But Filippo (that was his name) had enjoyed reading *Vroom with a View* so much that he sent me an email telling me that when I came to Cagliari I should look him up. What impressed me most about his email was his absolute certainty that not only would I return to Italy after my first Vespa odyssey through the country but that I'd get to Cagliari as well. He was right of course, but I didn't know that at the time.

Filippo lived in Poggio dei Pini, a suburb of Cagliari just south of the lagoons. We arranged to meet at the local cemetery – it was easy to find, he said – and as I made my way along the narrow spit of land between the coast and the shallow lagoons I saw two things I thought I'd never see. The first was a dead flamingo in the middle of the road. (I'd always considered flamingos too exotic to end up as roadkill.) The second was a sign for an old persons home offering the protective services of Padre Pio as an incentive to prospective customers. The Padre had only been a saint for a few years and it seemed he had already sold out.

Filippo was already waiting at the cemetery. He sat on a beat-up PX he used as his everyday bike and waved as I approached.

'My wife rang to tell me you were coming,' he said. 'She was on her way to work and saw you riding along Sulcitana, the main road.'

Like all partners of people with a 'hobby', Filippo's wife had acquired a complementary set of skills that she neither wanted nor needed. Now she could spot a GS from a TS and a GT from an ET and change the points on each of them if she had to. Even now, on her way to work as a nurse at Cagliari hospital, she had glimpsed a Rally 200 out of the corner of her eye and rang to tell her husband.

Whenever I get a little trainspotterish about Vespas Sally calls me a Ves-bore. She came up with the term herself – something that she's inordinately pleased with herself about – but I have noticed her look up whenever she hears that distinctive two-stroke sound.

Filippo had two daughters, Elisabet, eleven, and Maria, nine. He ran his business from home and looked after the girls on the days his wife worked. Mostly that involved getting them ready for school, dropping them off and picking them up at the end of the day.

It was school holidays, though, so instead he had to keep them entertained the whole day. They greeted us excitedly as we rode up the steep driveway to Filippo's home, then all three of them took me on a tour of the Museo di Vespa in the basement under the house.

The girls were as proud of their father's collection as he was. They showed me the restored 1948 Vespa 125 and the yellow Rally 180 that graced the homepage of the Sardinian Vespa Club website. They pointed at the various piles of Vespa parts stashed away in the corners of the room and told me exactly which kind of Vespa they were from.

Filippo's office was at the back of the basement and it too was resplendent with Vespa memorabilia. A bookshelf groaned under the weight of a complete set of Vespa technical manuals and various other books written in Italian, English and German about the marque. The walls were dotted with framed collections of Vespa-themed stamps and cigarette cards. In the corner of the room there was a huge silver cup that the club had won for travelling the most kilometres to a rally in Milan. The girls insisted I take a photo of their father holding it.

The plan was to have lunch at Filippo's home and then drive along the coast to Santa Margherita di Pula, the beach just after Nora, the town where Sant'Efisio had his head lopped off. Nora was abandoned in the fifth century after being sacked by the Vandals, and most of what remained is now submerged beneath the sea. But Filippo assured me the beach was one of the finest on the island.

We made our way up to the living area where the girls showed me photo albums full of pictures of their family – and Vespas – while Filippo quickly rustled up lunch. He rummaged through the fridge and tossed out a selection of cold cuts, olive oil and the weird toasted bread that comes in packets in Italy. Dessert was a couple of packets of Kinder Buenos. His wife used them to bribe the kids to help with the housework. Filippo tossed them in as his idea of a balanced meal. He admitted that he wasn't a great cook. Like most Italian men his mother had always fed him. When he finally left home – to get married – his wife took over his mother's role.

It wasn't the most sophisticated dining experience I'd had on my journey so far but it was easily the most fun. Filippo loved his daughters and they clearly loved him. It was chaotic and lively and each time a plate was passed it came with a joke or a smile. After a concerted campaign from the two girls we each got another Kinder Bueno to finish the meal (given only after they promised not to tell their mother). I hoped that one day I'd have a relationship like that with my daughter.

Filippo patted his stomach and announced that it was time to go to the beach. He and the girls would go in their restored 1968 Kombi van – Filippo was also president of the Sardinian Kombi club – and I would follow on Marcello.

The road along the coast to Santa Margherita di Pula was stunning. It hugged a rocky coastline topped by olive-green gorse and was lapped by a sea that was an impossibly bright shade of turquoise. Each bend revealed a new vista of craggy coves or white sandy beaches more lovely than the last. We were only 30 kilometres from Cagliari, the biggest city in Sardinia, and yet it felt like we were in the middle of nowhere.

We didn't actually go to Santa Margherita di Pula. Filippo said it was too commercialised. We stopped instead at an unnamed beach just before it, surrounded by braided fields of freshly harvested hay. The only sign of civilisation was a camping ground with a small kiosk where Filippo bought everyone an ice cream. The girls couldn't believe their luck – two Kinder Buenos and an ice cream on the same day. Elisabet declared it the best day of the holidays yet.

I spent the rest of the afternoon swimming in the clear sea, watching Filippo horse around with his daughters. It made me think of my two girls back in London – Sally and my unborn daughter – and when I got back to Cagliari I popped into an internet café down by the harbour to send them an email before the ship to Sicily sailed.

I'd emailed Sally the photo of the *carabinieri* Carlos and Ed pointing to the helmet and she'd replied, only half joking, that she expected more from the father of her unborn child. Her exact words were that if I tried another stunt like that and crashed she'd personally switch off the life support. Carlos had only threatened to fine me.

There was another one from my friend Rob back in Sydney. He'd emailed me while I was in Nuoro asking me how I was finding the thought of becoming a father. I'd told him I was finding the whole pregnancy thing all rather surreal.

'Of course it's bloody surreal,' he replied. 'You're about to become a father for the first time and you're riding around Sardinia on an orange Vespa!'

I sat in the internet café in Cagliari and silently nodded my head.

He had a point.

CHAPTER SEVEN

PALERMO

PATRON SAINT: SAINT ROSALIA

The overnight ferry from Sardinia to Sicily was called the *Emilia* and she was a floating version of a rundown tenement building in the Bronx. The lower decks were dark and dingy. The cabins were cramped and worn. And the hallways echoed with the muffled sounds of men fighting, babies crying, dogs barking and couples shagging. I half expected to get a knock on my cabin door from someone called Jimmy 'Two-Fingers' Ragatoni, asking for a *pizzo*, a small bribe, to ensure nothing happened to me on the crossing.

The communal areas on the upper decks of the ship were just as dismal. The carpets on the floor were threadbare and the paint on the walls chipped. The single television in the main lounge broadcast a hissing blizzard and the bank of fruit machines that lined one wall were all switched off. The only place that sold coffee, a grimy café in a corner of the lounge, closed half an hour after we sailed.

The *Emilia* was so bereft of entertainment opportunities that I spent a good part of the night looking at the black and white photos that lined the corridor leading to the chief purser's desk. They chronicled the building of the ship and I was pleased to note that the workers wore breeches and flat caps and looked like extras out of Martin Scorsese's film *The Gangs of New York*.

Most of the other passengers were out on the deck feverishly thumbing text messages and making frantic calls on their cell phones. At first I feared that I'd missed an announcement to abandon ship. The desperate way the Italians were trying to contact loved ones suggested that some sort of disaster had befallen us – a fire in the engine room or a rogue Mediterranean iceberg perhaps.

It was worse than that. The mobile phone signals were fading and the ship wouldn't be back in range of phone towers again until we approached Palermo. As the coverage ebbed away the Italians moved about the boat searching for spots that still had reception, before gathering at the rear of the boat to stare dumbly at their cruelly silent phones.

★

The journey to Palermo in Sicily was scheduled to take just over thirteen hours. My intention was to spend most of it sleeping but instead I was kept awake by a guy thumping the wall of another cabin and yelling 'shut the fuck up' in Italian. The constant flushing of the communal toilet didn't help either. It was right next to my room, about level with my head, and flushed with a loud sucking noise, just like the ones on passenger jets. It was also the only toilet in that section of the ship. Even though the ship didn't dock until 8.30 a.m., the morning ablutions of my fellow passengers started well before dawn.

And so it was that I found myself on deck as we approached Palermo.

It was beautiful. The air was incredibly still and the sea looked like it had been buffed to a stunning platinum sheen. Monte

Pellegrino stood regally crowned by a wisp of morning mist and the high mountain range that ran along the back of the city glowed in the early morning sun. The harbour was dotted with blue wooden rowboats and fishermen lazily dangling lines over the edge. The only hint of the city's dramatic history – Palermo is reputedly the most invaded city in Europe – was the dull thud of cannon fire from a fort to the west of the harbour.

I breathed in the thick sea air and felt invigorated. It was the kind of travel moment that stays with you forever, an ephemeral instant when sights, sounds and smells magically meld into one. A moment, I realised guiltily, I should have been sharing with Sally.

Soon the deck began to fill with other passengers. They pointed their phones in different directions trying to get reception. It had been eleven hours since we'd had any coverage and they were desperate for a fix. As we passed the Diga Foranea, the breakwater that marked the entrance of the main harbour, the phones sprang to life again, beeping madly with messages from people wondering where the hell they were. The relief among the Italians was palpable. They smiled and laughed as if a doctor had told them he wouldn't have to amputate their leg after all.

I had a message too. It was from Sally saying that she'd gone to bed early and had slept well.

Before I left Cagliari I had booked a room in a small hotel in Palermo called the Cortese. It was tucked behind the Chiesa del Gesù, the Church of Jesus, in the east of the city. I had spent most of my sleepless night journeying across the Tyrrhenian Sea studying a map and attempting to choose the best way to reach it.

The most direct route seemed to be up Via Francesco Crispi to Piazza Marina, the old town square where tournaments, theatre performances and public executions were held during the Middle Ages. From there I could head south along Via Vittorio Emanuele before turning left at Fontana Pretoria onto

Via Maqueda and nipping down Via dell'Università. It seemed remarkably straightforward and I knew immediately that it was destined to end in tears.

For one thing the map in my guidebook hadn't indicated that most of the streets in Palermo were one way. In the case of my chosen route, heading in the wrong direction. Nor did it indicate that on Saturdays all the lanes around the hotel were closed and filled with stalls of the weekly Balerò market. When I finally got within a block of the Cortese my way was blocked by hundreds of stalls, tightly packed together under a sea of tatty canvas umbrellas, selling plastic colanders, big pants and the occasional slab of freshly caught tuna.

In most places the lanes I had planned to ride along had shrunk to a tiny pathway so narrow that people had to shuffle sideways to get through. Occasionally the produce from a particular stall overflowed onto that pathway and people were forced to jump over a pile of artichokes or melons. I was only a couple of hundred metres from the hotel so I decided to chain Marcello to a pole, lug my bag the rest of the way and retrieve him at the end of the day when the market had closed.

Out of the corner of my eye I noticed a guy on a scooter ride into the mass of stalls and negotiate his way through the scrum of people. I expected him to be abused, maybe even set upon, but people stepped aside and let him through. The owners of the stalls that overflowed onto the path even shifted their produce momentarily so he could pass. I thought the rider must have been a one-off – a market official, perhaps, collecting stall fees. But over the next few minutes at least half a dozen other scooter riders plunged into the chaotic scrum of market stalls. So I decided to give it a go myself.

That's the beauty of a Vespa. It's not much wider than a person and not nearly as tall. In theory, anywhere a human can go a Vespa can too.

That was part of the design brief given to Corradino D'Ascanio, the aeronautical engineer whose task it was to create the Vespa. Back then most Italians lived in towns and villages that were knotted with tiny lanes and alleyways. It was no use having a cheap, affordable means of transport if it didn't take you right to your door. A door that could be at the end of a narrow pathway wedged between buildings thrown up in the Middle Ages. Or, in my case, the other side of a busy Saturday morning produce market.

I revved Marcello a couple of times, took a deep breath and plunged in. I wasn't as skilful as the locals but I made good progress. I clipped a watermelon as I passed a fruit and vegetable stall, but luckily the owner was quick enough to catch it before it fell. And at one point I had to wait while a guy unloaded ice from the back of a scooter to a stall selling tuna. (A coughing chorus of protest saw me switch off the engine until he was finished.) But soon I was winding my way past plastic colanders and cheap plastic radios like a local.

The only major incident I caused was when I ran over a Turkish carpet. The owner of the carpet stall refused to move it and the people stuck behind me on foot bullied me into just riding over it. I realised immediately that the locals had egged me on solely for their own entertainment. The carpet seller sprang from behind his counter and chased after me waving his fist. Everyone else creased up with laughter.

Ten minutes later I popped out on the other side of the markets. Adrenaline was pumping furiously through my veins. That had been some of the most exhilarating minutes of my trip in Italy. I very nearly turned around and went back through again, just for the hell of it.

I found the hotel on a quiet corner just the other side of the market. I clambered up the marble staircase still exhilarated from my market ride and accepted the key to *camera cento dodici*, room 120, from the manager with a cheery *grazie molto*.

The room had only just been cleaned. Indeed the cleaner held the door open for me to enter. It was surprisingly big for a single and I kicked back on the wide bed luxuriating in my good fortune. I had a quick shower and then hit the streets of Palermo, heading away from the markets and the Chiesa del Gesù to the narrow lanes in the south of the town.

Palermo's golden age began in 831 AD when it fell under Arab rule. For the next 200 years, and then under the Normans who followed, it was regarded as one of Europe's greatest metropolises. It rivalled Cairo and Cordoba in beauty and its educational institutions were considered the greatest of the era. The Arabic influence is still apparent in the architecture of the churches and in the palm trees that grace the parks and streets.

The city again flourished in the seventeenth and eighteenth centuries, during the Baroque period. Its influence is seen the highly ornamented stylings of various civic and religious buildings like the Santa Cita and San Domenico churches.

Palermo's strategic position in the middle of the Mediterranean saw it bombed heavily during the Second World War. Only pockets of its former glory remain and the rest of the city was rebuilt quickly and shoddily. The funds that had been earmarked to rebuild it were siphoned off by the Mafia. Now, 60 years later, people were still living in their patched-together homes next to the craters created by Allied bombing over half a century before.

Despite this – or maybe because of it – I immediately took a shine to Palermo. It had an energy, a *brio*, that suggested its citizens were living for the moment rather than preparing for some illustrious future that may or may not come. I rode past men selling shoes off blankets on the bonnets of their cars, food stalls set up in the ruins of crumbling buildings, and women selling embroidered tablecloths from the windows of their homes. The women passed the neatly folded purchases

through the black and pink flags of the local football team that hung from lines strung between the buildings about them.

Most visitors to Palermo begin their sightseeing at the Teatro Massimo, posing on the grand stone staircase where Francis Ford Coppola shot the dramatic final scenes of *The Godfather: Part III*. Others make a beeline for the Palazzo dei Normanni to admire its Arabic architectural flourishes and marvel at the mosaics and frescoes in the Capella Palatina, regarded by many as the jewel in Palermo's crown.

Me? I was heading to the Capuchin Catacombs out on Via Cappuccini. I wanted to check out the air-dried remains of 8000 of Palermo's former citizens.

Capuchin monks seemed to have a thing for displaying human remains. At the Santa Maria della Concezione dei Cappuccini in Rome they made patterns from the bones of their brothers when they passed away. Here the monks hung the fully clothed bodies in niches in long underground halls, like a grisly human version of flying duck ornaments.

The monks first started hanging bodies here in 1599. For the first century or so the honour fell to Capuchin monks only. But word spread and soon requests came from the monks' benefactors to be interred there after they died. The first was Don Carlo Formatura, a Palermo aristocrat. The catacombs became known as 'The Capuchins' Great Burial Place' and soon after Don Carlo was interred there, it was opened to the public. The response was so great that it had to be divided into sections: Monks, Men, Women, Professionals and Priests.

Each new resident was prepared the same way. The bodies were placed in cells situated along the passageways called 'strainers'. The conditions here helped dry out the bodies. Eight months later they were taken out of the cells and dipped in vinegar. Then they were dressed in the clothes they had left especially and placed in a niche in the whitewashed walls in the section appropriate to their gender and profession. The men wore suits and ties. The females were decked out in their best dresses, thoughtfully padded with straw so it looked like they still had breasts.

The monks responsible for displaying the bodies amused themselves by arranging the bodies in a manner that suggested they were doing something. Two men were turned to face each other so it looked like they were in the middle of a conversation. Another was hunched over, clutching his ribs like he was laughing. Another had his mouth forced opening in a screaming pose like he'd just jammed his foot in the door. The captains of ships wore caps that made them look like Johnny Depp in *Pirates of the Caribbean*. The children had an entire section to themselves, dressed in a variety of tiny outfits that made them look like a ghoulish doll collection.

I was surprised by how much the bodies of the children upset me. I wasn't even a father yet but the thought of losing my soon-to-be daughter at such a young age gnawed at the pit of my stomach. I stood before the remains of a mother and daughter, dressed in matching blue and white dresses, contemplating just how horrible it would be.

I was still lost in my thoughts when a living monk asked me a question in Italian. I hadn't heard him come up behind me and jumped with fright. He apologised for startling me and asked the question again, this time in English.

'Is she talking to you?' he asked.

I thought he meant in a metaphorical sense, so I said that yes, the sight of these bodies had made me contemplate my own mortality and the great responsibility of fatherhood that lay ahead of me. He shook his head and pointed to the mouth of the woman.

'No,' he said quite insistently, 'did she say something to you?'

Noticing my confusion the monk introduced himself as Brother Benedetto, formerly of Trápani, and told me that he was responsible for dusting the crumbling whitewash off the bodies. Apparently the woman I'd stopped in front of had the reputation as a 'talker'.

'Talkers' were the mummies that some people believed could commune with the living. This talker's first conversation was with a young rebel called Carlos during the time of Spanish rule.

'Carlos was on the run from the authorities and had taken refuge in the crypt,' explained Benedetto. 'The guards found him here and he was dragged away to Piazza Marina where he was hanged.'

Carlos knew such a fate awaited him and had wanted to know what a prayer to the dead was.

'She told him it was like a warm March sun,' said Benedetto. 'A fine day that dispels the rainy winter.'

There were quite a few talkers in the collection apparently. Most simply nattered with the visitors as a way of passing eternity. Others, like Father Urban of Monreale, spent the afterlife moaning about never becoming a saint.

'He says it's because the brotherhood never gave him the mass they owed him,' said Benedetto.

I asked Benedetto if he believed the bodies talked and he shrugged his shoulders. Most of the time people imagined it, he said. Sometimes the ropes that wrapped around the waists of the bodies and tethered them to the wall slipped, causing the bodies to move.

'Some people think they are leaning forward to whisper something in their ear,' he explained.

The talkers are not the only supernatural thing attributed to the catacombs. In 1646 Palermo was gripped by a severe drought. The locals arranged a religious procession through the streets of the city to try and break it. As they passed the convent, 44 friars came out with their hoods lowered to hide their faces and joined them. When the rain came, a delegation from Town Hall visited to thank the monks for taking part. And yet the monks didn't know what they were talking about.

I left Brother Benedetto with his dustpan and brush and headed to the chapel where the remains of twoyear-old Rosalia Lombardo lay.

The last person to be entombed here using the traditional methods was Brother Riccardo from Palermo in 1871. But in 1920 Rosalia was embalmed using new techniques pioneered by a Doctor Solafia. Rosalia lay in an open coffin like a perfectly preserved wax model, looking exactly as she did the day she died.

It is believed that various chemicals were injected into young Rosalia's body but no one knows for sure. Doctor Solafia took the secret of his methods to the grave. Considering Rosalia is an alarming shade of orange that is probably a good thing.

I spent the rest of my first day in Palermo undertaking more cultural pursuits. I dropped by the Norman Palace to see the mosaics – the central apse crowned by the mosaic of Christ Pantocrator had me considering a life in the priesthood – and then back to Fontana Pretoria and the nude statues that have led to it being christened the 'Fountain of Shame'.

My attempt to admire the freshly renovated interior of Teatro Massimo was thwarted when the girl on the ticket counter told me they only did a tour in English if enough English speakers turned up. I was welcome to sit in the foyer and wait for another nine Anglophones to appear but decided to spend the afternoon cruising the streets of Palermo on Marcello instead.

I soon discovered that riding a bright orange Rally 200 along the thoroughfares of Palermo is regarded by the local Vespa riders as an invitation to race. They rode up beside me at traffic lights, revved their engines and set off with a squeal of rubber when the lights changed. It was the Italian equivalent of Porsche drivers back home being challenged to a drag race by hoons in their hotted-up Holdens.

I knew that I had the horsepower to beat them. Most of my challengers rode PXs – the boxy, reliable Vespa that has been in production since 1977. Marcello was a Rally 200 – the model considered by purists as the 'hotrod of Vespas'. PXs topped out at 100 kilometres per hour. Marcello could do 116. But as a soon-to-be father I took the more responsible option of conceding defeat, suffering their leering grins in the knowledge that if I'd let him, Marcello would have smacked them down.

I returned to the Hotel Cortese and discovered that I couldn't get into my room. The key slotted into the lock but it wouldn't turn. I looked at the number on the key tag and noticed that the manager had given me the key to room 112. I went down and showed the key to the manager, giving him a patronising smile at his mistake, and handed him the key to change. He looked at me like I was mad.

'*Si, cento dodici*, one hundred and twelve,' he said. 'It is your room.'

Shit. When I'd checked in I'd thought he'd said 120. Three weeks into the trip and my Italian had progressed to the point where I didn't double-check anymore. I was so cocky about my Italian skills that I didn't bother to compare what I *thought* I'd heard to the actual number on the key. The words 'pride', 'fall' and 'before' sprang immediately to mind. Not surprisingly, in English.

The manager's English was about as good as my Italian, so with the aid of my phrasebook and the Italian/English dictionary he kept at reception, I explained what I had done. The situation was so ludicrous that it took a while for him to comprehend what I was trying to say. Room 120 was a double room. Any moron would have noticed that. When the scale of my stupidity finally dawned on him he guffawed in disbelief.

I offered to pay extra for the room but it wasn't an option. A couple from Rome had booked it and were due to arrive at any moment. Instead he accompanied me to the room and tutted as I gathered all my things together. Then he yelled down the stairwell for the cleaner to come back and clean it. Again. She gave me a look even darker than the manager had and muttered something in Italian. I think she said I was a stupid foreigner but my linguistic confidence was now shot to pieces so I couldn't say for sure.

The next day was Sunday. The weather was good so I decided to follow the lead of everyone else in Palermo and headed to Mondello, a seaside town wedged between Monte Pellegrino and Monte Gallo, 10 kilometres to the north of the city.

Mondello became a summer playground for the citizens of Palermo back in the nineteenth century when wealthy citizens built ornate art nouveau villas here. It became a kind of garden city, a place to escape the summer heat. Even today it is a popular place for the people of the city to take their *passeggiata*.

I took the scenic route up over Monte Pellegrino. The road rose steeply from Acquasanta, cutting back on itself and offering stunning views over the city. Once again I was happy for Marcello's extra power. He bounded up the mountain road like an eager puppy, still bursting with energy when we reached the Santuario di Santa Rosalia at the top.

Saint Rosalia is the patron saint of Palermo. She was the pious niece of William II and in 1159 fled to the mountain to renounce all worldly things. The sanctuary consists of a small chapel built in the cave where her remains were discovered five centuries later. The discovery coincided exactly with the end of a plague that had struck Palermo, a miracle some said, and it is celebrated twice a year with a triumphant parade.

Like most sacred sites in Italy the entry to the sanctuary was lined with tacky souvenir stalls where I was able to pick up a Saint Rosalia fridge magnet to add to the collection on the inside of Marcello's glove box. I would have liked to have caught a glimpse of the statue of Saint Rosalia that no less a person than Goethe had described as 'natural and pleasing'. Or dip my hands in the miraculous water that ran down the inside of the cave. But there was an unseemly scrum of pilgrims around both, and a pile of banknotes beside the altar that suggested a rather hefty 'donation' was expected.

Instead I clambered up a path at the back of the chapel that led to the top of the mountain. The peak was marked by another statue of Rosalia and I sat beside it looking towards Mondello. It was silent here, unlike the clamour in the chapel below, and the smell of lavender hung in the light breeze. I could understand why Rosalia liked it up here.

Mondello, on the other hand, would have Rosalia turning in her grave. Italians of all shapes and sizes and in various stages of undress were wandering along the streets slurping on gelato. The small sandy beach was packed solid with beach huts, set in lines perpendicular to the water so that more could be squeezed in. Scattered among them lay the Palermitans – grannies, families, couples, kids and teenagers – all the same shade of nut brown.

The street that ran along the beach was filled with gelato shops and lined with the scooters of the sunbathers. Young boys ran along tapping their handlebars to set off the alarms and then laughed at the owners when they came running from the beach in their swimmers with sand on their bellies. The boys stopped to admire Marcello and when they saw me watching them promised not to touch such a *bella moto*.

I bought a gelato and walked back towards the harbour in the south of the town. Here it was easier to imagine what Mondello had been like before the masses arrived – a tiny fishing village centred around a crumbling fifteenth-century tower. Brightly coloured fishing boats jostled in the harbour before the massive grandeur of Monte Pellegrino. I finished my ice cream content that I had found the seaside Italy that I had come to see.

I took the direct route back to Palermo. On the outskirts of Mondello the *carabinieri* had set up a roadblock to book people riding without a helmet. As a member of the EU, Italy was obligated to enforce laws that it had previously let slide. Young teenage boys on motor scooters in Palermo obviously didn't feel the same allegiance to Brussels because every one of them zipped around the *carabinieri*, laughing at the officers frantically blowing their whistles for them to stop.

I was wearing a helmet but I was still pulled over. I think the harried-looking policeman stuck his hand out because as a helmet wearer I was the kind of person who would obey him. He flicked through my papers and when he saw that they were in order sent me on my way with a sigh. I'd like to think I made him feel that he hadn't completely wasted his Sunday, but I'm not sure I did.

That night I caught up with a friend of Marco's called Sergio. He was a painter and Marco had felt he would give me a unique slant on the city.

'Sergio will show you the city through the eyes of an artist,' he said.

Sergio was my age. He was tanned, muscular and had a shaved head. A pair of stylish sunglasses rested on top of his shiny pate even though it was already dark. They stayed there for the rest of the evening.

We met on the steps of the Teatro Massimo. Sergio said foreigners seemed to like meeting there. I'd parked Marcello just outside the gate and Sergio insisted on seeing him.

'So this is the famous Vespa!' he said, looking at him admiringly. I couldn't help think that Sergio would have looked cooler on Marcello than me.

We were heading to a bar on Via Candelai, a street lined with cheap bars and restaurants. It was a popular early evening meeting spot for young Palermitans and the perfect place for an aperitif. It was a couple of blocks back down Via Maqueda. Sergio jumped on the back of Marcello without a helmet and said he'd give me directions. I hesitated, not at all sure about riding up a busy one-way street in the wrong direction, but Sergio told me not to worry.

'The drivers will see this Vespa coming,' he said with a laugh.

A few life-threatening moments later we arrived at the bar Sergio had chosen. We sat at one of the tables outside under umbrellas. Sergio ordered two beers and asked me if I spoke Italian. After my experience at the hotel I confessed that I didn't.

'Good!' he said with a smile. 'I am sick of people practising their bad Italian on me. Tonight I want to practise my bad English on you.'

Via Candelai was full of young people gathered to laugh, flirt, hang out and have fun; guys slouching against their scooters, trying to impress the girls.

I'd parked Marcello in the middle of them. Looking across at him that night it struck me that he was the perfect bike to slouch against. He stood out. He looked cool. And if you got involved in a little snogging action he was solid enough not to topple over.

I was momentarily distracted by the television in the bar. The evening news featured a report on a traffic jam in Bologna. It looked grey and dismal and a million miles from the buzz and warmth of this night in Palermo. It looked distant, otherworldly, and probably meant as much to Sicilians as a report on a traffic jam in Sydney. Sicilians watched the same TV as the rest of Italy. They had the same shops as the rest of Italy. But somehow it felt different.

'People here think of themselves as Sicilians first,' explained Sergio. 'We are also very suspicious of outsiders.'

I said I hadn't found that to be the case and he said it was because of Marcello.

'Your Vespa disarms us!' he laughed.

Sergio asked when my daughter was due, and when I told him he said that he had a daughter too. She was nine but he hadn't seen her for three years. He'd split with her mother. The pressure of having a child and an unstable profession proved too much. It was a messy separation and the mother refused to let him see his daughter. He told me he was thinking of calling his ex to try and see his daughter again and I told him he should. He nodded sadly.

After our beers we jumped back on Marcello and headed north up Via Vittorio Emanuele, this time in the right direction. We'd been to the street to be seen. We'd drunk in the bar to be seen. Next stop was the restaurant, a favourite with the more bohemian residents of Palermo. There was a ritual to a night out in the city, Sergio said. In that way Palermo *was* like everywhere else in Italy.

We turned up a tiny lane at the back of the Fountain of Shame, wove our way down a series of cobbled lanes that shook my fillings loose, and emerged onto a square overlooking the Chiesa San Francesco d'Assisi, a church that was built in the thirteenth century and keeps its medieval bearing. On the other side of the square sat an elegant outdoor restaurant where the beautiful people of Palermo chose fresh seafood from a display and drank expensive wine at tables overlooking the floodlit church. I asked with surprise if this was where we were eating and Sergio let out a contemptuous 'Pah!'

'We are going to the Stella,' he said.

Trattoria Stella was further in, deep in the Kalsa quarter, built by the Arabs in the first half of the tenth century. Here the lanes were darker and grottier. Cats fought on the street. Raised voices came from the apartments and the sound of bottles smashing echoed along the walls. I felt like I was back on the *Emilia* again.

A hand-painted sign on a hoarding surrounding an old building announced that we had arrived at the Stella. It pointed down an ancient stone tunnel lined with 44-gallon drums and bags of cement and a tower of tyres. The tunnel led to a flagstoned courtyard backed by a crumbling building covered in vines.

It looked like a film set. Candles of various shapes and colours were wedged into niches, creating shadows that danced madly on the walls. A motley collection of tables and chairs were scattered under two huge oleanders that dropped flowers on diners underneath. The kitchen was outside too, under a tin roof covered in creepers.

I told Sergio it reminded me of something I'd read, about Palermo being a city of beauty and lamentations. We were dining among the rubble of ruined buildings, with nothing but the stars above our heads, and it was beautiful.

The food, as you can imagine, was simple. Pasta. Grilled meat. Salad. But that night, in those surroundings, it felt like a feast.

Dessert was pineapple doused in *grappa*, the local firewater. A group of young people, one holding a dish covered in aluminium foil, the rest clutching bottles of wine, wandered through the restaurant into the decrepit building for a party. It was a reminder that people still lived among the ruins.

We finished the meal with a shot of *grappa*. Then another. It seemed to make Sergio contemplative.

Then he looked me in the eye as if he had something very important to say.

'You are about to enter one of the most exciting, beautiful and frightening periods of your life,' he said intently. 'Grab it with both hands.'

I told him that was one of the reasons I was doing this trip now – so I could spend more time with my daughter after she was born.

'That is smart,' he said.

After the meal, I gave Sergio a lift back to my hotel. He lived nearby, he said, and could walk home from there. I thanked him for the evening. He shook my hand and said *buonanotte*. Then he set off down one of the dark cobbled streets.

When he was a hundred metres down the lane I saw the screen on his mobile phone illuminate.

I hoped that he was texting his ex-wife to arrange to see his daughter again.

CHAPTER EIGHT

POGGIOREALE

PATRON SAINT: SAN ANTONIO DA PADOVA

I have a Sicilian accountant. His name is John Stillone and he runs his practice out of a busy office in the southern suburbs of Sydney. Whenever I mention where he is from people feel compelled to do bad Marlon Brando impersonations and make jokes about horse's heads. To my knowledge he has never sent an equine extremity to the tax office on my behalf. However, I should point out that I always get a refund.

John was born in Poggioreale, a small farming town in the heart of Sicily's rural north-west interior. It sits on the southern slope of Mount Castellazzo and commands views over the Belice Valley. Some believe the town was built on the site of an ancient settlement built by the Trojans when they fled the destruction of their city by the Athenians, although archaeological digs throughout the valley have not been able to confirm this.

John and his family emigrated to Australia in 1953, 15 years before Poggioreale was destroyed by an earthquake. It came early on the morning of 14 January 1968 and wiped out the 11 other communities in the valley as well. All told, 370 people died, thousands were injured and 70,000 people were left homeless.

The Poggiorealesi who stayed lived in tents and temporary huts called *barracca* until a new town was built a few kilometres to the south-east in the Mandria di Mezzo quarter. The old town was abandoned and remains untouched, a crumbling ghost town popular with directors making films about the Second World War. When John found out I was going to Sicily he insisted I visit his home town. He gave me detailed directions on how to get there and arranged for Gioacchino Coco, an architect from the *Comune* (local council), to show me around. John had gone to so much trouble on my behalf, it would have been rude not to go. There was also the important consideration that my financial wellbeing was in his hands.

I didn't go directly to Poggioreale from Palermo. I took a more circuitous route through the dry, barren mountains south of Palermo to Corleone instead.

Before Mario Puzo wrote *The Godfather* and chose the name Corleone for the main character in his book, few outside of Sicily had heard of the town. It was just another rural town in the dry interior of an island many people had left after the Second World War. But after the success of the book – 20 million copies sold and counting – and the even more successful movies – nine Oscars all told and US$250 million ticket sales in the States alone – there are very few people who haven't heard of it.

Mario Puzo didn't just stick a pin on a map to choose a name. Corleone has been a Mafia stronghold for over 50 years. In the first four years after the Second World War it had one of the highest murder rates in the world – 153 out of a population of 18,000 – and ever since then the local police have been pulling bodies out of the rocky crevices that surround the town.

Many of the *capo di tutti capi* (boss of all bosses), hail from this neck of the woods. Salvatore Riina, at one time the most wanted man in Italy, operated his 'business' from here until he was arrested in Palermo when his driver squealed. Bernardo Provenzano, known as 'the Real Godfather' or 'the Tractor' for the blunt way he dealt with enemies, ran a multifaceted crime empire for 43 years from a shepherd's hut high in the hills here.

Provenzano was regarded as the last of the Corleonesi, the rural Mafia, now seen as slightly old-fashioned. His business included extortion, drug trafficking, smuggling and public works contracts, but it was run 'the old way', where loyalty and the Bible were more important than driving around in a flash car. He was finally captured in 2006 after police followed his laundry delivery to a tiny hut in the hills. The hut was simply furnished, and fresh chicory picked from the hills nearby was cooking on the stove. Provenzano looked to all intents and purposes like a simple shepherd. Mafia experts like Attilio Bolzoni claim this was a deliberate choice – an example of Mafia ethics in the face of the flash 'Americanisation' of the Family.

After riding through the fertile valley of the Conca d'Oro, the golden bowl (or valley), Corleone appeared like a dry scab in the crevices of the mountains. Most of the houses remained half built with rusty reinforcement rods sticking out of the top for extra storeys that would never be built. Sergio had told me that as long as a house remained unfinished in Sicily the owners didn't have to pay tax on it. Power lines were draped between floors and between buildings. Jojoba and prickly pears sprouted among the dust and the debris. Nothing about Corleone gave any indication that it was the hub of a €6 billion crime empire. It looked tired, dishevelled and incontinent – a bit like 'the Tractor' when the *carabinieri* finally picked him up.

The only part of the town of any distinction was a rocky column that rose from the crevices of the valley. It was a column of granite, topped by a couple of old buildings and a grove of cypress pines. The 100-metre drop from each side looked like the perfect way to dispose of those who had broken the *omerta*, the code of silence that has protected the Mafia for so long.

My arrival in town was watched intently by the old men sitting outside the Associazione San Giuseppe, a social club where every man over 60 in Corleone gathered. They all wore dark glasses and as I passed, their heads swivelled in a line like the clowns you feed ping-pong balls to at a carnival. The old fellow on the end took out a mobile phone and punched a message to someone somewhere alerting them to the news that I had stopped at the Sweet Temptations *pasticceria* and was making a rather messy attempt to eat a *cassata*, a sponge cake filled with sweet ricotta, pistachios, liqueur and candied fruit.

Sweet Temptations was the only place in Corleone that acknowledged the *Godfather* phenomenon, and even then they did it in a decidedly understated manner. There were a couple of black and white stills from the movies on the back wall and a signed photo of Al Pacino behind the counter. I'd hoped for a range of suitably named confectionery – a Don Corleone *cannoli* perhaps – but I was left disappointed. It was as if the city fathers had decided to give the tourists that breezed through here something to justify a visit, but not enough to make them want to stay.

I wasn't the only interesting thing happening in Corleone that afternoon. A stage had been set up in the tiny square opposite for a concert later in the evening and the band was doing a sound check.

The band was called The Phom and they went about the business of setting up with a nervousness that suggested it was either their first gig ever or perhaps the fate of a close relative depended on their performance. The lead singer tapped the microphone anxiously and mumbled 'Testing 1, 2, 3' in Italian. Then the band crunched out a couple of songs from their set.

The men outside Associazione San Giuseppe ignored the band and continued to watch me instead. When the guitarist stood too close to his amp and set off a squall of feedback they didn't even flinch. They could have had their hearing aids turned down but I suspect that in Corleone a guy riding a loud, lairy Vespa beats a band playing a very bad cover version of 'Walk of Life' by Dire Straits every time.

I was staying in the Belvedere, the only hotel in Corleone. It sat high on the southern outskirts of town, looking out across a series of rolling hills stretching to the west. It was so new and shiny that I decided it had to be a front for some money-laundering scheme.

My suspicions were further aroused by a notice taped on the door saying that the hotel was closed and listing a number to call if you wanted to check in. The notice had yellowed and faded, suggesting that the Belvedere was very rarely open. I called the number and twenty minutes later a woman turned up holding a tiny dog in her arms. She let me in, flicked on a bank of lights, handed me a key to a room on the third floor and then turned around to leave. I asked if breakfast was included and she showed me a storeroom filled with bottles of mineral water and packets of biscotti. Apparently I was to help myself.

It was quite eerie having an entire hotel to myself. I padded about the empty halls, poking my head into various rooms and wondering what lay behind the doors that were locked and why I hadn't been given a room on the first or second floors. I decided that they were used for more nefarious purposes – an amphetamine lab perhaps or a safe house for illegal immigrants smuggled up from Africa. The reality, I suspect, was that the Belvedere had very few guests and the management simply put guests in new rooms rather than employ a cleaner to tidy up the rooms that had already been used.

I showered, rested and headed back into town as the sun set to watch The Phom. The old men had abandoned their chairs outside the Associazione and decamped to the benches in the square. Everyone else sat in cars that had been parked nose-first all around the square.

The locals didn't get out of their cars. They didn't even wind down the windows. They just sat and watched the band through their windscreens. I had the fanciful notion that it was to facilitate a quick getaway should the concert prove to be a ruse, a gig put on by the *carabinieri* to lure the local crimelords out of their rural hideaways for a big night out. It was probably just how things were done in these parts, but I was careful to park Marcello in a place that didn't obstruct their vision or their getaway route.

In the far corner of the square there was a bronze statue of Padre Pio. Earlier in the afternoon his outstretched arms had looked like a welcoming embrace to the sick and the needy. But that night it appeared as though the good Padre was reaching out to the band, pretty much in the manner large-breasted girls do while they are riding on the shoulders of jocks in Beach Boys film clips. The way the lights danced across his face also gave the impression that the Padre was smitten by The Phom.

I took my cue from the locals and sat on Marcello to watch the band, flipping down the glove box lid like an airline table to hold some rotisserie chicken and chips that I'd bought from a shop opposite the square. It wasn't exactly authentic Italian food. Nor was it a dish that Corleone is famous for. (The local ricotta cannelloni is particularly well regarded.) But that night, with a balmy breeze at my back, a bottle of Birra Moretti in my hand, and 'Eye of the Tiger' ringing in my ears, it really hit the spot. And I wasn't the only one who thought so. The old guy sitting in the beat-up Fiat I'd parked next to wound down his window and asked me where I'd got it from.

The next morning I foraged for my breakfast, left my room key at the unmanned desk and then headed west to Poggioreale, taking an extra bottle of water with me. There was no direct road between the two towns, just a series of minor roads that wound through the lonely hills that separated them. I didn't pass another vehicle or see another living soul. I simply rode through an expanse of nothingness, more immense than anything I'd seen in Italy before.

The new town of Poggioreale sits surrounded by farmland beside a lonely road leading directly to Palermo, 61 kilometres to the north. At 393 metres above sea level it is considerably lower in the Belice Valley than the old town, which sits – just in view – a couple of kilometres away.

The new town was finally finished twenty years after the earthquake. It's centred on three 'round' town squares, each encircled by rings of residential buildings. As with many planned towns, high concepts had been put ahead of practicalities when it was designed. I could see a hodge-podge of architectural styles that just didn't gel as a coherent whole. There was a neoclassical nod here, a medieval-style tower there, an African-looking sculpture and a pair of staircases that ascended into an optical blindspot like an Escher print. As my father would say, Poggioreale didn't know whether it was an arm or an elbow.

I arrived in the new town just before lunch. The streets were deserted and I puttered around the circular roads for a good ten minutes before I found someone to ask where I could find Gioacchino Coco. Eventually I found an old man – wearing dark glasses of course – but he simply shrugged his shoulders and said that he'd never heard of him. The next man I came across said the same thing, as did the middle-aged woman struggling home with a bag of shopping.

It could have been my pronunciation of Gioacchino. My Australian accent and uncanny ability to put the emphasis on entirely the wrong syllable made it difficult for even the most patient listener to understand. I suspected the residents had simply closed ranks to protect their local architect. They weren't sure what Gioacchino had done, but a stranger with a funny accent was asking after him by name. They weren't going to be the ones that gave him up.

I found a small *tabbachi* shop and explained to the owner where I was from, who I was looking for and who had sent me. He called out to a small boy loitering outside, gave him a stick of gum and told him to show me the way.

The boy looked like the kid out of *Cinema Paradiso*. He wore a tatty T-shirt and shorts and shot off from the shop like a greyhound. He bounded through the town, tearing across the Piazza Elimo along pavements cracked and filled with weeds. I had to stick to the road, riding along circular streets that I was sure had looked good on the town planner's easel but were useless for getting anywhere quickly. I tore around them, keeping one eye on the kid and another on the unexpected bends and dead-ends that kept appearing. It took every one of Marcello's 200ccs to keep up with him.

The new town of Poggioreale was home to only 1711 people but the town hall looked like it serviced a thriving metropolis. The grand entrance was curved and featured a series of tall glass doors flanked by columns three storeys high. Beyond that, a long corridor lined with offices (one for each inhabitant it seemed) ran to an infinite spot in the distance. Gioacchino's office, naturally, was right at the end.

The dress code at the Poggioreale municipal offices was as casual as the security. Men in short-sleeved shirts and jeans tousled the boy's hair as we passed and women in T-shirts and jeans pinched his cheeks. No one asked who I was or why I was there. Gioacchino didn't seem particularly surprised by my arrival either. He gave the boy a couple of euros, said something to him in Italian, and then indicated for me to sit down.

'I've been expecting you,' he said with a smile. He'd already had half a dozen calls telling him that a guy on an orange Vespa with Livornese plates was looking for him.

Gioacchino's secretary made us an espresso each and he asked me if I'd come from Palermo. I said Corleone and he raised his eyebrows.

'That is a long way on a Vespa,' he said, impressed. He was even more amazed when I said that I had got to Corleone by way of Sardinia.

As Gioacchino's secretary cleared away our cups, he grabbed his coat and beckoned for me to follow. He told his secretary that he was going to do some 'fieldwork'.

Fieldwork for the architectural professional in Poggioreale involves eating a simple lunch of tomatoes, mozzarella and salad leaves prepared by your wife and drinking a couple of tumblers of robust red wine poured from a flagon. Then, after a shot of the local rocket fuel for digestive purposes, a short journey into the hills to visit the ruins of Poggioreale Vecchio, the town destroyed by the earthquake. Gioacchino drove in his car. I followed on Marcello.

The ruins of the original Poggioreale sit high on the southern slope of Mount Castellazzo, surrounded by fields and overlooking the new town below. It is now a designated archaeological site, surrounded by a fence and with an entrance gate that is locked every night at dusk. Gioacchino parked his car outside the gate and jumped on the back of Marcello.

'It will be easier for us to get around,' he said.

We rode up Via Umberto I, with crumbling buildings either side of us. It felt like I was riding through a newsreel from the Second World War. The only building that had been built after 1960 was the public library and it had crumbled easier than most. The rest looked like they had been hit by allied bombers.

The Sicilian director Giuseppe Tornatore also picked up on the wartime vibe. He filmed his war epic *The Star Maker* here. And he also used the town for a few scenes in his movie *Malena*, notable for introducing Monica Bellucci to the world. Only a few weeks beforehand an American crew had been filming a *Band of Brothers*-style telemovie here. As we rode through the town Gioacchino pointed out a wall they had knocked down during the shoot. It had caused a great deal of anger in new Poggioreale but if he hadn't pointed it out I wouldn't have noticed.

Soon we reached the original Piazza Elime and the broken staircase leading up to La Matrice, the 'Mother Church', and its striking campanile. Every street, piazza and public building in the new town took its name from its equivalent in the old town but, sadly, none of its charm.

The church bell tower has become a landmark, a symbol of the old town. The fact that it still stands is seen as something of a miracle. Gioacchino pointed out some cracks and said that it was in danger of collapsing.

'People from Poggioreale who live in your country and the United States are raising money to make it safe,' he said. While I'm no building expert, I suspect they haven't got much time to do it.

Gioacchino pointed to a pile of stones that had once been his family's home. He was only five when the earthquake struck but he still has very clear memories of the night. A series of tremors came first and the local brigadier, a non-commissioned *carabinieri* officer named Antonio Rubuano, persuaded everyone to leave their homes. They fled into the surrounding countryside, huddling together against the freezing conditions.

'I remember seeing the buildings swaying from side to side,' he said. 'A woman was crying "San Antonio! San Antonio!"'

San Antonio da Padova is the patron saint of Poggioreale. I asked Gioacchino if people had lost faith in San Antonio after the earthquake. He looked shocked.

'Oh no!' he said. 'San Antonio saved us!'

Of the 370 people who died in the quake only two lived in Poggioreale.

'A fat lady who got stuck in the door trying to get out,' explained Gioacchino. 'And her husband trapped behind her.' The house collapsed on both of them.

The government's emergency and relief efforts were as devastating as the earthquake itself. Casualties were left unattended. Thousands were left homeless. And bodies trapped under the rubble were eaten by pigs as authorities dithered over what to do. The incompetence of both the national government and the local authorities were there for everyone to see. Poggioreale, and the Belice Valley, became a synonym for corruption in the wake of natural disasters. A new phrase entered the Italian political lexicon: 'I won't let this become another Poggioreale.'

For the first six months after the earthquake, the survivors lived in tents in the hills around the town. It was the middle of a particularly wet winter. Violent winds and rain turned the refugee camps into quagmires.

When the money came from the central government and international donors it was hijacked by the Mafia and corrupt politicians. The new site for Poggioreale was chosen not for its position but rather because the landowner was a friend of the local Don.

The survivors weren't averse to a bit of wheeling and dealing themselves. Each person had been promised the same-sized home in the new town as they'd had before. If they had a four-bedroom house in the original Poggioreale they would have a four-bedroom house in the new town. Gioacchino said that the townsfolk snuck into the ruins at night and built dividing walls in the wreckage of their homes so that it appeared they'd had more rooms than they did.

Until the new town was built, the survivors moved into temporary buildings called *barracca*. They'd been thrown up by the government six months after the quake and were meant to be a short-term solution – they didn't have baths or toilets – but in the end they were home to most of the town's inhabitants for eighteen years. The lucky ones escaped and started new lives in countries like Australia and the United States.

Most of the *barracca* were eventually knocked down but one remained. It sat on a hill behind the old town next to a stone staircase leading to nowhere and flanked by mature palm trees. The old woman who still lived there refused to move. It had been home for so long that she was determined to die there.

Back in the old town, Gioacchino pointed out a stone fountain near the eastern gate. He used to ride the family donkey there each day so it could drink.

'My friends rode their family donkeys here too,' he said. 'We would always have a race.'

Gioacchino laughed as he remembered. He said he could almost hear the clack of the hooves on the cobblestones. I said couldn't imagine the same thing happening on the streets of the new town. For one thing there wasn't a straight road in the place.

I parked Marcello beside the fountain and Gioacchino and I picked our way through the ruins and the thick brambles that had engulfed them to a cobbled street that ran down a gentle hill called Via Pavone. This was the street my accountant had grown up on. Gioacchino stopped outside a row of identical houses, gutted and empty and overgrown with weeds.

'This was Casa Stillone,' he said reverentially. I took a few photos, observed a minute of silence and then we moved on. It was a surreal moment considering no one had actually died here.

We finished the tour of the old town outside the old town hall on Via Umberto I. It was made from a reddish stone, and with its striking columns and grand staircase it reminded me of the treasury building in Petra, Jordan. The Nabataean ruins in Petra date from before the time of Christ. Poggioreale had been abandoned less than forty years before. But, strangely, it felt as ancient.

Poggioreale wasn't the only town destroyed by the earthquake. In all, 12 communities were destroyed. One was Gibellina, 7 kilometres to the west. Whereas the ruins of Poggioreale had been left, a snapshot in time, an entirely different approach was taken with the ruins at Gibellina. A local artist covered them in concrete. Gioacchino took me to see them.

The artist in question was Alberti Burri. The technique he used was called cretti. Previously Burri had created monochrome pieces made from paste and left to dry, the cracks and fissure that appeared being the art. When Gibellina was abandoned he covered the whole town. The fissures of the streets became the cracks of his work. The concrete masses of the building pointed to a time when the old town existed. And the integration of the rubble into the concrete reminded one of the earthquake's effects.

Well, that's what the panel said when Alberti Burri was awarded the Italian Order of Merit in 1994. That afternoon with Gioacchino, it looked to me like the hill had been covered in white icing and someone had got to it with a giant cookie cutter. I did like the way the irregularity of the concrete streets echoed the irregular pattern of the vineyards in the hills behind it, though.

From Gibellina I trailed Gioacchino along a road that followed the contours of the mountains and through a field of wild fennel to a plateau of rich farmland. (The Poggiorealese are so fond of fennel that they are also known as *finocchiari*, fennel eaters.)

Our destination was a farm in the hills that produced cheese. Not because there was anything particularly special about the cheese. It was made from sheep's milk which was common in these parts. We were heading there because the cheese maker, Gianni, had gone to school with my accountant. He stood at the end of a long drive waiting for us. After a cursory wave towards the shed where the cheese was made he led us to a table under a tree where a bottle of wine and glasses were waiting for us.

'To be honest, I can't remember much of him,' he said as he poured the wine. When I showed John a photo of Gianni when I got back to Sydney he couldn't remember him either. But that afternoon it didn't matter. We were sitting under a tree in the Sicilian countryside drinking a nice but robust red. In that way, the Sicilians weren't any different from other Italians. They'd use any excuse to take a break and have a drink.

We drank in silence, listening to the light breeze rustling through the trees and the tweet of the swallows as they dive-bombed insects around the shed. We were on our second tumbler of wine – my third for the afternoon counting the one I'd had at lunch – when a man came walking up the long drive. He wore breeches and a straw hat and his name was Francesco.

He was the local madman and he supported himself by picking wild oregano and then selling it in smaller bunches for €5 a time.

Francesco took an instant shine to Marcello. He danced around him excitedly and, after laying his oregano aside, gave him a hearty double thumbs-up. After ascertaining that Marcello belonged to me, he told Gioacchino that he wanted to show me his secret oregano patch.

'You are very privileged,' laughed Gioacchino. 'No one else knows where it is.'

Gioacchino declared that his fieldwork was over and headed back to work, leaving me with Francesco to guide me to the secret oregano patch and then to head back to the small B&B that Gioacchino had arranged for me to stay in.

Soon Francesco and I were zipping along bumpy roads in the empty hills with the sun on our backs. Francesco wildly waved his arms to give directions, choreographing me around herds of sheep that blocked our way until a grumpy shepherd herded them out of the way. He laughed like a child at the thrill of being on the back of my Vespa. At the end of a dirt road we stopped and clambered up some rocks to where his secret herb stash grew. He picked it. I held it. Just a whiff of oregano takes me back to that afternoon instantly.

On the way back Francesco started doing a charade of a motorcyclist twisting an accelerator in an attempt to make me go faster. I did and he giggled. The next corner I leaned into like I was Valentino Rossi. I did the same with the next one. It was covered in pellets of sheep dung.

I'm sure if you asked an Italian they'd tell you that there was a special way to ride a Vespa around a corner covered in freshly dropped sheep dung. If you pushed them, they could probably instruct you on how to do it while adjusting your Dior sunglasses in the side mirror at the same time. But on a lonely country road in the mountains of central Sicily, the only person I could ask was Francesco and he was sitting behind me, desperately clasping a couple of bales of oregano and trying hard not to fall off. I instinctively employed a 'hang on for dear life' strategy that proved ungainly but effective – equally so when we came upon the flock responsible on the other side of the bend.

I dropped Francesco off on a dirt road in the hills above the new town and made my way back to my room in the B&B. I enjoyed a meal with the family and went to bed exhausted.

The next morning I met Gioacchino at the local chapter of the Associazione Giuseppe. I'd been in Sicily for less than a week but the whole idea of the Associaziones intrigued me. They were more prominent here, with more 'members' than elsewhere in Italy, and looked like secret societies to which I'd never be admitted. What happened inside them? Why did all the men wear dark glasses? I'd mentioned my interest to Gioacchino the day before and he laughed.

'They are full of old men gossiping and playing cards,' he said. 'Nothing interesting goes on there.' The Associazione Giuseppe in Poggioreale served the best espresso in town so he decided to humour me.

The Associazione Giuseppe was like every Associazione I'd seen so far in Sicily. A gaggle of old guys with dark glasses and walking sticks sat outside in plastic chairs. And as I walked up to the door I was greeted by a wall of smoke and a hubbub of voices. This time, however, I was accompanied by a local, so I was able to go inside.

So what does one find inside a Sicilian Associazione? More old blokes in dark glasses. Most of them, as Gioacchino had said, playing cards. There was a moment of silence when I walked in, but as soon as they realised that I was the guy on the orange Vespa they turned back to their games.

'You are already old news,' laughed Gioacchino. The local barber had arrived back from Palermo that morning with a new car and the old men of the town were more interested in how he could afford it on their lousy tips.

All the other things that I had interpreted melodramatically were equally as innocuous. The dark glasses were to protect ageing eyes from the harsh Sicilian sun. The canes provided support for limbs worn out from tending rocky fields. Even the way my every move was watched was explained.

'These people live very boring lives,' said Gioacchino.

Gioacchino introduced me to two old guys at the back and asked if we could sit at their table. The fat one wore dark glasses, had a cane and smoked a fat cigar. The skinny one wore breeches like he'd just come in from working the fields. When Gioacchino went to the counter to order our espressos the fat one took out his cigar and spoke to me.

'What part of Sydney are you from, mate?' he asked.

His accent was as unexpected as his question. It was pure Italian/Australian – the sort of thing you hear on Norton Street in Sydney or on Lygon Street in Melbourne. I told him I grew up at Rossmore on the south-west edges of Sydney and his face split into a smile.

'My brother had a poultry farm in Leppington,' he said.

The Don's name was Franco and he reached out across his ample belly and shook my hand. He'd lived in Sydney for forty years and had come back to Poggioreale when he retired. I shouldn't have been surprised. There are more people living in Sydney who were born in Poggioreale than live in Poggioreale itself.

'It is much cheaper to live here,' he said. Especially with the amount of money he'd got for his house in Five Dock when he sold it at the height of the Sydney property boom. He also got an Australian pension.

Franco asked me if I knew the Campesis in Austral or the Labruzzos in Kemps Creek. I shook my head. I had a crush on girl called Vivian Rizzo when I was eleven but I think she was originally from Naples. And I mentioned the Cinis who ran a pig farm down on Rossmore Crescent.

'Calabrians!' he said with a sniff and ordered us all another shot of espresso.

Soon it was time to head west to the port of Trápani and the Egadi Islands anchored just offshore. I had enjoyed my time in Poggioreale. Riding through the fields of fennel and exploring the old town had been a highlight of my trip so far. But Marcello was restless and so was I. We needed the smell of the sea again.

Before I left Poggioreale, Gioacchino arranged for me to meet John Maniscalco, the man who had been mayor at the time of the earthquake and during the building of the new town. It was something every visitor from overseas did and even though I had no direct family links to the town it would be considered bad form if I didn't.

Former mayor Maniscalco lived with his wife in a second-floor flat in the centre of town. It looked modest from outside but inside it was lavishly furnished with the kind of over-the-top furniture advertised on late-night television. Gioacchino introduced me to the former mayor and then excused himself to go back to work. I couldn't be sure but it looked like he bowed as he left.

The former mayor and I sat on gilded chairs at an ornate dining table in silence. The cuckoo clock on the wall ticked loudly and a series of loud clanking noises came from the kitchen. An old lady emerged from the kitchen hunched over a silver tray and served us coffee in espresso cups with gold rims. When she left the room again the former mayor asked me if I was a journalist. I told him I wrote travel books and he relaxed, standing up from the table and beckoning for me to follow.

He opened a cabinet and showed me the trinkets from his tenure: a photo of him and the Pope touring the ruins, a citation from the national government for his services to the community, and a medallion presented to him when he visited a San Antonio festival in Sydney arranged by expatriates from Poggioreale. The medallion, it seemed, was one of his most treasured possessions.

He had attended the festival a number of times, he said, and he was going again next year. He showed me a photo taken of him there and the way people were in deference to him suggested that he was once the big man in these parts. Just how big I couldn't be sure. But in this part of Sicily you didn't become mayor unless you knew the people who mattered.

The thing that had impressed the former mayor when in Australia was the business links forged between the Poggiorealese living there. They used their common heritage to form a network of skills and trades. He wished that a similar network existed between those who had remained in Sicily, he said.

'People move to Palermo or the mainland, and cut all ties with the town,' he said.

The former mayor moved to the far side of the room and unlocked the most ornate cabinet in the house. Inside were two *squartucciatu*, bread sculptures, made especially each year to embellish the altars celebrating the festival of San Giuseppe in March.

The artistry of a good *squartucciatu* is breathtaking. The bread is rolled, cut and shaped into intricate designs of flowers, birds and other things of natural beauty. Each one has to be made without breaking the dough (symbolising the unbroken communion between Christ and the Church.) It is a skill particular to Poggioreale and passed down through the generations to only a handful of women. One of the perks of being the mayor was that one of the women showed him how to do it.

It is said that to create a *squartucciatu* requires time, enthusiasm, an artistic flair and a true spirit of faith – not life skills I'd normally associate with a hard-nosed former mayor. But ex-mayor Maniscalco was as proud of his bread swan and bread jasmine as he was of the photo of him and the Pope. He insisted I took photos and was delighted when I showed them to him on the LCD screen on the back of my digital camera.

'*Bellissima!*' he said. 'You must send me a copy!'

The exertion had wearied him. He shuffled over to the table and sat down, his large frame hunched. It struck me that in his day he must have been a feared man. Yet here he was, in his dotage, getting excited about bread art.

His frail state didn't stop me scribbling his address in my notebook. Or underscoring the sentence 'Must send photos' three times.

I'd be no use to my new daughter if I ended up swimming with the fishes.

CHAPTER NINE

MARSALA

PATRON SAINT: SAINT AMAND

On Sundays in June there is only one vehicle ferry a day between Trápani and Favignana. It leaves at 2.30 p.m. and arrives at the island a little over half an hour later. Tourists without vehicles can take one of the more frequent hydrofoils but I was travelling with Marcello so my only option was to catch the solitary ferry. I missed it because I was eating a bowl of seafood couscous.

In my defence I should point out that it was the best seafood couscous I'd ever tasted. In Trápani it is spelt *kuscus*, as much an indication of the port's rich Arab heritage as the Moorish architecture and wide streets lined with date palms. The sauce is made using tomatoes, parsley, garlic and a secret mixture of herbs and spices known only to the chefs of the town. It doesn't hurt either that the seafood used is pulled out of the ocean only hours before it is cooked.

When I'd ordered my meal in a dishevelled restaurant down by the harbour I hadn't held out much hope that it would be any good. My order was taken by the chef, who wiped his hands on his apron before pulling a notepad from the back of his trousers and a pencil from behind his ear to write down what I wanted. He also brought the meal to me, making no attempt to wipe away the sauce that dribbled over the edge of the bowl when he had slopped the couscous into it.

I'd chosen the restaurant because it was almost directly opposite the wharf from which the ferry to Favignana sailed. I could actually see the ferry from my table and watched out of the corner of my eye as the cars from Favignana drove off and the ones going there drove on. I saw a guy in blue overalls wave the last passenger on. But I kept eating. The couscous had a hold over me, rooting me to the chair.

I probably could have wiped my mouth, thrust a €20 note into the restaurant owner's hand, torn off on Marcello and still made it to the dock. If it was a Jackie Chan movie I probably could have used one of the carts holding fishing nets as a ramp to roar off the wharf and land safely on the deck. But the chef, responding to my *umms* and *aahs* of delight, brought over the pot and offered me seconds. I took him up on his offer. It was the last boat of the day. I'd booked and paid for the ticket. The greatest compliment I can give his meal was that I didn't care in the slightest.

I backtracked instead to Èrice, an ancient stone town that crowns the mountain that towers over Trápani and the bay. Known in the ancient world as Eryx, it was the site of a temple dedicated first to Aphrodite, then Venus under the Romans. Some say the temple was home to sacred prostitutes who carried out sacred prostitution. And it is interesting to note that it was left to its own devices by every invader who took the town. The Romans actually stationed 200 soldiers to protect it.

The road leading to Èrice zigzagged up the dry mountain like a tightly wound spring, switching back on itself a number of times before it reached the top. Marcello attacked it with relish, powering around the tight corners and overtaking RVs struggling up the hill. They had to park in the car park outside the walls of the town along with every other vehicle. On Marcello, however, I could proceed through the Trápani Gate, one of the three gates in the thick city walls, and pick my way along the polished cobbled streets to the Piazza Umberto I in the centre of town.

I was greeted at the gate by one of the organisers of the town's annual Slow Food Festival. It had been held that weekend and, with the shadow thrown by the fourteenth-century campanile lengthening, it was coming to a close. He handed me an official Èrice Slow Food goodie bag and I hung it from the hook under the seat. It was a black pouch emblazoned with the Èrice Slow Food snail and contained a guide to the festival, coupons that could be redeemed at the stands and a glass to taste a complimentary selection of wines. It usually cost €20 he said, but because there were only a couple of hours left – and I owned such a magnificent Vespa – I could have it for free.

The narrow lanes of Èrice were full of well-dressed people tasting wines from small tables set up outside restaurants, bars and family homes. The owners of the food stalls were packing up and sampling the wine too. It had deteriorated into a slowly getting drunk festival.

I found a room in a small pension towards the edge of town called the Santa Lucia. Its stylish rooms had stunning views over the valleys to the east and the rugged coastline to the north. Normally such a room would be out of my price range but the lady running it took such a shine to Marcello that she offered me a good rate if I agreed to stay for at least two nights. As an added incentive she said I could keep Marcello in an old manger just inside the city walls that she had converted into a supply room.

With my lodging for the night sorted and Marcello safely tucked away beside piles of cotton sheets and thick bath towels,

I grabbed my pouch and plunged back into the town eager to use some of my free coupons before the festival ended.

I followed a group of people into a small hall where glamorous representatives from the Fazio winery were plugging their stuff. A woman who looked like Monica Bellucci spotted the official festival wine glass in my hand and poured some of Fazio's award-winning Moscato Passito into it. After I had taken a couple of self-conscious sips she asked me what I thought of it. I made some appropriate noises – basically a more dignified version of the ones I emitted while eating the couscous – and said that my Italian wasn't up to describing how good it was. Strangely, I wasn't offered another glass.

Even with the crowds that had descended on the town for the festival it was startlingly easy to get lost in Èrice. Within moments of leaving one wine-tasting event I found myself in a deserted lane with no idea how I'd arrived there and no idea how to get back. I tried retracing my steps but ended up instead at the Castello di Venere, the castle built in the twelfth century on the site of the old temple to Venus – looking back across the valley to the coast. Another time, I found myself at the Duomo above pine-clad hills enjoying views of the saltpans of Trápani and across the straits to the Egadi Islands. My guidebook said the islands looked like whales, but at dusk, with spray of the sea fudging, smoothing and rounding their coastlines, they looked like a school of Loch Ness monsters.

I eventually found my way back to Corso Vittorio Emanuele and its colourful *pasticceria*. The last of the festival-goers sat at wooden booths set up outside on the cobbled street, tucking into coronary-inducing pastries before heading home. The ones that looked like bread rolls full of chocolate cream seemed the most popular choice. I even saw the woman who had poured me the Moscato Passito tucking into one.

The *pasticceria* also sold *dolci di badia*, the almond-paste sweets shaped like fruit that Èrice is famous for. They were arranged artistically in the windows, their hyper-colours reminiscent of a Botticelli painting. When I was a kid my Italian friends had them at their birthday parties and, as a clueless Aussie, I'd eat them thinking that they'd taste like the piece of fruit they resembled. It was like eating a gobful of wedding cake icing. But it didn't stop me doing it every time I saw one.

The sun plummeted quickly behind the Egadi Islands and the last of the festival crowd disappeared into the night. I ate at a restaurant recommended by my landlady, a place on Via Chiaramonte that she said made 'the best artichoke pizza in Italy'. I emerged just after 9 p.m. with my belly full and wandered the deserted lanes back to my hotel. The only other living soul I came across was a man with a sign around his neck declaring 'I'm a drunkard and a divorcé'. I saw him again the next morning, this time wearing a pair of foam wings and a sign that said he was the Archangel Gabriel. He was haranguing the postman to check if there were any letters in his sack for him. Apparently he was expecting a message from God.

Over the next few days I decided I liked Èrice a lot. It was peaceful and relaxing and I enjoyed the peculiar sensation of feeling like I was perched on top of the world. My room was comfortable. The food was great. And I got acquainted enough with the Archangel Gabriel for us to nod at each other as we passed. He spotted me on Marcello one day and called me over to say that he had a Vespa just like it in heaven.

My unexpected stay in Èrice gave me a chance to visit the places that I'd missed in my rush to get from Poggioreale to Trápani in time to catch the ferry. I particularly wanted to visit Segesta and a Doric temple that many believe is the most magnificent in Sicily.

My journey to Segesta took me on a pleasant ride through the patchwork of fields I could see from my room in Èrice. Here farmland was tilled and tended in a manner that hadn't changed for centuries, with dry stone walls delineating allotments worked by men with leathery faces and mules in need of a good meal. The roads that passed through them were seldom used by anyone other than locals. As I rode by, an old farmer looked up and doffed his flat cap as I passed.

The Elymians started building the temple of Segesta in 430 BC and, it has to be said, they knew how to pick a building site. The temple enjoys a setting as dramatic as Èrice, one of their earlier projects. It sits beside a deep canyon, backed by granite-flecked Monte Barbaro and surrounded by fields lined with grapevines or covered in bright yellow flowers.

The temple itself was never finished. The Elymians got into a spat with Selinunte just down the road and blew the building budget on trying to get the Carthaginians to back them. The 36 sturdy Doric columns, pitted and worn by time, are topped by a sturdy entablature and pediment to hold a roof that was never built. Stone studs that were normally removed on completion still line the stylobate, the top step. Swallows nest where the fluting for the columns should have been. But rather than detract from the temple these things simply add to its grandeur.

It helped, of course, that I had the site to myself. Elsewhere in Italy such a magnificent ruin would be overrun with tourists. But that day, halfway through a hot, dry morning, it was empty. A light breeze played a mournful tune through the columns. Swallows darted and dived after insects drawn towards the fields of flowers just over the rise. And I had a wide-screen view from a seat shaded by a pair of wattle trees. It was perfect.

It couldn't last. A minibus arrived and a handful of tourists clambered up the path towards the temple, fanning themselves with their guidebooks. But for half an hour it was just me and the swallows and the lizards scampering over the stones. I jumped on Marcello, twisted the accelerator and headed back to the cool heights of Èrice, lathering my arms and the tops of my legs with sunscreen in an attempt to lessen my chances of getting a Vespa tan.

And so it was that on a Wednesday, three days after my first attempt to catch a ferry to Favignana, I was back in Trápani trying again.

I had set off early from Èrice, ostensibly to make sure I got the ferry, but in reality to ensure I had enough time for another bowl of seafood couscous. The chef recognised me by my slurps of delight and again brought me seconds. I made the boat but only seconds before a Jackie Chan jump would have been necessary. I parked Marcello on the car deck, made my way to the passenger lounge and promptly fell asleep.

I woke up in a Robert Louis Stevenson novel. A tall, bare mountain rose dramatically from a bay, towering over the tiny town that sat opposite it. It was topped by a sinister stone building – a prison apparently – and around its base a vaulted nineteenth-century fishery sat abandoned and derelict like a shabby string of pearls that had long lost their lustre. It felt like the ends of the earth, not an island 15 kilometres off the west coast of Sicily. I decided immediately that I liked it.

Favignana is best known for *la mattanza*, the annual ritual slaughtering of blue fin tuna that come to mate here every spring. It is held between the end of May and early June and has been practised for over 2000 years. Using skilfully crafted nets and urged on by 'priests' known as *Capo Rais*, the local fishermen arrange their boats in a manner that channels the fish into a *camera della morte*, chamber of death. When there are enough fish trapped inside, the fishermen launch a frenzied attack, six or seven of them attacking each tuna with a gruesome hook and dragging them onto the boats.

Not surprisingly, the number of tuna – and their size – is declining each year. That's what happens when you interrupt a species with a bit of ritual slaughter when they're meant to be shagging. But it hasn't stopped *la mattanza* from becoming a tourist attraction, with the more sadistic paying top dollars to be on board to witness it up close. You'll find some of Japan's top chefs on the island then too. Over 90 per cent of the tuna caught are transported immediately to Tokyo.

I had missed la mattanza by a week. I'd considered leaving Palermo early to see it, but remembering the gruesome *mattanza* scene in Roberto Rossellini's movie *Stromboli*, I decided against it.

Favignana was in a post-*mattanza* lull. The clobbered tuna were on a refrigerated freighter back to Japan and the hordes of tourists that descended on the island during the height of summer were still over a month away. The weather was good though, and the locals used the time to repair their fishing nets or apply a lick of whitewash to the houses they would lease for over-the-odds prices to people from the mainland.

The downside was that all the hotels and B&Bs recommended by my guidebook were closed. One, an *albergo* run by sisters that my guidebook said served the best food in Sicily, had a sign in three languages saying they wouldn't be open until August.

I puttered around the town and the western part of the island growing more and more frustrated, but thankful that I was on the back of Marcello and not on foot.

I returned to the dock and asked a fisherman repairing his nets if he knew of anywhere I could stay. He pointed to the Marina Residence. It was an unremarkable building right on the harbour with an institutional air that I had assumed provided lodgings for homeless sailors. The fisherman assured me that they also rented rooms to tourists and pointed to a door that he said led to the reception.

The reception, naturally enough, was unattended. I rang the bell on the counter and after a few minutes a fat middle-aged man wearing a straw hat and dark glasses emerged from a doorway at the back of the room. He wasn't happy about being disturbed and when I asked if he had any rooms available he shook his head and said all the singles were closed until the summer. There were only doubles and apartments available.

He turned to leave, certain this news would get rid of me. I asked him how much a double cost and he swore under his breath.

'Thirty euros,' he mumbled. It was only €5 more than a single cost. I said I'd take it for two nights.

The checking-in process was long and painful. When the manager took twenty minutes just to photocopy my passport I began to suspect he was hoping I'd throw up my arms in frustration and walk away. I'd obviously broken an unstated rule that although the Marina Residence looked like it was open, it really wasn't. Each moment I didn't take the hint and leave his curses got louder and more profane.

When I asked if I could pay by credit card I thought he was going to explode. It wasn't an unreasonable request. The office was covered with Visa stickers and the little machine that accepted the card was on the desk and switched on, with its green light blinking. But he insisted on cash. When I gave him two €50 notes to settle the €60 bill, he spluttered with rage and told me to go and get change.

Now it was my turn to get a little pissed off. I told him it was cash, like he asked for, and if he didn't have change he could give a discount rate so the bill came to €50 even. He called me a *ladrone*, thief, pulled out a fat wad of notes from his pocket and, peeling off the change, tossed it to me with my passport and the keys to my room. He disappeared back through the doorway before telling me where my room was.

An old drunk showed me the way instead. He was one of the residence's 'long-term' guests and stood beside me as I opened the door so he could get a glimpse inside. The manager had given me one of the apartments, a quirky little place set over two floors with a metal spiral staircase, TV, air conditioning and a kitchen with a fridge and microwave.

It was the room they all aspired to, the drunk said, and the only reason I'd got it was because the cleaning lady was in Trápani. None of the other rooms had been cleaned since *la mattanza*.

The town of Favignana was tiny. The long, straight design of the Marina Residence meant that the town's two main attractions – the harbour and the town square – were immediately accessible depending on which door you chose to exit from. The harbour was reached from the front. If you wanted the square you went out the back.

I chose the front door and spent the afternoon sitting on the wharf with my legs dangling over the edge watching fishermen paint their boats and repair their nets. A boy stood on the end of the concrete breakwater fishing, getting tips from his father whenever he cast his line, and as dusk approached other fishing boats returned and loaded their catch of fish into waiting *Apes*.

After I'd showered and evening fell, I chose the rear door, emerging onto the town square as the orange streaks from sunset slowly darkened and the street lights flickered to life. The air was thick and warm and I sat at a table outside a restaurant drinking beer from a bottle dripping with condensation. Somewhere on the square a radio played a song from the new Kings of Convenience album. I can't tell you how impressed I was. Not just that the radio station was playing a Kings of Convenience song, and a song off an album that had only just been released, but how perfectly the languid piano line matched the mood of Favignana that night. Even now when I hear that song I'm immediately transported back to that evening.

The restaurant was popular with the locals so I decided to stay and eat a meal there as well. The menu was heavily tuna-based. *Spaghetti alla Favignanese* turned out to be spaghetti with tuna. *Linguine alla Zia Domenica* was, you guessed it, linguine with tuna. *Tonno Ammuttunatu* was a tuna casserole. In the end I plumped for *tonno all'araba*, figuring that the pistachio nuts, toasted almonds, capers and minced chilli peppers would give the tuna steaks a suitably Middle Eastern zing. They did.

I finished the evening wandering the tiny alleys of the town eating an ice cream I'd bought from the *gelateria* on the other side of the square. The alleys were quiet and empty except for the one that was lined with fish shops. The shops were still open, and busy with local women stocking up on fish fresh from the boats. A gang of cats sat outside waiting for scraps.

The next day I rode through a tunnel underneath Monte San Caterina to the west side of the island. It was less developed than the eastern side but the waiter at the restaurant had told me that this was where his favourite swimming spot was. It was on a rocky point just south of Punta Ferro, he said, next to a sheep farm surrounded by a low stone wall. If he hadn't given me such specific instructions I would have given up at the tufa quarry, but I continued and was rewarded with a rocky cove where the sea was a startling shade of blue.

There was no sand of course. If there had been it would have been covered in deckchairs and umbrellas and guarded by someone demanding €5 to step upon it. Instead I clambered down onto a rocky ledge and dived straight into the sea, swimming out far enough to avoid being dashed upon the shore.

The water was warm and salty so I lay with my arms outstretched, bobbing with the ebb and flow of the sea. I'd parked Marcello among the rocks and looking back at him, it struck me how much the scene looked like a Vespa ad from the seventies. By that point Piaggio was shamelessly pursuing the youth market and every piece of advertising seemed to feature a brightly coloured Vespa and a girl in a bikini. Sometimes it was on a rocky beach like this. At other times it was on a sandy beach and the girl wore cheesecloth.

The message was always the same. A Vespa was elemental. When you rode one you were at one with the air, the sun and the sand. One ad featuring an electric blue Vespa ran the headline '*Oggi son il mare*' – 'today I am the sea'. That day, floating in the clear, clean aqua waters off Favignana, I knew exactly what they meant.

I wasn't the sea though. I was a husband and I was about to become a father. And I was reminded of that as I rode back towards the town and spotted a bronze statue of a woman holding a baby. It was in the middle of a field just before the tunnel that cut through the mountain, and there were a couple of rows of stone benches set out in front of it. It was an outdoor chapel – the site of a miracle, a vision perhaps – and I felt compelled to pull over. I sat on one of the benches and contemplated the responsibilities that lay ahead of me once I got home. I called Sally on my mobile phone and caught up with the news that our little one was kicking like Bruce Lee. The sun was dropping below the horizon when I finally rode off.

*

I often find myself on little quests when I'm on one of my journeys. On my last visit to Italy it was to find a Kinder

Surprise holding the little green Vespa toy I'd seen advertised on the box. I don't set off with a particular quest in mind. They just kind of happen. *Lonely Planet* publishes a book called *Experimental Travel* that eulogises setting yourself a quest to make your journey more rewarding, but the idea seems a little contrived. It makes a travel quest sound noble rather than recognising it for what it really is – an early indicator of a troubled and twisted mind.

My quest in Favignana was to find Benito Ventrone. Benito's picture was on every can of Il Tonno tuna. He had a full white beard and wore a black and white striped long-sleeved T-shirt. A bandana topped what I suspect was a shiny pate and he had more gold chains around his neck than Mr T. A stall owner in the markets of Palermo had told me he was the King of Tuna and that he lived in Favignana.

As impressive as being sovereign of an entire species of fish undoubtedly was, that wasn't what started me on my quest to find Benito Ventrone. It was the fact that he looked like Kenny Rogers. One of my favourite websites is called MenWhoLookLikeKennyRogers.com. The guy who created it has a theory that all men over a certain age start to look like Kenny Rogers and encourages people to send in photos of people who do. My plan was to get a photo of Benito to prove that the theory holds true in Sicily as well.

My contact told me that once I got to Favignana I would find Benito in La Casa del Tonno, the House of Tuna. It was a store just off the main square that sold all things tuna – including *lattume di tonno*, seminal fluid from male tuna, which the accompanying brochure said should be 'cooked with salt and consumed in slices with olive oil'. I went into the shop and asked if Benito was in. A shadow passed across the shop assistant's face.

'He died last year,' she said sadly. I offered her my condolences before sneaking a couple of pictures of a delicately arranged selection of cans of tuna bearing his likeness. I hoped that would be enough to impress the guys at MWLLKR.com to post it.

The next morning a heavy sea mist hung over Favignana, delaying the ferry that would take me back to Trápani by an hour. The mist was still thick when we left, and as we pulled away from the dock I imagined it was the sort of morning on which the *mattanza* took place. The boats lying in wait. The clunk of an oar. The clueless tuna coming in. The chamber of death. The first blow. The frenzy that followed. It was those thoughts – and the fact that I had a photo of a dead guy who looked like Kenny Rogers on my camera's memory card – that convinced me I should never live on a small, isolated island.

I resisted the siren call of another bowl of seafood couscous in Trápani and made my way south past saltpans and windmills to Marsala. The saltpans in the shallows between Trápani and Marsala have been worked since Phoenician times and the methods used today differ little from those used in antiquity. Bare-chested men still shovel the salt, which sits in huge piles along the banks. Windmills still power the Archimedes screws that take the water from basin to basin.

The colours here were strong and vibrant – the bright blue sky looking even more intense against the pure white salt. Again I was struck by how well Marcello fitted into this environment. Sophia would have looked meek and pale against the whitewashed walls of the windmills yet Marcello looked even more striking, his orange *duco* somehow richer and deeper. The scenery along the coast here did not overwhelm him – it treated him as an equal partner.

The road south of the saltpans hugged the coast and the huge expanses of muddy flats exposed by the receding tide. The seabed is littered with wrecks from a sea battle fought here in 241 BC at the end of the First Punic War. It is known as the Battle of the Egadi Islands and scholars regard it as a decisive engagement in Rome's ultimately successful attempt to wrest control of Sicily – and the western Mediterranean – from Carthage.

I studied the battle in ancient history at high school. Over fifty ships had gone down and I remember my teacher, Mr Purves, was particularly excited about one that had been raised from the sea, restored and put on show in the Museo Archeologico in Marsala. They found evidence of what the crews ate – deer, goat, horse, ox, pig and sheep, as well as olives, nuts and fruits – no surprises there. I also recalled they found traces of cannabis as well. The Carthaginians used it as a stimulant before going into battle. It's funny the things that stick in a seventeen-year-old's mind.

I'd always imagined such an epic battle would have taken place in an equally dramatic environment – somewhere rocky and treacherous and full of foreboding like the San Vito Lo Capo north of Trápani. Instead, as I approached Marsala I discovered the coastline was slimy and stinky from rotting seaweed left by the tide. That didn't stop the locals from pulling out their deckchairs and lying in it though.

Marsala is Sicily's largest wine-producing centre, famous for the sweet dessert wine that bears the town's name. Strangely, it was an Englishman called John Woodhouse who first recognised the commercial potential of the wine. He visited the town in 1770 and realised that, like a high-quality port, Marsala's local dessert wine could travel for long periods – and hence long distances – without going off.

In a roundabout way, Mr Woodhouse was the reason I was in Marsala. When I was growing up my dad loved Marsala. I was in town to buy him a bottle from the source.

My dad was introduced to Marsala by the Sicilian tradesmen he worked with as an apprentice plumber. (They also introduced him to olives, mortadella and a host of other smallgoods that were new to Australia then.) He wrote the name of the stuff on a piece of paper and my mother bought a bottle from the little Italian deli in Liverpool the next time she went shopping.

Dad drank it like port. Mum used it in cooking. As a special treat, we'd occasionally get a glass of Marsala with lemonade. It was sickly sweet and delicious. A bottle usually lasted a year and Mum always replaced it with one just the same – an Ambra Semisecco from the Casano winery in Marsala.

Then my parents became Seventh Day Adventists. Part of the faith was abstinence from alcohol. My mum still used Marsala in her famous peach slice – indeed it was the Marsala that made it famous – and kept a bottle strictly for cooking in a cupboard above the oven.

My dad still loved Marsala and would occasionally sneak some. My mum became suspicious and began to mark the label after she'd finished cooking. When she used it again and saw that the contents were below the mark she would confront my dad. He'd say it had evaporated and that she shouldn't keep it above the oven. It still makes me laugh to think about it.

Once I got to the centre of Marsala, the town, I parked Marcello and went in search of Marsala, the wine. I found a little general store on Piazza F Pizzo. It was called Gaspare Laudicina and, despite having an extensive selection of local wines, it didn't stock anything produced by the Casano winery, the makers of the Marsala from my childhood.

It was the kind of store my dad would have loved though. It was full of salamis, hams, olives, pickled onions and slabs of meat the origins of which I didn't even want to guess at. So I bought him the most expensive bottle of Marsala they had instead. It was called Terre Arse – which I hoped wasn't a health and safety warning – and it had a dark label directly printed on the bottle that was impossible to mark.

I rode south through the warehouses and factories on the outskirts of Marsala towards Mazara del Vallo, an old Arab fishing port where I planned to stay the night. I'd put the bottle of Marsala in a plastic bag and hung it precariously from the hook under Marcello's seat. When I rode across some disused railway lines, half-buried in the tarmac, the shock made the plastic bag tear.

What happened next can only be described as a miracle. The Marsala Miracle of Marsala, if you'd like. On hearing the bag tear I pulled Marcello to the side of the road and caught the bottle before it fell and smashed. Impressive as that was, it wasn't the miracle.

That was when I looked up and saw that I'd stopped outside the Casano winery. There on the gates was the crest held by two lions that had graced the label that my mother marked every time she returned her bottle of Marsala to the cupboard above the oven.

The factory was about to close for the day but I felt compelled to go inside. I wove my way through the workers leaving for home and parked Marcello in front of what I guessed was the main office. A man with greying hair wearing a short-sleeved shirt and trousers emerged and asked what a strange man riding an orange Vespa was doing in his winery at such a late hour. I explained I was from Australia. He said he was Mr Casano – the big boss – and he agreed to show me around.

As we wandered through the winery I told Mr Casano the story about my family and his Marsala. He seemed bemused by the story but it might well have been the way I told it using an innovative combination of pidgin Italian and charades. He smiled when I acted out my dad's furtive sips from the bottle hidden above the stove, and translated what I was trying to say to his wife, who had come to see what was keeping him.

I spotted a bottle of the Ambra Semisecco and was pleased to see that the label hadn't changed over the last thirty years. I showed the Casanos where my mother would mark it and Mr Casano told me that they still exported it to Australia. He asked if I'd like to taste it, as well as one of their superior Marsalas. When I'd tasted both he asked me which one I preferred. I admitted that the superior one was more sophisticated. But my palate was in a nostalgic mood and I pointed to the Ambra Semisecco of my childhood.

'*Buone memorie*,' I said as way of explanation. Good memories. Mr Casano smiled and said something in Italian to his wife. She left the room, returning a few minutes later with a bottle of Casano Ambra Semisecco in a special gift box.

The Marsala Miracle of Marsala wasn't quite over yet. The gift box held two bottles, leaving a space for the bottle of Terre Arse. More miraculously, the hook under Marcello's seat fitted through the handle of the box, which was the perfect size to hang from the hook and wedged tightly against the floorboard.

Mrs Casano said that St Amand, the patron saint of wineries, was smiling upon me.

I took a photo of Mr and Mrs Casano standing beside Marcello as a memento of the miracle of Marsala and proof to my dad that the bottle came directly from the source. They wished me a good journey and stood and waved as I rode off through the factory gates, my precious cargo wedged safely between my legs.

I still had 1500 kilometres of my journey to go. There would be times when my resolve would be tested and I'd be tempted to take a few swigs of the Casano Ambra Semisecco myself. I made a promise that if I did I'd mark the label to show how much I'd drunk.

Just for old times' sake.

CHAPTER TEN

AGRIGENTO

PATRON SAINT: HERCULES

I wasn't sure what to expect of Agrigento. It sits halfway along Sicily's southern coast between the Hypsas and Akragas rivers, built above the site of an ancient Greek city founded in 581 BC. The Greek poet Pindar wrote that it was 'the fairest city inhabited by mortals'. The American historian and politician Henry Adams described it as 'Athens with improvements'. When I had dinner with Sergio in Palermo he said the place was 'a bucket of shit'.

The truth lay somewhere in between. The harbour at Porto Empedocle was dominated by an ugly cement factory and the nearby beach was overwhelmed by some of the most unlovely apartment buildings I had ever seen. Yet the Valle dei Templi, Valley of Temples, was as lovely as Pindar and Adams had suggested. A line of ancient ruins sat along a ridge overlooking the sea surrounded by wildflowers and oleander. The Temple of Concord, hewn from tawny stone and shaded by a lonely tree, looked the most artfully arranged.

I rode through the valley to the centre of Agrigento. It sat on a rocky hill above the ruins, surrounded by some of the poorest suburbs in Italy. It was in these suburbs that Sergio had spent his youth. The homes were shoddy and incomplete. The streets were broken. Even the stadium remained unfinished. The scaffolding had been left against the southern wall so long that it had rusted onto it.

The centre of the town had a dark charm. The townsfolk moved here in the Middle Ages after the city in the valley had endured one too many barbarian sackings. It was based on three interlocking piazzas, each linked by stone staircases and cobbled streets that afforded glimpses of the valley and the sea below. The grandest buildings were built during the time of the Normans, but if you looked closely in the nave of the church of Santa Maria dei Greci you could still see columns from the ancient Greek temple it was built on top of. The column stumps were incorporated into the foundations.

I was staying at the Bella Napoli, a cheap but cheerful hotel on Piazza Lena in the top part of the town. It was halfway up Via

Bac Bac, a one-way street going, unfortunately, down rather than up. I spent half an hour riding through a maze of one-way and pedestrianised streets trying to find where it began but always ended up back at the bottom. In the end I rode up the street the wrong way, arriving at the hotel just as the manager came outside to smoke a cigarette. He greeted my arrival with a friendly *buona sera*, seemingly unconcerned that I had broken the law to reach his establishment. The only time he expressed surprise was when I checked in and handed him my Australian passport.

'You are not Italian?' he asked, perplexed. When I shook my head he asked if I had Italian family. I shook my head again.

'It is your Vespa then,' he said with a laugh. There had to be some kind of Italian influence at work for me to ride up *senso unico* the wrong way.

I tossed my bag in my room and rode back down the hill to the Valley of the Temples. It was late in the afternoon but the hotel manager said that it was the perfect time to visit. It was cooler. The busloads of tourists were gone. And the limestone tufa used to build the temples glowed from the softer light of the setting sun.

I parked Marcello under a tree near the tourist office. Officially the spot was out of bounds but the young guy selling tickets didn't seem to mind. Unlike the cranky old lady at *Nuraghe Santu Antine* he liked Marcello and by the simple act of riding such a Vespa I went up immeasurably in his estimation. When an officious tour guide tried to push ahead of me to buy a ticket the young guy told him and his wealthy private client from Milan to wait until he served me.

'He is, how you say, a wanker?' he said as he handed me my ticket. I smirked at the shared joke. The tour guide gave us a filthy look. He didn't know what had been said about him but he knew it wasn't complimentary.

The site was divided into two zones and set in a vast parkland of dry rocky ridges, jojoba plants, prickly pear and *macchia*. I headed straight up a dusty path to the remains of the Temple of Hercules. In its day it was regarded as one of the most beautiful temples of antiquity. Now all that remains are eight broken columns of different heights put back in place by the Englishman Sir Alexander Hardcastle in 1924.

I'd like to say my interest in the Temple of Hercules was sparked by something I'd learned studying ancient history at high school. Perhaps the fact the temple was the oldest in the valley or that its partial reconstruction was funded by Sir Alexander Hardcastle out of his own pocket. Sadly, the origin of my interest was more lowbrow than that. It sprang from the TV show *Hercules: The Legendary Journeys*.

Hercules: The Legendary Journeys was filmed in New Zealand and introduced the world to *Xena: Warrior Princess*. It was a camp mix of action, arch anachronisms and, OK, I admit it, girls in chainmail bikinis. I can still quote the opening monologue verbatim and especially loved the line describing antiquity as a time 'when the ancient gods were petty and cruel and plagued mankind with suffering'. I've always felt that the rhythm of it makes it almost poetic.

Hercules was played by Kevin Sorbo. He invested the part with a cheesy nobility. Every episode featured some minor goddess throwing herself at Hercules and Hercules respecting the memory of his dead wife by refusing to take the girl up on her offer. My all-time favourite line from any movie or TV series was when he spurned Nemesis, played by Kimberley Joseph. She asked Hercules if he was always this noble. Herc's reply of 'I try to be' was so cool that I've stored it in my memory banks for when I get asked the same question. That day hasn't come yet.

I backtracked along a rutted Greek road to what remained of the other temples and noted with delight that they too were dedicated to ancient gods that had featured in the Hercules television series. There was the Temple of Hera, the pissed-off wife of Zeus who spent most of the series trying to kill Herc because he reminded her of her husband's infidelity. It sat on a high rocky ledge overlooking the site. The Temple of Castor and Pollux, the twins that Zeus fathered with a woman called Leda when they both morphed into swans. And the Temple of Concord – named after a Latin inscription found in the area, not a character from Hercules. It's the pretty one that features on all the postcards and was restored to its original classical form in 1748.

All that remains of the temple dedicated to Hercules's old man, Zeus, is a pile of rocks. At 113 metres long and 36 metres wide the Temple of Olympian Zeus was thought to be one of the largest temples built in ancient times. It was the first temple invading armies razed to the ground and the first the locals rebuilt when they got the chance.

The temple features a pair of *telamones* holding up the roof. In ancient architecture a *telamon* was a sculptured support carved in the shape of a man. They are also known as *atlantes*, named after Atlas, the Titan forced to carry the world on his shoulders for eternity.

Only one *telamon* remains and it lay on a bare patch of dirt beside the ruins. Its features were worn. All that was left was a basic human form in stone. The arms were bent back to hold up the roof above it, but now, out of context, it looked like the giant stone figure lay with its hands behind its head, having a kip. Things like that amuse me and I nearly filled my memory card taking photos of it.

I returned to my hotel as dusk approached, riding up Via Bac Bac the wrong way again and parking Marcello in the small square outside the hotel. I showered quickly and then plunged back down into the centre of the town on foot. Many of the streets in Agrigento are closed to traffic in the late afternoon and the locals use it as an opportunity to go shopping or take a stroll in much more convivial circumstances. My stroll down Via Atenea was particularly agreeable, past bookstores, jewellers and boutiques, and finished with the mandatory visit to a *pasticceria*.

Occasionally I'd duck down a cobbled lane just to see where it led. More often than not I stumbled upon a hidden vantage point with a stunning vista across the valley below. On Via Giambertoni I found a cheap restaurant called L'Ambasciate di Sicilia that had a balcony looking south over the ruins and the sea. The seafood pasta was not the best I'd had on my travels but the view was dramatic. I watched the sun set and the floodlit temples illuminate over a *macchiatto* and a shot of grappa which I didn't order but drank all the same. And wondered what had happened to Sergio here to colour his opinion of Agrigento.

The next day I headed inland to Piazza Armerina. I rode through rolling hills and past jerry-built towns. I thought back to the unfinished houses of Corleone. I could see that the definition of 'unfinished' differed from one province to another, maybe something to do with the available tax breaks. Sometimes all it took was tacking clear sheets of plastic onto a window frame instead of using glass. Here, in the hills of central Sicily, the definition was stricter. The local authority demanded roughly laid bricks, the concrete oozing between the joints, and strands of steel reinforcement sticking out of the roof like uncooked spaghetti.

Thankfully the wild barren hills that surrounded these towns were lovely. The sandy-coloured fields stretched into the distance and the hills were topped by stone villas as picturesque as those in Tuscany. The occasional pump dredging oil from a rocky field spoiled the mood, but more often than not it was just me, Marcello and a lonely stretch of bitumen, lined by trees so perfectly gnarled and ancient that they looked like they had been grown especially that way.

Just past Barrafranca I got stuck behind a truck attempting to break the record for carrying the most watermelons in a single journey. The melons within the tray were placed in neat rows. Once the pile reached the top they tapered into the shape of a pyramid. The driver must have been going for degree of difficulty bonus points because he had decided against using a tarpaulin.

A winding mountain road. A truck full of melons. A guy on a Vespa following right behind. I knew instinctively how it was all going to end. It had all the makings of a scene from a slapstick Italian movie from the seventies. I should have pulled over to the side of the road and let the truck disappear into the distance.

Instead I rode along mesmerised by the melon at the apex of the pyramid. I watched as it rocked from side to side, certain that the next corner would be the one that tipped it over the edge. When it finally fell – as I knew it would – I watched dispassionately as it split on the road in front of me.

I remember thinking that the splash of pink coupled with Marcello's bright orange paint looked very tutti-frutti. Then my mind wandered and I wondered what tutti-frutti actually meant.

Then Marcello's front wheel hit melon rind and I was confronted with the more immediate concern of staying upright. Marcello wobbled, I stuck my legs out wildly for balance, and the people in the car behind me laughed. All it needed was a swirling Hammond organ soundtrack, a camp *tu-tu-chi-chi-tu* chorus and I would have had a box office hit.

I'd come to Piazza Armerina especially to see the mosaics in Villa del Casale. Set in the hills 3 kilometres south-west of Piazza Armerina, the villa was at the heart of an immense Roman rural holding and built some time between the third and fifth centuries AD. Its fame – and UNESCO listing – comes from the mosaics that decorate every one of the 62 rooms. They are regarded as the most outstanding Roman mosaics in the world and were preserved thanks to a flood that buried them in mud in the twelfth century. They were discovered again in 1950.

I've always liked mosaics. I think it's the mixture of simplicity and sophistication that appeals. The nature of the medium creates so many restrictions. The tiles are small. You have to juggle the colours to get shade and light, details and overall impressions. But in the end this invests the mosaics with a beauty and simplicity that could not have been achieved with a brush and paint.

There is some debate as to when the villa at Casale was built and whom it belonged to. One theory dates the villa between the fourth and fifth century AD and insists that it belonged to the Roman senator Rufio Albio. He regarded this part of Sicily as a place of 'poetic tranquillity'.

GV Gentili, a historian who took part in the digs that uncovered the mosaics in 1950, believes the villa was built between the third and fourth centuries and was the hunting lodge for Emperor Maximianus Herculius. His theory is based on the fact that the boy in the mosaic in the vestibule has a squint. Chronicles from the time clearly mention that Maximianus's son Maxentius had a wonky eye.

Regardless, it was a massive undertaking. Teams of craftsmen from North Africa were drafted to lay over 3500 square metres of mosaics. Over 30 million mosaic tesserae were used. Working on the assumption that it takes one worker six days to complete a square metre of mosaics, the historian Paul MacKendrick calculated that 504,000 man hours would have been needed. It wasn't cheap either. In those days builders were paid 50 denarii a day. A mosaicist commanded 150.

It is not until you walk through the remains of the villa that you appreciate just how massive an undertaking it was. There are rooms for slaves. Rooms for doormen. A massage room. A pool. Cold baths. Hot baths. A domestic chapel.

A gymnasium. And each is decorated with its own mosaic telling a tale from Ovid, Seneca, Novaziano or Grattio. Even the floor of the toilet was covered in a spectacular mosaic of a leopard chasing a donkey chasing a rabbit chasing a pigeon. I wasn't sure what it meant or whether it had any relevance to the task at hand but it looked spectacular.

The level of detail is so extraordinary, archaeologists have built careers around analysing the footwear, hairstyles and clothes depicted. I've already mentioned Maxentius's squint. Every image exhibited that attention to detail. The great hunting scene that runs along the main corridor chronicles not just the hunt itself but the wild game being loaded on ships afterwards, blood dripping from their wounds. One mosaic in a room at the back features a girl with a bare butt sitting on the Emperor's lap. The look on his face – and hers – suggests that it's good to be the Emperor.

Perhaps the most famous room is the Hall of Female Gymnasts in Bikinis. It features a mosaic of female gymnasts in bikinis. Archaeologists claim it is a 'rare and precious record of fashions at the time'. Their 24th century counterparts will probably say the same thing when they dig up a copy of *Sports Illustrated*. I expect it's the sort of thing Russian billionaires are having done in their petro-rouble palaces at this very moment.

I left the villa through a patch of wild honeysuckle and lavender and headed back towards Piazza Armerina. On the outskirts of town an old man in a flat cap was selling peaches from the back of his *Ape*. They were plumpest peaches I'd ever seen and I bought two as an afternoon snack. The man threw in an extra one for free. He was impressed that Marcello was the same colour as his fruit.

I didn't stay in Piazza Armerina itself. My guidebook suggested a quirky *agriturismo* in the hills 3 kilometres south of the town. It was called the Agricasale and had marked the route to get there with signs featuring a little red fox saying

'Follow me!!!' The signs began on the outskirts of town and popped up with alarming irregularity on trees and telegraph poles. I nearly gave up a couple of times but just as I was about to turn back another sign popped up. The three exclamation marks compelled me to keep going. They suggested something really extraordinary awaited me.

The Agricasale wasn't the sort of place I would normally stay in. It was built in a hacienda style round a huge pool with tennis and volleyball courts set to the side. The driveway was lined with flagpoles flying flags from different countries and the glass entrance doors displayed an array of international icons that suggested they accepted credit cards, domestic pets and people with wheelchairs. Bicycles and campervans were welcome too, but seemingly not motor scooters. Well, not specifically.

It was all very whitewashed and terracotta'd and I half expected to be greeted by a holiday rep in a red uniform telling me that my type wasn't welcome here. Instead I was welcomed by a man who looked like Raul Julia and hugged me like a long-lost relative. He told me a room including breakfast and dinner would cost me €50 before knocking the price down to €40 and giving me one of the private villas in the hills a couple of hundred metres away.

'Business is slow,' he said with a magnanimous smile. 'You may as well use it.'

The villa sat alone at the end of a long drive cloaked by cypress trees. It was set over two floors with a balcony that looked across the empty hills to the south. I stood for a moment soaking up the solitude, listening to the coo of a dove and the chirping of the crickets. I'd feared the worst when I approached the Agricasale but this was one of the best places I'd stayed in on my journey so far.

I unloaded my bag from the rack on the back of Marcello and realised that I'd lost my boots. I'd taken to riding in sandals since reaching the warmer climes of Sicily and had been tying my boots to the back rack by their laces. They were the only covered shoes I had so I decided to retrace my steps, hoping to find them lying forlornly by the side of the road.

The last time I remembered seeing them was when I stopped to take a photo of the Second World War statue of soldiers climbing up a bronze hill and falling off the end of it in the centre of Piazza Armerina. It was just before I saw my first fox sign and set off into the countryside.

My boots were dusty brown, the colour of the Sicilian countryside. Chances were that I'd drive straight past them. I'd already noted with alarm how similar pine cones looked to a pair of boots. In the right light, or half in shadows, they could be identical. I hadn't noticed how much rubbish there was beside the road either. Mostly it was the stuff you'd expect to see – plastic bottles, cigarette packets, flyers, hubcaps. I also came across two TV screens, a shirt and a solitary sandal. But, sadly, no boots.

In a perfect world my boots would be sitting neatly beside the road waiting for me to reclaim them. In truth, the odd shape of a boot meant they could have landed anywhere. If I had been going fast enough when they made their escape, they could have worked up enough momentum to bounce over an embankment into a field below. I imagined a farmer coming upon them as he ploughed his field – European size 42, just his size – and considering them as a miraculous gift from the Virgin Mary. Maybe he'd set up a little outdoor chapel, like the one I saw in Favignana, and the faithful could come and worship at the site of the Miracle of the Boot.

Soon I was back in town. On the intersection where I had turned off the main road I came upon an accident. Two cars had collided. One had been going straight, the other turning right into its path. The *carabinieri* were in attendance, removing their caps and scratching their heads the way police do the world over.

A horrible thought popped into my head. What if my boots had caused the accident? Maybe one of the drivers had swerved to miss them. I slowed as I passed, looking to see if my boots were jammed somewhere under the tyres. They weren't. Part of me was disappointed until I realised that my travel insurance probably didn't cover such an eventuality. I decided to let sleeping boots lie, and took the long way around the rear of the town and back to the *agriturismo*.

The restaurant at the Agricasale was famous for using fresh organic produce grown on the farms that surrounded it. My guidebook suggested making the effort to eat there even if you were staying elsewhere in Piazza Armerina. When I arrived at the dining room at the allotted hour it was empty but for the manager, sitting in a corner watching a football match on a wide-screen TV.

The manager jumped up and approached me with a sheepish grin. I was the only guest, he said, and I thought he was going to tell me that it wasn't viable for him to open the kitchen just for me. Instead he led me to a table set for one, and yelled to his wife in the kitchen. She emerged with a plate overflowing with marinated eggplant, meatballs, asparagus wrapped in swordfish, olives, tomatoes and slices of mozzarella. When I'd polished that off she returned with another plate with two slices of quiche and five arancini – deep-fried rice balls filled with minced meat, cheese and peas. It took some doing but eventually I had struggled through the whole lot.

My smirk of satisfaction vanished when the manager's wife returned with a bowl of pasta in a tomato and mushroom sauce and declared it was my *primi piatti*, first course. When I'd struggled through that, a *secondi piatti*, second course, was placed before me – a pork stew with olives, onions and balsamic vinegar. In Italy the second course is usually just a cut of meat or fish, but here it was served with a side of potato baked in cream. I took a couple of mouthfuls but couldn't eat any more. I was feeling sick as only a glutton can.

The manager, meanwhile, was eating watermelon as he watched the football. I thought that would be really nice. It looked sweet and light, just what I needed to settle the food that rested heavily in my stomach. I asked the manager if I could have a piece for *dolci*, dessert. He indicated for me to wait. My dessert was on its way.

The manager's wife emerged moments later with a pastry filled with ricotta, dusted with icing sugar, topped with fresh strawberries and cherries and drenched in a red sugary sauce. I struggled out the door and up the hill, but only after finishing a complimentary glass of almond wine.

The villa was only a couple of hundred metres away but I wished I'd ridden Marcello.

CHAPTER ELEVEN

SYRACUSE

PATRON SAINT: SAN LUCIA

I skipped breakfast the next morning and headed east through dry hills to Caltagirone. The hottest months of summer were approaching and the local farmers were using the slightly cooler days of June to burn back undergrowth that had grown in spring.

In Australia the local bushfire brigades usually perform such tasks, keeping a close eye on the fires so they don't get out of control. Here in the centre of Sicily the fires were lit and left to their own devices. They burned along the side of the road, creeping right up to the tarmac.

As I rode around one bend the wind fanned the flames so that they shot up around me. I whizzed through them like a stunt driver, emerging largely unscathed except for the singed hairs on my arm. And thankful that the bottles of Marsala swinging dangerously close to my crutch didn't ignite.

I grew up in a part of Sydney that was popular with Italian immigrants. They moved into houses, tore up the carpet and tiled everything. My parents thought they were mad. But whenever I visited my Italian schoolfriends on a scorching summer day, those houses were blissfully cool.

Caltagirone has taken that concept and executed it on a city-wide scale. Everywhere you look there are tiles or objects made from ceramic. Both sides of the Ponte San Francesco are decorated with ceramic flowers and crests. The stone balustrade around the *giardino della villa* is topped by ceramic jugs painted with pictures depicting everyday life. Even the Victorian-style bandstand is covered in tiles. If it can be painted, glazed and whacked in an oven, it has been. And if it can't be, it'll have a couple of tiles stuck on it or some ceramic piece of art stuck on top.

Caltagirone has always produced ceramics. Farmers constantly unearth prehistoric pots as they plough fields in the hills around the city. Before the great earthquake of 1693 levelled the city, 5 per cent of the population were involved in the tiled decoration of churches and public buildings. When the city was rebuilt even more turned their hand to moulding clay to meet the demands of its new Baroque stylings. In the nineteenth century they turned their hand to figurative work that remains popular today. The Arab name for the town, Cal'at Ghiran, can be translated as Castle of the Vases.

The city is famous for its distinctive polychromatic colours introduced to the local craftsmen with the arrival of the Arabs. The blues and yellows are particularly vivid. When I parked Marcello on Piazza Municipio beside a wall embellished with a gaudy ceramic coat of arms, he looked like an integral part of the scenery.

The city's most famous landmark is La Scala, the stone staircase built in 1608 to link Santa Maria del Monte cathedral at the top of the hill with the Palazzo Senatorio below. The risers on each of the 142 steps are decorated with hand-painted tiles, no two of which are the same. There are a few ceramic shops along it, but largely it is lined by the homes and workshops of locals.

I left Marcello in the square and clambered up the stairs to the church at the top. There were no other tourists. A woman hung out her washing. A little girl with curly hair played a skipping game that saw her hopping up and down the steps. A beat-up Vespa was parked on one of the lanes that led off the stairway. The ordinary and everyday embellished the extraordinary.

A young girl sat outside the cathedral drawing a poster to alert tourists that the bell tower was open. It had been closed for the past five years and the archbishop had decided on a whim to open it again. Despite her best efforts it looked like a school project with 'Visit the Bell Tower!' written in fat letters in crayon and decorated with pictures cut out of a guidebook and glued on.

I asked the girl if the bell tower was open now and she nodded. On hearing I spoke English she asked me if 'Visit' was the right word to use on the poster. She had been considering using the word 'Tour'. I told her that 'tour' suggested that there would be a tour leader and her eyes widened.

'Oh no,' she said. 'You must climb the steps yourself.'

Her answer astounded me. Not because I had to climb the bell tower without assistance. Rather because her voice was deep and gravelly. She was a young, attractive girl yet she sounded like Satchmo. It wasn't uncommon in Italy. Most Italian women seemed to have husky voices. On my last trip I'd watched the Italian version of *The Nanny* and noted that they had dubbed Fran Drescher's nasal tones with something altogether huskier and sexier.

The girl unlocked the door leading to the bell tower. The spider's web across the door suggested that I was the first visitor since it had reopened. The ceramic portraits of Mary that lined the walls were coated with a film of dust and every step I took on the spiral staircase left a footprint. At the top of the tower everything was covered in pigeon shit, including the bell. But the view was great – if you turned your back on the ugly phone mast at the back of the church – and the cool breeze was sensational.

I returned to Piazza Municipio and found Marcello surrounded by a pack of young guys. They wore jeans and trainers and had hair stiff with gel. They asked if the Vespa was mine and when I said it was they told me to jump on it and follow them.

They led me to a ceramics shop on Via Celso. It sold the usual tat – ceramic plates, jugs, vases – and I thought they had brought me here to buy something so they would get a commission. I told them that I didn't really have room on my Vespa for a giant ceramic umbrella-stand in the shape of a human head. They pointed to a red Vespa, just like Marcello, parked outside.

It looked like a Rally but the badges were missing so I couldn't tell for sure. The young guys called out to a man with a shaved head in the ceramics shop. His name was Joe and he told me it was a Rally 200. A 1974 model. One of the young guys wheeled Marcello over and parked him next to the red one. His mates hollered with delight. Then they clambered on both bikes, flashed a series of heavy metal hand signals and insisted I take a photo. I couldn't help but laugh.

Joe was impressed by Marcello's stripes and called across his friend who worked in the tattoo parlour opposite. He took photos of the stripes on his mobile phone and told Joe he'd make up a set for him. Joe looked over his friend's shoulder at the tiny screen, art-directing him, making sure he got it right.

Joe invited me into the shop for a cup of coffee. It belonged to his family and there was a workshop out the back where they made the stuff they sold. His father was working the wheel. His sisters were painting patterns on a pair of jugs. And his brother was reading the sports section of the newspaper.

'He makes the antiques,' Joe said enigmatically.

Joe made two cups of espresso from the coffee machine at the back of the workshop. (I think an inhouse espresso machine is an inviolable condition of every workplace agreement in Italy.) He cleared a space for me to sit on a bench, waving his hand dismissively over their stock and calling it 'touristic'. He explained how they made it but didn't expect me to buy. As a fellow Rally owner I was obviously a man of taste.

Joe was more interested in my trip. His eyes widened when I told him that I had ridden all the way through Sardinia and across Sicily. The furthest he'd been on his Rally was down to a beach near Gela, 34 kilometres away.

'Maybe I will go on an adventure with my Rally,' he said.

We returned to the bikes and the young guys were still sitting on them. Joe chuckled.

'It is a compliment,' he said. 'At least they are not calling us old men for riding Hondas!'

Before I left Joe gave me a ceramic Vespa painted in the distinctive Caltagirone yellow and blue.

'Souvenir,' he said with a laugh. It was nice but we both knew it wasn't a patch on our Rallys.

By the time I reached Syracuse all I wanted to do was sleep. I had ridden the length of Sicily under a relentless sun and it was taking its toll. I splashed out on a room in a hotel on the waterfront in Ortygia, the small island that hangs off the rest of Syracuse like a lamb cutlet-shaped appendix. I should point out that in my world splashing out equates to paying €70 a night for a room. Luckily the Hotel Gutkowski was the kind of hip hotel that wasn't quite hip enough to figure out it could charge extra the less it put into a room.

Ortygia has always been the focal point of Syracuse. Two and a half thousand years of history are crammed into a medieval maze less than 1 kilometre long and 500 metres wide. You'll find the city's most impressive buildings there, like the sixth-century Temple of Apollo and the stunning Baroque Duomo.

And the bars and restaurants are more lively than on the mainland, just the other side of the causeway.

I rarely ventured beyond the causeway. I dropped by the Basilica Santuario Madonna delle Lacrime to pick up a Saint Lucia fridge magnet. (Saint Lucia is the patron saint of Syracuse and her bones had just been returned to the city after a lengthy battle with authorities in Venice.) And I visited the Greek amphitheatre at Neapolis where 16,000 people watched opening night performances of plays written by Euripides and Sophocles back in the fifth century. The rest of the time I wandered the cobbled streets off Piazza Archimede or clambered down a steel staircase to the stony beach just off Lungomare.

Soon it was my last night in Syracuse. A cool breeze danced off the sea and well-dressed locals sat under palm trees in outdoor restaurants or strolled along the promenade that ran alongside the harbour. I'd spent three days in the town where Archimedes had done some of his best work and all I'd done was sleep, eat and swim. I decided it was imperative that I did something cultural. I'd seen a poster advertising a puppet show at the Piccolo Teatro dei Pupi, the Little Theatre of Puppets. It promised a '*spettacoli tradizionali*' and I decided it fitted the bill.

The woman at reception in my hotel grimaced when I told her I wanted to go. Puppet shows have been popular in Sicily since the fourteenth century. They invariably involve a storyline that sees Christian knights beating up Saracen invaders or, inexplicably, crocodiles. These days they're viewed as a little passé.

'We are more sophisticated in Sicily now,' she said.

'Crocodiles and swordfights are for children.' Nothing she could say would dissuade me. My heart was set on it.

I found the Piccolo Teatro dei Pupi on a tiny lane just off Via Maestranza. A chubby guy with a black beard was sitting against the counter with his head in his hands. The theatre was to the side. The wooden benches lined up in front of it were empty.

'Puppet show?' I asked hopefully. He nodded in a pained manner.

'We are waiting for many more people,' he said

I asked the guy a few inane questions to pass the time and learned that tickets cost €5, he was the puppeteer and he'd been pulling the strings since 1995. His name was Alfredo Vaccara, the name above the door and plastered all over the posters. He took great pains to point out that the Alfredo Vaccara was his grandfather. It was like he was warning me not to expect anything special.

'It was different in his day,' said Alfredo. 'Locals came to watch. It was the entertainment. Now there is TV. Playstation. I have to rely on tourists.'

A young couple walked in. I must have looked hopeful because Alfredo was quick to tell me it was his brother.

Another half an hour passed. I asked if July was a busy month and Alfredo said that it usually was. This year there had been very few tourists. It was something I had noticed too. Half an hour later no one else had turned up.

'There is another show tomorrow night,' he said. I told him I was heading for the Aeolian Islands and he gave me a resigned shrug.

Before I left I took a photo of a forlorn Alfredo inside the empty theatre. He made a joke about captioning the photo 'Waiting', and asked me to email it to him.

I wandered off into the night looking for something else to do. I'd seen some interesting pubs and bars earlier in the day. The 747 Bar was all orange and chrome – a very Marcello kind of establishment. And the Pub Vecchio, which looked suitably old as its name suggested, had also piqued my interest. But both were closing for the night now that the aperitif crowd were gone. I sauntered down a dark cobbled lane looking for

Piazza San Giuseppe and the Il Bagatto, a pub the woman from the Hotel Gutkowski had said might have a band.

The only other people on the street were two young girls in short skirts and high heels. They heard my footfall behind them and turned around to see who it was. When they spotted me, a scruffily dressed guy on his own, they clutched their bags and scurried down the street, trying not to trip up on the cobbles.

I never know what to do in such circumstances. If I sped up to pass them they might think I was chasing them and start screaming. If I dropped back I would look guilty. I contemplated calling out that my intentions were pure but given the paucity of my Italian I decided that wasn't such a good idea. God knows what I could have said.

In the end I turned down a tiny lane and hoped that it would lead me to where I wanted to go. It didn't. It brought me back out onto the same street, only this time in front of the girls and facing towards them. It looked like I had deliberately nipped down the alley to get ahead and ambush them, and they looked suitably alarmed. I crossed to the other side to show that I meant them no harm but that only confirmed in their minds that I had been caught out. I turned down another lane and hid, hoping they didn't call the *carabinieri*.

It struck me that if I'd ridden Marcello I wouldn't have found myself in this predicament. I wouldn't be stumbling around dark alleyways for one thing. And if I had happened upon the girls they would have wondered where the owner of such a cool Vespa was going, and maybe even have followed me. On foot I was someone to be avoided. Or worse, a stalker.

I found the Il Bagatto. The 'band' for the night was an unshaven guy wearing dark glasses who went under the alarming name of Kissing Tulips. He strummed a couple of tunes on his guitar between knocking back two bottles of red wine. The woman at the hotel had warned me it 'would not be fantastic'.

I tried a few more pubs and quickly realised that there isn't a tradition of sad guys on their own sitting alone drinking beer in Italy. Italians visit pubs in packs. They laugh and joke raucously among themselves. And they use their mobile phones to coordinate their arrival en masse so that no one endures the shame of being alone. I texted Sally and told her it wasn't as much fun without her.

I drank too much and staggered along Via Roma trying to remember the way back to my hotel. I spotted a kebab shop, the first I'd seen in Italy, and realised I hadn't eaten dinner.

I ordered a kebab and sat slumped in a plastic chair drinking Coke from a can as I waited for it to be prepared. It was a scene played out the world over every Friday and Saturday night.

But let me tell you something. Just because a kebab is made in Italy, it doesn't make you look any cooler when you're struggling to eat it as you make your way home.

CHAPTER TWELVE

MOUNT ETNA

PATRON SAINT: SAINT AGATHA

I left Syracuse in a hurry, hurtling past the faceless apartment blocks that surrounded the town and along the seaside highway lined with factories. I was anxious to get to the Aeolian Islands, a chain of volcanic islands sprinkled off the north-east tip of Sicily. They took their name from Aeolus, the ruler of the winds and master of navigation. Ancient poets described them as 'rocky jewels set in an azure sea' and the entire archipelago is a designated World Heritage Area.

I'd like to say that I was in a rush to get to the islands because Stefano Gabbana and Domenico Dolce had invited me to a party at their holiday villa there.

Naomi Campbell dances on the beach out front and Madonna sometimes drops by on a yacht. But it was much more urgent than that. It was the last day visitors could bring vehicles to the islands before they were banned for the summer. If I didn't get to Milazzo and on a ferry to Lípari, the largest island in the group, my plan to island-hop to Naples was dead in the water.

If I had been riding on Sophia I wouldn't have even considered trying. Her ancient 125cc engine liked to take things at a more leisurely pace, trundling along for a few kilometres and then stopping at a café for an espresso or beside a field for a picnic. Marcello, on the other hand, liked a challenge. In that way he was a much more masculine Vespa. He didn't want to just cover the kilometres. He wanted to do them as quickly as possible and in a manner that got him the most attention.

By mid-morning I had reached the southern slopes of Mount Etna, Europe's most active volcano; a day rarely passes without a shot of steam and ash or a rumble underfoot. The eagle-eyed among you will have noticed that the lava on the planet Mustafar in *Revenge of the Sith* looked a touch Sicilian. George Lucas came here to get footage for the third episode of the *Star Wars* prequels. The Roman poet Virgil had witnessed Mount Etna erupt and described 'globes of flames, with monster tongues, that lick the stars'. That morning it looked more like a benign uncle sitting in an armchair, sucking on a pipe.

I'd made good time that morning so I decided to ride to the summit. Marcello raced up the steep mountain like he was on a life-saving mission. The road cut back and forth over a black river of igneous rock. It was the cooled lava from the last eruption and was peppered with bright wildflowers. It looked like an ancient flow, one that had been part of this stark landscape for thousands of years. Then I rounded a corner and noticed the roof of a house poking through the rocks. The satellite dish on top suggested it had gone under some time after Virgil's visit.

I couldn't go any further than the entrance to the Rifugio Sapienza tourist complex. A posse of emergency vehicles blocked the way. The monitoring equipment on the mountain had registered a dangerous gas emission from a vent on the Bocca Nuova crater and the complex was closed. I noticed that the heavy machinery used to clear the roads after an eruption

were the exact same shade of orange as Marcello. If I'd been wearing a reflective safety vest the *carabinieri* manning the roadblock probably would have let me pass.

I took a few photos and set off back down the mountain. I stopped for lunch in Nicolosi, a small ski town perched on the southern slope. In 1669 a vent opened on the edge of the town, spewing lava directly onto the streets. I could see the reddish cinder cone from my table at a small restaurant called Piccolo Mondo Antico (the Small Ancient World).

I'd chosen the Piccolo Mondo Antico because I could park Marcello on the pavement and watch my bags from the huge stone windows. When the waitress brought me the menu she asked me if I was French. I shook my head and she asked if I'd come to the restaurant because I'd seen them on the internet. Again, I shook my head and shrugged my shoulders apologetically. I had spotted the restaurant as I was riding by and stopped on a whim. The impromptu marketing survey over, the waitress handed me the menu. Everything on it contained mushrooms.

Mushrooms grow wild on the slopes of Mount Etna. The locals have their own secret spots where they find the plumpest and juiciest specimens. In November, after the autumn harvest, festivals are held in all of Etna's villages where mushrooms are served in every imaginable way. That day I chose the courgette flowers filled with mushroom puree and a simple *fettuccine a la funghi*. Both dishes were excellent. The mushrooms were full of the flavours of the mountain and deftly cooked. But then you'd expect that from a chef who only cooked mushrooms, wouldn't you?

The waitress brought me a coffee and asked if her son could play on Marcello. He had been standing by a window watching Marcello as I ate, fidgeting as he waited for the chance to jump on. To an eight-year-old in a tiny Sicilian town, Marcello's bright colour and white stripes must have made him look like the Vespa equivalent of a coin-operated Bob the Builder tractor ride. I said OK.

The waitress pulled up a chair to watch her son. He sat twisting the accelerator and making revving sounds. His feet couldn't reach the running boards and he had to lean forward to get to the controls. He had a grin on his face as wide as a melon and his mother smiled as she watched him.

I asked the waitress what it was like living in the shadow of an active volcano. She shrugged and said that you got used to it. The very thing that threatened them – the ash and the lava – also nurtured them. The slopes of Mount Etna were home to some of the most fertile farmland in Italy. The rich volcanic soil was what gave the mushrooms served in the restaurant their distinctive flavour.

'Besides,' she said, pointing to a framed picture on the wall, 'we have Agatha to protect us.'

Agatha was the patron saint of Mount Etna. Or to be more precise, the patron saint of stopping eruptions on Mount Etna.

She was young, beautiful and rich. She had lived in Catania in the third century and had dedicated her life to God. When the Roman Emperor Decius outlawed Christianity she was rounded up and put in a brothel. When she refused to service the customers her breasts were cut off and she was rolled on hot coals. An earthquake struck as she died from the wounds, killing her tormentors.

Her reputation for interrupting eruptions came when a procession carrying her veil halted a lava flow threatening Catania in 253, the year after she was martyred.

The waitress pointed to a spot on the outskirts of town marked by a huge crucifix. Two years before, the local priest had planted a crucifix to stop the advance of another lava flow. He invoked the name of Saint Agatha and the molten lava stopped in its tracks. It was a miracle, she said.

The priest was lucky he hadn't tried to pull that stunt before 1983. Until then it was illegal to artificially divert the path of a lava flow. The law was passed after the 1669 eruption. A riot broke out on the slopes of Mount Etna between the citizens of Catania and the citizens of Paternò. The people of Catania wanted to divert the lava flow from their city. The folk of Paternò weren't happy that their town would end up in the lava's path instead. Fisticuffs ensued. Catania got fried.

From Nicolosi I followed the road that headed north around the base of the mountain. Here the slopes of Mount Etna were brocaded with lemon groves and pistachio farms. The waxy leaves of the lemon trees filtered the midday sun and the air was thick with the zesty smell of lemons lying crushed on the side of the road. It felt clean and fresh and it was easy to forget that it could all be taken away by a lazy burp from the mountain.

By mid-afternoon I hit the north coast of Sicily near the resort town of Castroreale Terme, and scootered along a curving entrance ramp onto the autostrada that linked Palermo and Messina.

I'd spotted the autostrada, which spanned an entire valley, as I approached from the south. The pale concrete columns, hundreds of metres high, were eerily reminiscent of the columns of the Greek temples I'd seen elsewhere in Sicily. Thanks to a particular Sicilian skill in extracting funding from the European Union the island was criss-crossed with modern autostradas that pushed the boundaries of engineering to span valleys, tunnel through mountains or hang suspended magically along the coast. I wondered if future generations would look upon them with the awe I had experienced viewing the temples at Agrigento.

I shouldn't have been riding Marcello on the autostrada. By law he needed to have an engine capacity of at least 250cc. But with a top speed of 101 kilometres per hour I decided that he was more than capable of holding his own. I just made sure that I stuck to the far lane as Alfas and Fiats hurtled past. It gave me the chance to peer out over the valleys and the rocky coast far below.

The turnoff to Milazzo was marked by an autostrada service centre, so I stopped to get some petrol for Marcello. I was pleased to see the big 'A' indicating there was an Autogrill too. Autogrills had been a real revelation on this trip. They are a restaurant, café, snack bar and produce shop all rolled into one and, unlike similar establishments in England or Australia, the food on offer is really quite good. I particularly like the sandwiches. The bread is fresh, a wide selection of exotic cheeses and hams are used for fillings, and best of all they never cost more than a couple of euros.

I returned to Marcello with a sandwich and a bottle of blood-orange juice and found a young *carabinieri* officer circling him and checking him out. My first thought was that the guy was looking for some indication of Marcello's capacity. The Rally 200 badge was obscured by my bag on the back rack. But instead of asking for Marcello's paperwork and fining me for riding an underpowered motor scooter on the autostrada, the young officer asked me about my trip. In particular, he wanted to know whether I was camping or staying in hotels.

He was disappointed when I told him I stayed mainly in hotels.

'With a Vespa like this I would camp beside the *mare*,' he said wistfully. 'To wake up listening to the waves, to smell the air, it would be wonderful.'

I ate my sandwich and drank my juice. The *carabinieri* watched me ride off and waved as I (illegally) got back on the freeway and (illegally) rode down the ramp towards Milazzo.

I arrived in Milazzo an hour before the last vehicle ferry left for Lípari. Lípari is the name of both the island and its main town. The town is the largest in the archipelago and the hub of the Aeolian ferry system. My plan was to base myself there for a few days before hopping north through the other islands to Naples.

A young Aussie couple waited on the dock loaded down with plastic bags full of groceries. They had stocked up for a nuclear winter, not a short trip to an island, and I wondered if they knew something that I didn't. I considered popping across to the COOP supermarket across the road to buy a 2-litre bottle of Coke just in case. I decided to take a chance that cola would be readily available on the islands and sat in the shade on a pile of steel girders under one of the date palms at the back of the dock instead.

Soon we were joined by two old German backpackers, a man and a woman. Like the Aussie couple they had shunned the more expensive option of catching a hydrofoil to Lípari and were catching the cheaper car ferry instead. They were both in their seventies and stooped under the weight of their enormous backpacks. I shifted along the steel girder I was sitting on and indicated that they could sit in the shade. The old bloke told me to go fuck myself.

I blinked at the Germans in shock. It wasn't the kind of language I'd expected from an OAP and the surreal nature of the tirade short-circuited my normal reaction of telling the guy to do the same to himself. Instead I gave him the benefit of the doubt. Maybe I had misunderstood him. The German accent sounds quite brusque even when it is not meant to be. I offered again. This time the old man made sure I understood him by giving me the finger.

The Germans found another tree and sprawled out on the ground. They had the attitude of world traveller types a quarter of their age. They leaned against their backpacks with a practised slouch, glaring at everyone else waiting for the boat. We weren't proper travellers, it seemed. I was riding a Vespa. And the Aussie couple had spent more money on groceries than the Germans had on their entire trip.

The ferry came and the Germans pushed ahead to make sure they were the first aboard. It was a quick trip across. I barely had enough time to watch an episode of *McLeod's Daughters*, dubbed in Italian, on the televisions that hung from the ceiling. (I was struck by how much the dry fields of Australia looked like the interior of Sicily.) The ferry pulled into the port at the town of Lípari just as the sun was setting.

Lípari looked exactly like a fishing port from an old Italian movie. It was set in a rocky bay, crowned by a church with a thin spire at one end, and dominated by a squat castle on a dramatic knoll at the other. A line of buildings with wrought-iron balconies overlooked a promenade dotted with date palms. Colourful fishing boats bobbed along the marina and young boys dived for coins off a bridge leading to the dock used by hydrofoils. All that was missing was a young Sophia Loren in a peasant blouse flirting with an equally young Marcello Mastroianni.

The car ferry docked at the larger port on the far side of the castle. A group of old men in flat caps were waiting to greet

the ferry. They half-heartedly waved flyers and business cards at the cars and motorbikes disembarking. They didn't seem fussed if you took one or not. They were going through the motions to keep their wives happy. Then they'd return to the nearby café for a game of cards and a shot of grappa. That didn't stop the OAP German backpackers from aggressively brushing them aside and heading straight to the public bus. The old men appeared as stunned by their antics as I was.

I'd rung ahead and booked a room in a *pensione* run by a South African woman called Diana Brown. She had married a local fisherman called Massimo some years before, and had promised to send him to collect me at the dock. Massimo was a small, wiry man who yelled 'Mr Peter! Mr Peter!' when he spotted Marcello. I'd told Diana that my Vespa was orange and impossible to miss.

Massimo jumped on the back of Marcello and directed me to the hotel. We zipped up tiny cobbled lanes, dodging carts loaded with fishing nets and sending cats scurrying away from fish scraps left for them by fishermen. Within two minutes we were at the hotel, which was tucked up a lane decorated by lines of washing that ran parallel with Corso Vittorio Emanuele, the main drag.

Massimo introduced me to Diana and she led me to my room. It was bright and spacious and had a small balcony. After I had showered and washed the grime of the day's travel from my skin I sat outside at the small table and listened to Lípari. A cat wailed. A bottle clinked. A metal sign creaked in the light breeze. Somewhere in the distance someone played an accordion. The Aeolian Islands had taken some getting to. But I was already glad that I'd made the effort.

CHAPTER THIRTEEN

LÍPARI

PATRON SAINT: SAINT BARTHOLOMEW

For a sleepy island adrift in the Tyrrhenian Sea, Lípari has had a hectic history. In Neolithic times it was a centre for obsidian, a hard black volcanic glass that could be fashioned to have a sharp cutting edge. At various times the Etruscans, Greeks and Carthaginians took control of the island. The Carthaginians used it as a naval base during the First Punic War. Then the Romans turned it into a place of retreat, therapeutic baths and exile. In the sixth century AD the holy relics of Saint Bartholomew, one of Jesus's twelve disciples, were brought to the island's cathedral.

Things heated up again in the ninth century when Saracen pirates started terrorising the Tyrrhenian Sea. In 839 most of the population was slaughtered in a Saracen raid, prompting church officials to move the relics of Saint Bartholomew to Benevento on the mainland. (They are now in Rome and Canterbury Cathedral in England.) The raids continued intermittently until 1544 when the pirate Barbarossa, better known as Redbeard, razed the town and it was abandoned completely. Charles V repopulated the town with his Spanish subjects in 1556, building the massive walls that surround the castle to provide sanctuary. But piracy continued unchecked throughout the Mediterranean and the island sank into obscurity.

Even now, with the population swelling with tourists for the summer months, Lípari felt positively sleepy. On my first morning, I wandered through the tight laneways and up the steep stone staircase to the cathedral without seeing another soul. A handful of kids sat on the stairs selling shells, black rocks and ashtrays made from Coke cans. They laid out their 'products' on blankets on the shady side of the stairs, moving their stock as the sun moved.

I was visiting the cathedral to get a Saint Bartholomew fridge magnet. Although his bones were long gone the cathedral still did a brisk trade in Saint Bartholomew memorabilia. Bartholomew would be my first disciple and I wondered what protection he would afford me and Marcello. Apparently Jesus had said Bartholomew was incapable of deceit. The old lady who sold me the fridge magnet told me he was the patron saint of bookbinders, butchers, cobblers, leather workers, plasterers and shoemakers. More importantly, he also looked out for those suffering nervous disorders, neurological diseases and twitching. My mental state was fine here on the islands but who knew how I would react to the traffic chaos in Naples?

I ate lunch at one of the outdoor restaurants that lined the harbour. A huge canvas umbrella protected me from the sun and a cool sea breeze tickled my brow. I watched a group of boys diving off the dock for coins. They looked like scamps from an old black and white movie, cheekily asking anyone who passed to toss them a coin. When they'd got enough money together they raced across to the nearby *gelateria* to buy an ice cream. The manager chastised them for leaving a puddle of water in front of his shop, but always served them nonetheless. I think they were his best customers.

There was a definite pecking order among the kids. The bigger ones got most of the coins. They were faster and more experienced. The smaller boys paddled in the water, duck-diving periodically to get the coins the older boys missed or of a denomination deemed not worth the effort.

My table was right on the waterfront and two of the boys came up and spoke to me. One was older. The other was one of the young apprentices. He was one of the smallest boys diving, but he seemed to be having the most fun.

'You speak English?' the little one asked impishly. 'One coin, please!'

I rummaged through my pocket and found a one euro cent coin. I showed it to the boys and tossed it into the water. The older boy gave me a filthy look and walked away. The cheeky little one dived in for it anyway. (It is testament to how clear the water was that he found the tiny brown coin in a matter of seconds.) I rewarded him by tossing a €2 coin into the water. He retrieved it in a flash, scrambled out of the water and held the coin aloft triumphantly to show the other boys. They hollered and stamped that it wasn't fair but he ignored them and ran straight to the gelateria. With a €2 coin he could buy an ice cream immediately.

Lípari has a total surface area of 37.6 square kilometres. There are four main villages. It wasn't long before Marcello and I had explored every corner of the island. I dipped my toes in the hot sulphur-bicarbonate springs at the old Roman thermal baths in San Calogero. I checked out the scene at Spiaggia Bianca. And I happily tootled along the coastal road that hugged the cliff below the pumice mines where the fine white dust billowed off the mountain like smoke. More often than not I'd end up at the lookout at Quattrocchi, gazing across at the picture postcard view of the crater on Vulcano, the island only a kilometre away. Quattrocchi means 'four eyes'. Massimo said it was named after the newlywed couples that went there to have their photos taken.

My afternoons were much more relaxed. I would begin with lunch, taken by the harbour and consisting of fresh seafood, usually with the capers that grew like weeds in these parts. Then a siesta, leaving the balcony shutters open to catch a languid Aeolian breeze. When the shadows began to lengthen I would ride Marcello to a wild corner on the western side of Lípari and watch the sun set over the sea, dropping like a coin between Salina and Filicudi, two of the other Aeolian Islands.

My favourite spot was at the end of a tiny lane hidden by an ancient stone wall covered in wisteria. The lane serviced a gaggle of small farms before petering out into a goat track that led to a green plateau on top of massive volcanic cliffs.

I discovered it quite by chance. The first time I ventured out along the lane I passed an old farmer lugging a bag of grain on his shoulder. He looked at Marcello suspiciously – orange Vespas were rare in these parts – so I greeted him with a cheery *buona sera*. He smiled and asked if I could help him with the grain. He placed it across the seat behind me and walked beside Marcello holding it while I rode slowly along. His farm was only a couple of hundred metres away, but the help was appreciated. He pointed to a path where he assured me the view was *bella*.

There is a scene in the movie *Il Postino*, filmed on Salina, the island I'd visit next, where the young postman asks Don Pablo, the famous poet, how to become a poet. Don Pablo tells him to 'walk slowly along the shore as far as the bay and look around you'. Nature would reveal the poetry. And the poetry would reveal what was important in life.

My secret spot on top of the cliffs had the same effect. I lost all track of time sitting there. I'd listen to the waves crash on the rocks far below. Or listen to the gulls as they circled the cliffs. Other times I'd spot a hydrofoil leaving a wake in the still sea that looked like a cut in silk. Sometimes it was so quiet I could hear the chirp of crickets. And I'd think. Not about what I was going to have for dinner. But about the life that lay ahead of me when I got home. I felt surprisingly calm.

It also dawned on me that it was less than two weeks before my birthday. Sally and I had discussed the possibility of her coming to Italy to help me celebrate it. It would be in the thirtieth week of her pregnancy, just within the timeframe airlines allow you to fly. Between the thirty-first and thirty-fifth weeks they let you on board grudgingly, but only with a letter from your doctor stating your due date and certifying that you are fit to fly.

Sally had dismissed the idea as impractical. I was travelling by Vespa. She had joined me for two weeks in Tuscany on my last trip but she didn't have a baby bump then. That evening as I watched the sun turn into a fiery red ball and sink below the horizon I realised that my birthday would be meaningless unless I could share it with the person – soon-to-be persons – who meant the most to me.

I hatched a plan. What if we chose a place and just stayed there? My time on Lípari had given me a taste of slowing down and taking it easy. We could get a room somewhere on the Amalfi Coast, Positano, maybe, and relax. After all, it would be the last time for a very long time that there'd be just the two of us. I rode back to town, popped into the internet café/*gelateria* and booked Sally on a BMI flight for Naples. I was so excited I ordered a bowl with three scoops of ice cream to celebrate.

My journey had a timetable now. Sally would be in Naples in just over a week's time and I still had the rest of the Aeolian Islands to see.

The first island I visited was Salina. It is dominated by two dormant volcanoes that make the island look like a discarded bikini top floating aimlessly in the sea. It is the most fertile of the Aeolian Islands. Capers grow profusely here and are exported all around the world. It is also the only place growing *malvasia* grapes of any quantity in the archipelago, and hence the only place to taste authentic *malvasia* wine. The wine was honey-coloured and sweet, but even my sweet tooth had trouble adjusting to the distinctly sulphuric aftertaste.

Once you get beyond the main port at Santa Marina Salina the island feels wild and lonely. Much of the movie *Il Postino* was shot here and it is not difficult to imagine that, like in the movie, you are back in the 1950s again.

Ironically, the extraordinary success of that movie is destroying the island's charm. The beach near Pollara, where the above-mentioned scene was shot, is disappearing, a victim of erosion caused by the engines of thousands of motor boats that descend on it each summer. When the movie was made it was a 10-metre band of grey sand and white pebbles stretching down to the sea. Now it is only 4 metres wide. Worse, the huge cliff behind it, known locally as Il Costone, is beginning to crumble. Rocks fall onto the heads of movie buffs with such regularity that the local council is having trouble getting public liability insurance.

I headed instead for Rinella, a small port at the bottom of an extremely windy road. The beach there is reached by clambering down a steep rocky path lined with jojoba and prickly pear.

I was alarmed to discover that it was a pebble beach – doubly alarmed that the pebbles were big as emu's eggs and just as black. I've never understood what you're supposed to do on a pebbly beach. They're too uncomfortable to lie on. Walk along them and there's a real risk of twisting an ankle or a knee. Worse, these pebbles held the heat and seared the soles of my feet as I hopped down to the water. It was pleasant enough when I reached the crystal clear sea and floated suspended above the rocks. It was cool and refreshing too. Then I realised I had to clamber across the hot rocks and back up the steep path again.

Back at Santa Marina Salina the ferry master wouldn't let me on the ferry back to Lípari. He spotted Marcello's Livorno number plates and said that only vehicles belonging to residents of Lípari were allowed on board. I told him I was staying on Lípari but it didn't make a difference. The date for non-residential vehicles entering Lípari had passed.

If I couldn't take Marcello on board I'd have to leave him on Salina. And I wouldn't be able to get him off Salina until early September, a few weeks before my daughter was born. I was in a jam. Just as the panic began to bubble in the pit of my stomach my newfound Zen calmness, forged high on the cliffs of Lípari, kicked in. I remembered that the ferry I was catching to Naples called into Salina on the way. I could pick up Marcello then.

The ferry master interpreted my silence as profound sadness. The beatific look on my face spooked him. Afraid I was in the middle of some sort of aneurism he suggested an Italian solution. If I could show him the ticket for my trip over that morning he would allow me and Marcello on the ferry. I thanked him like a Hare Krishna, astounded that it had taken me this long to discover that this Zen stuff really works.

The next day I went to Vulcano. I rested my newfound spiritual powers and left Marcello behind. I only wanted to climb the Gran Cratere and take a therapeutic dip in the *fanghi* (mud baths). Both were within walking distance of the tiny harbour at Porto di Levante.

Diana at the hotel warned me that I might have problems getting a hydrofoil to Vulcano. The local fishermen were on strike and blockading the harbour. It was a typically Italian dispute. Ten years earlier the fishermen had been given an EU-funded payout to stop driftnetting. Now stocks were depleted and it was getting hard to catch fish, they wanted to start drift-netting again.

I'd seen fishermen tacking up posters the day before. My Italian wasn't up to reading them but the clip art they'd used – fireworks and champagne bottles – hinted at a celebration rather than a call to arms.

The blockade too was a very Italian affair. The fishermen blocked the entrance to the harbour and made rude hand gestures to the captains of the tour boats trapped inside. The tour boat captains called the fishermen sons of whores and gesticulated back. After ten minutes one of the fishing boats moved aside and let the tour boats past. The *carabinieri* stood on a police boat just to the side, leaning back against the cabin, adjusting their aviator sunglasses and picking their teeth. They were never called upon to intervene.

The hydrofoils docked on the outside of the harbour so a group of fishermen chained themselves to the passenger shelter outside the ticket office to disrupt the service. Massimo was among them and waved when he spotted me. He beckoned me to come over, dragging up the arm of the guy he was chained to in the process.

'*Ciao*, Peter!' he said cheerily and asked me where I was going. I told him Vulcano and he told me to come back in half an hour.

'The boys are getting bored,' he whispered conspiratorially. 'We will be going to the bar soon to plan our next move.'

Massimo was as good as his word. Half an hour later I was on a hydrofoil for the five-minute journey across the Bocche di Vulcano to one of the two active volcanoes in the archipelago.

The Gran Cratere volcano rises menacingly over Porto di Levante. Orange and red sulphates streak the base like open wounds and the yellow-rimmed crater hints at bubbling toxins within. It looks threatening but the truth is that the old girl is on her last legs. The last major eruption was in 1888. There is a possibility she will erupt again, but for the moment the Gran Cratere wheezes and hisses like an asthmatic.

The path to the top of the crater starts on the southern outskirts of the town. Tourists were treating it like an afternoon stroll. They walked up the scree in flip-flops like they were off to the beach. Men walked bare-chested. Women wore shorts and tank tops. One older Italian woman, with skin as brown and leathery as a handbag, attempted the climb in her bikini. I felt distinctly overdressed in jeans, a T-shirt and a new pair of walking boots I'd bought especially before I left Syracuse.

The climb wasn't as easy as it looked. It was hard enough getting a footing in the scree wearing boots, let alone a pair of flip-flops. None of the pseudo-volcano climbers had brought water with them and one by one they gave up on reaching the top. I passed them as they gasped with their hands on their hips or sat resting on rocks, ignoring the signs requesting people not to sit or lie down. When I reached the summit at 386 metres, I found that I had 'Al Cratere' to myself.

I didn't stay long. The views across the mouth of the crater to Lípari were stunning but the smell of rotten egg gas was overpowering. I walked around the path that followed the rim, peered into a few hissing cracks that looked like open sores oozing pus, then scrambled back down the scree into town.

Vulcano's other tourist attraction is the *fanghi*, the volcanic mud baths that sit under a spiky *faraglione*, rock tower, beside the sea. My guidebook described the mud baths as 'a thick yellow soup of foul-smelling sulphurous mud'. The mud is famed for relieving arthritic conditions and skin problems, especially psoriasis. A notice tacked on the fence surrounding the pools gave instructions in five languages on how to get the most from the baths. It read like the side of a shampoo bottle. Rub in mud. Let it harden. Then jump into the sea to rinse it off. Repeat as necessary.

I stripped down to my board shorts and hobbled across the hot caked earth to the baths. I sat in the foul gloop and immediately felt depressed. Not only did it stink like a carton of rotten eggs, my fellow bathers looked like people with arthritic conditions and skin problems – *chronic* arthritic conditions and skin problems.

It suddenly dawned on me that I had no idea why I was there. I didn't have any conditions that needed curing. My eyes were stinging from the sulphur fumes. And my board shorts would stink like a fart for the next three months.

I decided that I didn't need to do it. I jumped out of the pool, rinsed off in the sea and jogged back to the changing huts like a man who had just seen a vision of God.

My elation was short-lived. As I got dressed I noticed that my white-gold wedding ring had turned an alarming shade of yellow. I checked the sign on the fence again. At the bottom, in what I regarded as very small type, there was notice warning bathers not to wear jewellery in the baths.

This was not good. Sally had bought me the ring from a jeweller perched high in Sydney's posh Strand Arcade. Now it looked like it had come from an arcade machine. Worse, Sally was arriving in Naples in less than a week's time. I took the ring off and rubbed it furiously with the bottom of my T-shirt but nothing changed.

I considered telling Sally that I had lost it. Then when I got back to Sydney I could buy a new one and tell her I had found it again. But that would open up all kinds of questions about why I had taken it off in the first place.

When I got back to Lípari I went straight to the internet café. No one seemed to worry that I smelt like a rotten egg. I did a search but surprisingly there weren't any websites devoted to how to rescue wedding rings tarnished by volcanic mud pools.

In desperation I put the ring in a glass tumbler and soaked it in Coca-Cola overnight. My mum had placed a tooth I had just lost in a glass of Coke when I was a kid in an attempt to turn me off the stuff and by morning the tooth had been dissolved. That night in Lípari my wedding ring just turned a more alarming shade of yellow. I'd have to confess to Sally that I had ruined it and hope that she didn't see it as some kind of metaphor for our marriage.

I took one more boat trip before I left the Aeolian Islands. It was a tour offered by the Gruppo di Navigazione Regina that took in the islands of Panarea and Stromboli. The brochure promised it would be 'a cultural event, a tale about the history of men in the Mediterranean'. My fellow passengers, however, were more interested in working on their tans. They were Italian couples mainly, and already a deep shade of brown. The M/N *Viking* had barely pulled out of Lípari harbour before they had stripped down to their swimwear, rolled out their towels and lain on the deck.

The brochure promised a refreshing swim in the crystal clear waters in the Cave di Pomice on the east coast of Lipari. I was the only person who wanted to swim so the captain continued straight on to San Pietro on Panarea.

Panarea is the smallest and prettiest of the Aeolian Islands. It is dotted with whitewashed buildings that many people feel give the island a Greek flavour. The way Punta del Corvo rises dramatically behind the town and the bougainvillea tumble over the terraces, I thought it looked more like the South Pacific.

I spent my allotted hour in Panarea climbing the terraced laneways and dodging the golf carts that were the only vehicles allowed on the island. They were square and white and dorky and rattled along with an anaemic whir. The locals, being Italian, still invested them with just enough flair. The local *carabinieri* threw theirs around like it was a super-charged Ferrari. And a society matron, resplendent in flowing white chiffon and Gucci sunglasses that took up her entire face, drove along chatting on her mobile phone, imperiously unaware of the tourist she sent diving for cover. She only just missed running over my foot.

From Panarea the M/N *Viking* set off manfully across the limpid seas towards the island of Stromboli.

I can't tell you how excited I was to be going to Stromboli. Stromboli is the quintessential volcanic island. It is a perfect cone, 924 metres above sea level, and one of the most active volcanoes in the world, erupting continuously for over 2000 years. It issues a near constant stream of smoke and the top of the cone dances with incandescent cinder and lava bombs. Volcanologists call these 'Strombolian eruptions', and the term is used to describe similar activity on other volcanoes around the world.

Amazingly, people live on the island. The main settlement of Stromboli clings to the lower slope on the northern side, just around from the Sciara del Fuoco (Stream of Fire), a grey scar of scree where rocks and lava plunge from the top of the volcano directly into the sea.

The savagery of the island has always appealed to creative types. Professor Lindenbrook emerged from Stromboli's crater in Jules Verne's *Journey to the Centre of the Earth*. Roberto Rossellini filmed his iconic movie *Stromboli* here. The house he shared with Ingrid Bergman while filming – they were both married to other people at the time – is the island's only bona fide tourist sight. Domenico Dolce and Stefano Gabbana have a summer home here and on any given night during the warmer months you'll find the world's rich and beautiful dancing on the black sand out the front with a soundtrack and light show provided by the volcano behind them.

The M/N *Viking* pulled into the small harbour and the captain said we had two hours to have dinner and to explore the town. I didn't bother. I scrambled down a wall and onto the black sand beach, walking until I reached the end, beyond the last of the houses. I went into the water and it was here that I spent my time in *Stromboli*, lying on my back in the lukewarm waters, watching the volcano that rose dramatically in front of me. It wasn't dark yet so I couldn't see the incandescent explosions on the summit. But I could hear them. They sounded primal.

On the way back to Lípari the captain stopped the boat in front of the Sciara del Fuoco. It was getting dark now and the explosions were easier to see. Red sparks flew into the air, dislodging rocks that then tumbled down the scree and into the sea. Everyone 'oohed' and 'aahed' like they were watching fireworks on New Year's Eve.

I felt something more elemental. In Rossellini's movie Stromboli, the volcano forces Ingrid Bergman's character to reflect on who she is and what she believes in. Pregnant and trapped in a loveless marriage, she tries to escape by walking across the island. The volcano thwarts her every step of the way, stripping her first of her luggage and then of her pride. In the end she is reduced to sobs, calling to God for help.

OK, I'll admit the volcano didn't reduce me to a sobbing wreck. But in a funny way I did see it as a metaphor for my current situation. The volcano was like my unborn daughter, the 'good explosion' that people had told me was going turn my life upside down. I was like the people living here and on the slopes of Mount Etna. I knew a seismic event was coming, but I didn't know whether it would be a minor dislocation or a major one. I just had to take a leaf out of their book and make peace with it.

If I got nervous or twitchy thinking about it, I always had my Saint Bartholomew fridge magnet to console me.

CHAPTER FOURTEEN

NAPLES

PATRON SAINT: SAN GIUSEPPE MOSCATI

According to Dean Martin, Naples is a city where the moon hits your eye like a big pizza pie. The world seems to shine like you've had too much wine. Bells ring ting-a-ling-a-ling. And people find themselves inexplicably singing *'Vita bella!'* That's why I was a little surprised to find myself riding Marcello along the harbourfront with a scruffy Australian backpacker on the back.

The backpacker's name was Joe. He was a first-generation Australian/Italian. I met him on the ferry from Lípari to Naples. One minute I was staring out to sea contemplating the life-altering changes ahead of me. The next I had an Aussie standing next to me calling me mate and asking me if I knew the footie scores. I wondered how he knew I was an Aussie too – I wasn't carrying my Qantas bag – and he said he didn't.

'You didn't respond when I spoke Italian,' he explained. 'So I tried again in English.'

The ferry to Naples was the last overnight ferry I'd be catching on my journey. It was also the worst. It shuddered and creaked and groaned like a dying beast. The fluorescent lights flickered erratically and the carpet tiles that lined the floor came up so easily that some bored children started using them as Frisbees. I'd booked too late to get a cabin and had to be content with a hard plastic seat in the lounge. It was too uncomfortable to sleep on so I created a little nest in a corner. The constant chatter of the Italians, the bright spasmodic light and the dying groans of the ferry had sent me to the deck in search of darkness and solitude.

Joe was doing a grand tour of the old country. He was staying with relatives he had never met and visiting the places his family had spoken of with nostalgia as he grew up. He was open and friendly and struck up conversations easily. When I told him I was riding around Italy on a Vespa his eyes widened in disbelief.

'You're crazy!' he said with a grin. Then he asked me if I was sure there wasn't an Italian somewhere in my family tree.

I wasn't the only person Joe had befriended on the trip. As we stood chatting on the deck a middle-aged Italian woman with glamorous blonde hair waved and smiled flirtatiously at him.

'She is having problems with her husband,' he said, by way of explanation. Apparently the husband didn't listen to her, but Joe did.

In Lípari Joe had befriended an American woman who had been brought up in Italy as a child, but had spent her adult life in New York. She told Joe she felt torn between two cultures. She was neither completely Italian nor American. Joe told her to embrace the best parts of both worlds.

'It's like me with the World Cup,' he explained. 'I'll support the Socceroos until they get knocked out. Then I'll get behind the Azzurri.'

There were times on Joe's journey that his openness had got him into trouble. He met a gay guy in a bar in Rome who bemoaned how complicated his love life had become. Joe told him about a poem he'd seen on the side of a bus in Positano.

'It said "You can live a life without love, but to live life with love for one day is like living a thousand lives,"' he told me. Someone had told Joe since that it was something Che Guevara had said. It certainly struck a chord with the guy in Rome. He had been texting Joe ever since saying how much he wanted him.

On the chaotic road that ran along the Bay of Naples that morning Joe proved to be a godsend. He had been to the city already so he gave me directions while I concentrated on avoiding a collision. We hurtled along Via Nouva Marina, weaving in and out of the traffic, before plunging into the confusing maze of lanes that made up Spaccanapoli, the heart of the old city.

Here Joe directed me through a maze of one-way streets to the central train station on Piazza Garibaldi. When I swerved at the last moment to avoid an African guy setting up his stall selling sunglasses he yelled in my ear that I was an absolute legend. It was exhilarating, the best introduction to Naples possible. I could ride like a local, get the adrenaline buzz and not have to worry if I was heading in the right direction. I would heartily recommend Joe to anyone contemplating a scooter tour of Naples.

Joe was catching a train north to Rome. He felt obligated to let his admirer know that he wasn't that way inclined. His train wasn't leaving for another hour so we pulled up outside a café that Joe said was cheap and good. More importantly there was a bench outside where we could sit and keep an eye on Marcello and our bags.

Piazza Garibaldi is the transport hub of Naples. I found it refreshingly grubby and disordered, although I could have done without the noise of the jackhammers digging up the traffic roundabout in the middle of it. This had once been the heart of ancient Napoli. It was entirely possible that the workmen would come upon an ancient Roman artefact. Their haphazard work methods suggested that they were as concerned about doing damage as the drivers going within millimetres of them.

The area around the station was thick with hawkers selling sunglasses, handbags and the latest Madonna CD. The road that headed north, Corso Garibaldi, was lined with international call centres and dusty stores selling specialties from Africa and Poland. The clocks on the wall of the call centre indicated that their clients were fake bag salesmen from Africa and prostitutes from Eastern Europe. The clocks didn't show the time in London, New York, Paris and Tokyo. The times in Yaounde, Kinshasa, Lagos, Moscow, Kiev, Sofia, Dakar and Algiers were displayed instead.

Soon it was time for Joe to go. I told him to let his friend in Rome down gently, and buzzed down Via Mancini to a cheap unnamed hotel that Joe had recommended. I'd barely switched Marcello's engine off before a young street urchin darted across the street and started tugging at my straw hat, tied to the front luggage rack.

The street kids of Naples are known as *scugnizzo*. They live by their wits, doing errands in return for food or money. They were popular with the GIs based in Naples during the Second World War who sent them to buy black-market cigarettes or arrange a date with their sisters. The cheeky urchin with a heart of gold was the staple of old Italian movies set in the city.

Life on the streets is harder and more dangerous now, but this boy had the same mischievous spirit. When he couldn't dislodge the hat he tapped the lock on the glove box to see how easy it would be to break into. I swatted his hands away with a smile and looked him straight in the eye.

'If you touch this Vespa again Padre Pio is going to shove red hot pokers up your arse for eternity,' I said. 'Do you understand?' He nodded his head and gave me a wide-eyed 'Si!' As soon as my back was turned he was checking out the padlock I'd used to chain the bike to a pole.

The rest of Italy rarely has a good word to say about Naples. They regard it as a lawless and lazy city, full of people living off state funds paid for by their taxes. (Even if many of them avoid paying taxes themselves.)

Personally, I think they are simply jealous. The Neapolitans still have that Italian *brio* that is being rubbed out by the rules and regulations imposed on the country since it joined the European Union.

Consider this popular Italian joke. A businessman visiting Naples from Milan finds a boy sleeping on a bench and asks him what he does for a living. The boy says that he fishes. The man from Milan says that if he were the boy he wouldn't sleep, he'd fish until he could afford a boat. Then he'd keep fishing until he had a fleet of boats and a nice big house. Then, eventually, after years of hard work and dedication he would be able to retire and put his feet up. The boy laughs and says, 'But I'm already doing that.'

Neapolitans live their life for the moment. Behind the wheel of a car or on the back of a scooter, they live it for the split-second. I know this sounds crazy, but I couldn't wait to throw my bags in my room, jump back on Marcello and plunge into the maelstrom of the Neapolitan road system. I threw myself into the traffic swirling around Piazza Garibaldi with a vague intention of heading up to the stout Castel Sant'Elmo and the hills of the Vomero district, famous since antiquity for its scenic beauty and therapeutic climate. In the end I just went with the flow.

The buzz of riding a Vespa in Naples is one of life's most exhilarating natural highs. The streets are thick with traffic yet the traffic moves at a disconcerting pace and motor scooters attack from all angles, like viruses looking for a chink in an immune system.

In Naples, the Highway Code has been condensed to a single line: Every man for himself. Yet, astoundingly, it rarely results in bloodshed. Just as you think you are about to be forced off the road and into a pile of rubbish that hasn't been collected for a month, the traffic parts and you squeeze through the gap like Moses and the Israelites crossing the Red Sea. The real danger came from the cobbled roads. They were pockmarked with sink holes where the cobbles had been stolen by locals to help build a house.

The Vespa of choice in Naples was the PX. Filippo from Livorno had a friend who bought old PXs throughout northern Italy and shipped them to Naples. Like the citizens of Palermo in Sicily, the Neapolitans appreciate the simple lines and reliability of the PX.

'You could shoot a PX with a shotgun and it would keep going,' Filippo said. The way he said it suggested that in Naples that was an admired and much-needed quality.

Neapolitans also have a particular way of riding their Vespas. They take the protective cowls off the sides of the bikes and leave the engine – and the spare tyre – exposed. I asked Filippo if it was because they were afraid the cowls would get stolen or dented and scratched by careless drivers. Or whether they thought by removing the cowls they'd gain an extra couple of millimetres to squeeze through the traffic. He shook his head.

'They say it's because it's hot down there,' he'd said. 'But really they do it because they think it looks cool.'

Removing the cowls certainly went against the wishes of the man who designed the Vespa, Corradino D'Ascanio. In a radio interview four years after the first Vespa was built he admitted that he had never liked the tangle of exposed parts that 'common' motorcycles had. It resulted in dirty hands and trousers, which he regarded as 'the most conspicuous inconvenience' of the marque. He designed the Vespa to keep all the messy stuff like carburettors and oil filters out of sight and out of mind. He'd even anticipated a problem with overheating and addressed it with the simple but brilliant idea of fixing a fan to the flywheel.

Having said that, I've got to admit that the PXs of Naples had a battered charm in keeping with the city they called home.

I finished the day with a (relatively) gentle ride up Corso Umberto I, the long, straight road that runs directly from the stout Castel Nuovo to the craziness of Piazzi Garibaldi in front of Central Station. Just past the university I noticed there were Africans selling sunglasses. They had knock-offs of all the latest styles, including a pair from Christian Dior that made everyone except Italians look like Spiderman. If they didn't have the style you wanted, they simply took you to the window of a genuine sunglasses shop, asked you to point out the pair you liked and then went to their 'supplier' and got you the exact pair.

As I scootered around the statue in the middle of Piazza Nicola Amore, the Africans scooped up their sunglasses in a second and ran off down the tiny lanes that radiated off the road.

At first I thought it was because they'd seen me coming. I'd nearly collected one of their brethren on the same stretch of road that morning. I had the fanciful notion that they saw the bright orange Vespa and thought I was in the employ of Donatella Versace – a crazy, scooter-riding vigilante dealing out retribution on behalf of the fashion eyewear industry.

Then I spotted a pair of policemen patrolling the pavement on foot. I was surprised to see them. The enforcement of copyright protection is notoriously lax in Naples. It's not hard to pick up a copy of the latest Windows operating system for a couple of bucks and a pretty good fake Louis Vuitton bag for a tenner. I noticed they were wearing Gucci Aviator sunglasses. Even from the road the gaudy logo was visible on the arms. They weren't genuine. A real pair cost €300. These guys were just doing a bit of 'shopping'.

The next morning I decided to explore the Centro Antico on foot. I wanted to soak up the atmosphere and figured that a stroll through Spaccanapoli, the city's busiest and most architecturally rich quarter, was the best way to do it. I wandered down streets closed to traffic, popping down the tiny lanes that fanned off them. Grandmothers dressed in black argued with young guys wearing tracksuits. A young woman haggled passionately over a melon from a fruitseller. A girl watched her father playing poker with men on the street, whispering in his ear when she saw his opponent's cards. I felt like I had stumbled into a Fellini movie.

On San Gregorio Armeno I came upon the craftsmen who carve shepherds and other figures for the traditional Neapolitan nativity scenes. The Christmas crib, or *presepe*, is central to the celebration of Christmas in Naples, and although the festive season was still over five months away the craftsmen were doing a brisk trade. The windows of their shops were lined with tiny carved donkeys, Josephs and Marys, as well as Pulcinella, the stupid but cunning clown who is the stock comedy character when Neapolitans want a laugh. The craftsmen didn't limit themselves to traditional characters. Judging by the window displays, members of the current Napoli football team were popular, as was Padre Pio. It seemed the people of Naples also had a soft spot for Princess Diana. In one store there was a whole shelf of tiny wooden Dianas.

The *presepe* was a reminder that Neapolitans are among the most fervent Catholics in Italy. And that like the wooden figures they decorate the cribs with, their Catholicism isn't the most traditional form of the religion. Miraculous cults have always been popular here and in the seventeenth century there was a brief obsession with worshipping the dead. Even today there is a small chapel hidden on Via Tribunali with an underground cemetery where parishioners gather to worship souls stuck in Purgatory.

This populist approach to religion means that the churches are always full. It's as though the street life of Naples spills into the church. People continue conversations and even arguments as they enter, dipping their hands into holy water and then wagging them to continue making their point.

The liveliest church I visited was the Gesu Nuovo on the piazza of the same name. The church was originally a palace which was bought and converted by Jesuits in 1584. The facade of the church is covered in a distinctive diamond-point rustication that doesn't quite work. I suspect a travelling salesman called by just after the Jesuits had bought the place and sold them some very grey, very shoddy cladding.

Things got cheerier inside. The Baroque interior was all multicoloured marble, vivid frescoes and ornate works of art. Mass was being held and the over-the-top styling matched the mood of the congregation perfectly. The benches were full and people were clambering over each other to listen to the priest. Long queues snaked through the church to open-sided confessional boxes where the priests sat like gypsy women giving tarot readings. Except the priests had a Bible in their laps rather than a deck of cards. One parishioner wasn't happy with the penance he was given and argued the point with the priest he'd just confessed to.

'I see your point, Father,' he seemed to be saying, 'but by my reckoning that should be five Hail Marys not seven.'

Just as I thought it couldn't get any crazier, a pair of policemen dragged in an African bag salesman off the street and deposited him and his contraband in a chapel to the side of the main hall. They frisked him, searched his bags and picked out a pair of sunglasses each. Then, as one policeman held the African, the other got out his radio and called headquarters. One of the priests went over to complain about the noise. The police tossed him a pair of sunglasses and he left them to continue.

I returned to fetch Marcello and made my way to the basilica of Santa Maria della Sanita. It was situated in the heart of a working-class area on the wrong side of the old city walls, at the far end of a busy street market as chaotic and crowded as the one I had ridden through in Palermo.

The basilica houses a famous image of the revered saint Vincenzo. The locals know him affectionately as *o munacone*, the big monk. More importantly, the African bishop Settimo Celio Gaudioso was buried here in a cave in 452 and a gruesome catacomb has grown around his tomb. Visiting the last mortal remains of monks had become somewhat of a theme to this trip.

A sign out the front of the basilica indicated that there were tours of the catacombs every day and listed the times. According to the sign a tour started in ten minutes. A young guy sitting at a table at the back of the church sold the tickets but said that they only conducted a tour if there were at least two people. No one else turned up so I offered to buy two tickets.

'It doesn't work that way,' he said, without explaining why not. 'There is an Italian tour group arriving in fifteen minutes. You can go with them if you'd like.'

The Italian tour group didn't show up. The young guy called a bored-looking girl over and told her to take me through alone anyway. I had thought she was his girlfriend, waiting for him to finish work so they could go somewhere more exciting.

She led me to the entrance to the catacombs at the back of the central nave. It was protected by an unsightly padlocked metal gate which she unlocked with a key that looked like it was from the Middle Ages. A muddy passage led to a dank cave and she beckoned for me to follow.

The cave was decorated with real skulls, embedded into the walls. Over time the front of the skulls had broken off. Only the embedded rear half remained, looking like a gruesome chocolate mould. In one place a whole skeleton was used. And once again only the embedded bits survived. Elsewhere skeletons were drawn in, but like the frescoes in other sections of the cave they were worn and difficult to make out.

It was a quick tour. The girl couldn't speak English. She simply pointed at things and let me divine their meaning myself. The cave was also very cold. The girl was only wearing a T-shirt and hugged herself against the chill.

That evening I returned to Spaccanapoli in search of a genuine Neapolitan pizza. Pizza was originally a peasant dish, made simply from dough, olive oil and tomato. It was sold from stalls on the street and was eaten at any time, day or night.

Pizza is so inextricably linked to Naples that it's surprising to learn that it was first introduced in the 1800s. Before that the peasants ate cabbage. The upper classes ignored it completely until 1889 when Queen Margherita, wife of Umberto I, decided to give it a go. Mozzarella and basil were added to the dish to create the colours of the Italian flag (red, white and green) and the Margherita pizza was born.

Pizza purists recommend Pizzeria di Matteo on Via dei Tribunali. They serve pizza by the slice, folded a *fazzoletto*, like a handkerchief, and you eat it standing at the counter. Some eat it on the street, like Bill Clinton did when he called by with his posse of secret service agents on a visit to Naples.

I ate at Pizzeria Sorbillo. It was a few blocks further into the heart of Spaccanapoli on Via dei Tribunali and broke with tradition by allowing patrons to sit at a table and eat. It was founded in 1935 by Anna Sorbillo and is regarded as one of the best pizzerias in the city. I did a Google translation of their Italian-language website and was presented with the alarming information that in between making pizzas, Anna had borne twenty-one sons. Each one of them became a *pizzaiuolo*, pizza chef.

There was a queue for tables, which I took as a positive sign. The sign above the door proclaiming that they served '*la vera pizza napolitana*' – the real Neapolitan pizza – was encouraging too. To display such a sign a pizzeria had to conform to strict government guidelines. The stickers on the door heralding the approval of the Associazione Pizzaiuole Napolitani and Associazione Vera Pizza Napolitani impressed me less. I had noticed the crests of both associations on the website. When I clicked on them I was simply redirected back to the Pizzeria Sorbilla homepage.

Within ten minutes I was ushered in. My table was against the rustic stone wall and had a marble top and a clear view of the *pizzaiuolo* at work. He took a lump of dough and heaved it onto the marble counter, forcing air into the dough. Then he broke off a piece as big as an orange and gave it *la gestualita*, the movement, and twirled it in his fingers until it became a Frisbee of dough. In one deft movement he applied the toppings, placed it on a paddle and slid it into the oven. I got the feeling he knew what he was doing.

I ordered a Margherita pizza and within a few minutes it was placed before me. Compared to the Domino's pizza I occasionally have on a Friday night it looked quite bare. Tomato, oil, mozzarella and a few torn leaves of basil. All the ingredients were fresh, bought that day from the colourful food market sprawled across the lanes a few metres away. I'm sure you're not surprised to learn that it knocked a Meateor from Domino's into a cocked hat.

Before I ate, I asked the waitress if Anna Sorbillo had really given birth to twenty-one sons. She laughed.

'Yes,' she said. 'The Italian government gave them a commendation for producing so many *pizzaiuoli*.'

Finally satisfied, I left the pizzeria. Pizzeria Sorbillo had lived up to its motto of '*Qualità in Quantità*'. I set off for my hotel, glad that I had walked. It gave me a chance to work it off.

And so the days passed in Naples. With Marcello I could venture beyond the centre of the city to the Riviera di Chiaia, the seaside resort that looks like a 1950s postcard. More often than not I'd promenade along the seafront, past the fish markets and beaches packed with Italian sunbathers. This was Marcello's spiritual home. Indeed, early one evening as I sat watching the sun set an American tourist asked if she could take a photo of him.

'It's so Italian looking,' she said, showing her husband the picture on her camera's LCD screen. She didn't realise I could speak English.

At other times I'd tear up Via Umberto I and around the square at Piazza Garibaldi just for the fun of it.

This soon took its toll on Marcello, however, and his accelerator cable began to stick. The first time it happened I was waiting at a set of lights. The second was when I was manoeuvring to get around a garbage truck. I spotted a small motorcycle repair shop on Via Foria, just down from Piazza Cavour, and decided to have the problem fixed immediately.

The shop had an official Piaggio sign above the door. I hoped that it indicated the mechanic had passed a number of rigorous tests and that his shop had been inspected and deemed worthy by pernickety officials from the company. Within seconds of meeting the mechanic, a rough and ready fifty-year-old in blue overalls, I suspected he had won the sign in a raffle.

For one thing he didn't even bother taking Marcello into his workshop. When I told him the problem, he took off the cowl covering the engine and laid it on the pavement where I'd parked the bike. He braced himself against the running boards and tugged at the accelerator cable like it was a worm reluctant to be eaten by a bird. When it wouldn't give he decided to attack it from the other end, pulling out the speedometer so he could reach the cable at the point where it met the handle. He didn't use special tools supplied to him by Piaggio. He used whatever was at hand. He was so brutal and careless that I christened him the Butcher of Naples.

To be fair to the man, I'm sure most of his customers didn't give a shit what he did to their Vespa.

They were just a means of getting around. Indeed any scratches or damage he caused would just add to the bike's cachet of cool. But I couldn't bear to watch. Every scratch was like a knife against my own flesh.

A short round woman with big round hair came out of the shop. It was the mechanic's wife and she wanted to know if he was coming home for lunch. The mechanic had opened Marcello's glove box to get at the speedometer and his wife noticed all the saintly fridge magnets stuck on the inside. She gasped and crossed herself.

'You have Moscati!' she said.

The San Giuseppe Moscati fridge magnet was the latest in my collection. I'd picked it up for a euro when I visited Gesu Nuovo. There was a chapel there dedicated to Moscati. He was a doctor in the First World War and was famous for diagnosing an illness and prescribing a cure for it without ever having seen the patient. The chapel was lined with silver charms in the shape of various bodily parts: small gifts of thanks that reflected the wounds and diseases he'd healed. I'd chosen his fridge magnet over the more conventional choice of San Gennaro, the patron saint of Naples, because Moscati looked like a cross between the actor Ben Kingsley and the Pakistani president General Pervez Musharraf.

'He was a very good man,' she said of San Moscati. 'He will protect you on your journey.'

He couldn't protect Marcello from her husband though. After the mechanic finished fitting a new accelerator cable, he forced the speedometer back into place with a screwdriver, gouging out a big chunk of the paintwork below it. He only charged me €5 but the real miracle that day was that I didn't hit him.

The morning I left Naples I went to a lotto office and bought a ticket. The lotto is fanatically observed in Naples and winning it is seen as the ultimate triumph over the system. It was instituted by Ferdinand I in 1774, and many of the traditions remain. Now, as then, the draw is made at 12 noon on Saturdays, when a blindfolded child pulls out the winning numbers.

Five numbers between 1 and 90 are drawn out. You choose the numbers you want and the amount you want to bet. You can play a single number if you like, but the return is so small that most people don't bother. Playing two numbers is called an *ambo*. It pays you 250 times the amount you bet if you're correct. Three numbers is a *terno*. That pays odds of 4250/1. Four numbers is a *quaterna*. It pays 80,000/1. Playing all five numbers is called a *cinquina* and pays a whopping 1,000,000/1. There is a limit to how much you can bet on a *cinquina*, but those who think they are on a sure thing simply buy multiple tickets.

Naples being Naples, superstitions are rife around the lotto. Some people consult *Assisti*, guided ones, who claim to have supernatural insight into the winning numbers. Most Neapolitans, though, consult *La Smorfia*, a book that interprets dreams and events and gives you the corresponding number. It is updated regularly to keep up with the times. (If you dream of meeting someone on the internet, for example, the number is 43.) Most Neapolitans know the meaning of the numbers off by heart.

I got myself a copy of La Smorfia at a bookstore on Via Pessina after visiting the National Museum. The store sold academic books mainly, but had a whole shelf dedicated to the lotto and *La Smorfia*.

I returned to my hotel and with the help of La Smorfia and a tiny Italian dictionary chose my five numbers.

VROOM BY THE SEA

I was just about to begin a seaside holiday (16) with my Vespa (79) and my wife (11) who was pregnant (45) with my baby daughter (60).

It sounded like a winning combination to me. Regardless of whether I won any money.

CHAPTER FIFTEEN

POSITANO

PATRON SAINT: SAINT PANTALEONE

When Johann W Goethe visited the Amalfi Coast in 1787, the master of Germany's *Sturm und Drung* movement was rather taken by the scenery. 'When the inhabitants here go to heaven,' he famously wrote, 'it will be a day like any other day.'

It's easy to see why Goethe was so smitten. Gelato-coloured villages cling to the side of sheer cliffs like a painting. The sea is a different, somehow better, shade of blue. And the air is heavy with the smell of lemons and wild herbs.

What Johann neglected to mention is the perilous state of the road that clings precariously to the rock face around the coast. Chances are the locals will reach heaven quicker than most of us. The first sign I spotted when I rode onto the famous stretch of road just north of Salerno was in four languages instructing me to 'Give way to overtaking traffic'.

The road easily lives up to its billing as the most beautiful road in Europe. It is known simply as State Road 163. Less than a century ago it was little more than a donkey track. It winds its way along the side of the mountains, following every indentation and crevice, the ocean a sheer drop of a couple of hundred metres below. It is so narrow and treacherous in places that you'd swear all the road builders did was lay some tarmac on top of the hoof prints.

The road stretches 50 kilometres from Salerno in the south to Sorrento in the north. The Sorrento end is closer to Naples. And Positano is closer to Sorrento than Salerno. But I skirted around the back of the mountains to start at the Salerno end anyway. It meant I got to ride on a longer stretch of the road, and the stretch my guidebook said was the most stunning.

It became immediately apparent that riding a Vespa was the best way to see the Amalfi Coast. For one thing you don't get that terrifying sense of claustrophobia that people in cars and buses get. Even at its narrowest point the road was plenty wide enough for a Vespa. Sections that were too tight for two cars to pass presented no problem to a Vespa and a car. At a pinch I could squeeze between a crash barrier and a tourist coach.

Having said that, I quickly learned to pull over when I spotted one of the big blue local SITA buses coming in the opposite direction. The drivers threw the buses around the tight bends without any concern for the vehicle, their passengers or oncoming traffic. I wondered why the local authorities hadn't put up signs warning drivers to 'Give way to SITA buses'. I guessed that they figured that once you'd encountered one on the edge of a sheer rocky cliff you would as a matter of course.

Every corner came with a fish-eye mirror to show you what was coming the other way, a man selling strings of red hot peppers and bottles of *limoncello* from a wooden cart, and million-dollar views of the rocky coastline. I half expected to come upon Dean Martin and a broad in a headscarf coming the opposite way in an Alfa Romeo convertible.

The mood of my mid-morning ride was spoiled somewhat by the driver of a Mercedes Benz behind me. He was in a hurry for some reason and kept trying to overtake me at the most inopportune moments. He'd surge forward, push me towards the edge, before dropping back in the face of an oncoming car or bus. My relaxed pace aggravated him. I was enjoying the view too much to rush. After fifteen minutes of being tailgated I stopped at a particularly lovely viewpoint to take a photo and let him pass.

Soon I reached Amalfi. It is the biggest town on the coast and also one of the most popular with tourists. Tucked between the mountains and the sea, it's a picturesque jumble of towers, domes, staircases and laneways. It was also a powerful maritime republic and in the eleventh century rivalled Genoa and Venice in importance.

I wound my way down into the town and found it struggling to cope with the influx of summer tourists and the traffic they bring. It was crowded and chaotic and a municipal policewoman directing traffic was finding it difficult to keep control. She signalled for one driver to stop and he kept going, nearly running her over.

'*Grazie, prego,*' she yelled sarcastically after him.

Further up the road a male colleague was having more success. He had a handheld computerised gadget that dispensed fines immediately and was running around frantically punching in registration numbers of all the cars parked illegally along the main drag.

I wove through the scrum of vehicles and people and on to the other side of the town. A SITA bus had stopped to pick up passengers and my nemesis in the Mercedes couldn't get past him. I scootered around him, and then the bus, with a cheerful toot on my horn. The road was clear on the other side and I roared up the hill with great delight. The Mercedes never appeared in my side mirrors again so I guess he never got around the bus. Shame.

I rounded a bend and spotted Positano. It was love at first sight. The town looked like a glamorous movie star posing for a cover shot. The tutti-frutti houses that tumbled down to the ocean were her cleavage. The church with its mosaic cupola was a piece of expensive designer jewellery. The sea was an exotic gown that changed colour depending on which way you looked at it. The mid-morning sun provided the flattering lighting, the mountain a suitably dramatic backdrop.

In 1953 John Steinbeck wrote that Positano 'bites deep'. It was so popular with writers that at one time the sound of the sea crashing on the rocks below was drowned out by the clack of typewriters. Steinbeck also wrote that 'nearly always when you find a place as beautiful as Positano your impulse is to conceal it'. He didn't. In fact that very line was published in an article he wrote about Positano for *Harper's Bazaar*. A procession of artists, tourists and very rich people have been calling by ever since.

I turned off SS163 and onto Viale Pasitea. The tiny one way road wound its way down through the town, passing villas, small stores and the occasional car park where vehicles were packed in like sardines in a can. I was looking for Casa Soriano, and I found it, beside a tiny church with a thin spire and a palm tree in the courtyard.

I had booked a room in Casa Soriano while I was on Lípari. I'd picked it out of a DK Eyewitness Travel Guide. It was the first time I'd used a DK guide to find accommodation. Casa Soriano was described as an eighteenth-century villa with vaulted ceilings. Best of all, it was cheap. I called the number listed numerous times, at various times of the day and night, but all I kept getting was a fax machine. I suspected that it was too good to be true.

Then, the day before I left for Naples, an elderly man finally answered the phone. It was so unexpected that I got a little flustered with the dates. When I asked if he wanted a credit card number to hold the reservation he laughed. They didn't take credit cards. I'd have to use a *bankomat*, cash machine. It was so informal and slack it made me suspect even more that it was all an elaborate prank.

I buzzed the front gate fully expecting to be told the room had been given to someone else and that my soon-to-be-arriving heavily pregnant wife and I would have to find somewhere else to stay. Instead I got a crackly 'Mr Moore?' over the intercom and a clunk as the gate was unlocked to let me in.

The villa sat at the top of three sets of stairs. The stairs were covered by a canopy of lemon trees groaning under the weight of their fruit and led past three levels of terraces. The first was a vegetable garden full of tomatoes and cucumbers. The next, a family home, where I was greeted by an old man sporting a moustache and a straw hat. The third and final level was where the rooms were, at the back of a balcony with a pergola covered in purple bougainvillea and honeysuckle that looked directly over the sea.

'Wow!' I said without thinking. The old man laughed.

It was my turn to laugh when he showed me inside the room. It might have well been an eighteenth-century villa but the last time it had been renovated was in the 1970s. The bath had a bizarre step that you sat on – perfect for pregnant ladies, he assured me – and the curtains and bedspread were made from a bright floral print that looked like the frocks Agnetha from ABBA used to wear. I realised with a smile that it was Marcello, reincarnated as a room.

The old man asked for my passport. I gave it to him and told him that Sally was arriving the next day. He laughed. I pointed at Marcello on the street below and asked if it was OK to park him there and he laughed again. I decided he laughed a lot, which I guess isn't surprising when you wake up to a view like this every day of your life.

I stood on the balcony mesmerised by the view. It felt like I could reach out and touch the yellow, blue and green ceramic tiles on the dome of the Santa Maria Assunta. And Li Galli, the islets where the sirens tried to lure Odysseus to his death, floated in the ocean straight ahead. If I craned my neck I could make out the tutti-frutti-coloured houses above me and the craggy mountain beyond that. Below, the tiny grey beach was lined with brightly coloured umbrellas. When the sun set later that day they closed like sunflowers, waiting for the morning sun to open again.

I caught a SITA bus to Sorrento and then an airport bus to Naples Capodichino Airport. It took one and a half hours each way. I could have done it in half the time on Marcello, but it isn't really an option when you are picking up your wife who is over seven months pregnant. An article in a 1957 *Popular Science* magazine noted that scooter riders were 'either single or newly married' and that scooters were so conducive to romance that 'there is a fast turnover between these two categories'. It didn't mention how quickly scooters facilitated the turnover to the next category after that – parenthood. Or the consequences on your transport options.

I was feeling anxious about seeing Sally again. I still felt a little guilty about taking off on this trip while she was pregnant. I knew it was something I needed to do to be a better father. And Sally said she knew what I was like when she married me. But I couldn't help wondering if she felt the same way halfway through her third trimester without the father of her child around to massage her feet or make her a cup of tea.

Then I spotted Sally and she smiled. I know it's a cliché, but she really did glow. Her belly was twice the size it was when I'd last seen it. She wasn't carrying any extra weight so it looked like someone had stuck a basketball up her dress. I instinctively reached out and touched it.

'She's excited about seeing you too,' she said with a grimace. 'She kicked the whole way over.'

I took Sally's bag and led her out to the bus. She expressed mock disappointment that we weren't going by Vespa.

'I'm keen to meet this new Vespa of yours!' she said.

Positano is not the ideal place for a heavily pregnant woman. Most places are reached by steep staircases carved into the side of the mountain. So we spent the first few days relaxing in our bougainvillea-covered eyrie, passing the time reading and eating tomatoes grown in the garden below us, supplemented with fresh bread, ham and antipasto purchased from the tiny *alimentari* a little way down the hill.

We spent one morning discussing a name for our daughter. I showed Sally the list of 'typically' Italian names Sergio had written down for me in Palermo. Crocifissa. Catena. Concetta. Immacolata. Assunta. Incoronata. She was aghast.

'They sound like serious medical conditions,' she said, unimpressed.

I held up a piece of a pizza. 'What about Margherita?' I said.

Sally raised her eyebrow. I told her that it translated as Daisy in English and she agreed that was better. No concrete decision was made.

In the afternoons, when it was cooler, we'd clamber down the stairs to the town below. For all its fame and popularity, Positano still felt sleepy, even now during the peak summer season. In 1999 the mayor of the town signed a Slow City Charter, pledging to minimise noise and advertising hoardings and to promote the good things in life. It was working.

The staircase diagonally opposite Casa Soriano cut directly down to the town centre. It emerged to the side of the church of the Santa Maria Assunta. We'd have a chilled juice in one of the cafés overlooking the beach before wandering among the chi-chi boutiques selling Positano sandals and pastel linen suits. After deciding we didn't have the wherewithal to carry off the Italian beachside look we'd catch the little orange municipal bus to the top of the hill and walk halfway down again to our room. If we were lucky we'd just miss a bus and have time to buy an ice cream from the gelateria next to the bus stop.

Sally's belly got attention everywhere we went. The man in our favourite gelateria asked when the baby was due. A waitress in a café by the beach cooed and asked if she could touch it. Passengers on the bus stood up and gave her a seat with a smile. It reminded me of the way Italians reacted to Marcello. I think it reflects well on Italians that they respond so warmly to motor scooters and motherhood.

One morning we were clambering down the stairs to the beach. A middle-aged Italian lady was waiting for her friend who was struggling with the last few steps. Between sucking in lungsful of air herself, the woman noticed Sally was pregnant and clapped her hands.

'*Complimenti!*' she said. I wasn't sure whether she was congratulating Sally on the upcoming baby or for tackling the stairs in her pregnant state.

There isn't an awful lot to do in Positano. To be truthful that's part of its charm. But there are only so many times you

can walk by a boutique without being convinced that you really need a pair of Positano sandals. Every second day we went on an excursion. Nothing too adventurous – Positano was centrally located on the Amalfi Coast, so it didn't have to be. Just a short trip somewhere to get us away from the Positano House of Sandals.

Our first adventure took us to Ravello, perched high atop a mountain. The poet Andre Gide wrote that it was 'closer to the sky than the sea'. Its artistic credentials are as impressive as Positano's. A Ravello merchant named Rufolo is mentioned in *The Decameron*. DH Lawrence knocked out a couple of chapters of *Lady Chatterley's Lover* here. Wagner used it as inspiration for Klingsor's magic garden in *Parsifal*. Gore Vidal had a villa here too, until his bad knees forced him to sell it.

Getting to Ravello from Positano was a two-part process. We had to catch a SITA bus to Amalfi and then a small local bus up through the steeply cultivated hills to the top of the mountain.

The nearest SITA bus stop was at the top of Positano, at the junction where Viale Pasitea met the SS163 near Nuovo Chiesa. One of the things I loved about travelling by Vespa was that I wasn't beholden to timetables. I didn't have to buy tickets (not that the Italians did anyway). And I didn't have to worry about my bus or train being late. I could just jump on my Vespa and go. But that morning I realised the benefits of just sitting somewhere and watching.

The junction was patrolled by a young municipal policeman who was responsible for keeping the traffic on this part of the Amalfi Coast flowing. It wasn't as easy as it appeared. The corner immediately north of the junction was too narrow for two vehicles to get around. Delivery vehicles stopped to make deliveries to the shops here. And locals double-parked their cars while they nipped in for their morning espresso at the small café adjacent to the bus stop.

The young policeman approached the task ahead of him with gusto. He blew his whistle, windmilled his arms and indicated for drivers to stop by authoritatively showing the palms of his white-gloved hands.

A driver in a car with German plates didn't move when the policeman told him to. In a flash the young guy whipped out a pad from his back pocket and started writing a ticket. The driver pointed in panic at a delivery truck blocking his way and he was let off with a warning.

The policeman's greatest challenge that morning was moving the vehicles left unattended by the locals. Whenever he found one abandoned, inconsiderately blocking the road, he blew his whistle wildly until the owner emerged, invariably from the café, with a pastry in their hand and a mobile phone to their ear.

When he wasn't blowing his whistle or directing traffic the policeman paced restlessly around the junction. A small dog from a house nearby started following him. When he crossed the road, it did too. When he went back to the other side of the road, it went too. People waiting for the bus started giggling and the policeman realised with alarm that the dog was undermining his authority. When he tried to chase it away it came back yapping, thinking he was playing a game with it. The SITA bus came before we could see how the situation was resolved.

The small bus that took us up into the mountains from Amalfi was filled with old ladies returning from a shopping trip. They knew the bus driver. He did the same journey back and forth five times a day. In an attempt to entertain them and keep his sanity he gave a running commentary on the journey. The idiocy of the drivers he came across on the tight mountain road seemed to be his favoured theme. On one corner a woman had stopped to have a sip of her drink.

'Oh yes, *signora*,' he said sarcastically. 'A fine place to drink your red drink.' The Italian ladies behind us tittered.

'He's like a London cabbie,' said Sally. 'Got an opinion on everything.'

The bus dropped us off at Piazza Vescovado, right outside the Duomo. The church is dedicated to Saint Pantaleone, a fourth-century saint whose blood is supposed to liquefy once a year like San Gennaro's in Naples. The big event was only a week off and the priest was decorating the church with the help of two aged parishioners.

The *ambos*, raised pulpits, had a nursery vibe about them. The one used for reading the gospels was decorated with dragons and birds and was supported by six roaring lions. The one used for reciting epistles illustrated the story of Jonah and the whale. The designs tickled Sally's fancy and she lit a candle to our unborn daughter.

We cut across the main square and headed into the quaint village to find a restaurant. It was lunchtime and Sally needed to eat. We spotted a restaurant with a terrace overlooking a lush green valley to the sea.

Our waiter was an obnoxious man wearing a cream jacket two sizes too big for him. He decided immediately that we weren't the kind of customers who tipped generously and proceeded to ignore us. He lavished his attention instead on a pair of matronly American women.

'I know you told me not to ask,' drawled one, wearing what looked like a wig. 'But what would you eat?'

Fifteen minutes later the waiter still hadn't brought bread to the table. We told him we were leaving and all he did was shrug.

We returned to the main square and a small sandwich joint called *Il Panini*. It was extremely busy and the owner had to take orders, toast the sandwiches and take them to the table himself. He was rushed off his feet, but when he noticed that Sally was pregnant he asked when our baby was due. Sally told him the end of September.

'My sister is due on 21 September!' he said. He wished us well, and told us the quickest way to Villa Cimbrone, where we were headed.

Villa Cimbrone was built in the late 1800s by an Englishman by the name of Lord Grimthorpe. It is set on the furthest tip of Ravello's ridge and boasts a clifftop belvedere that offers arguably the best view on the coast. It is known as the Terrace of Infinity, and sits suspended over the valley below. The balustrade is topped by busts of famous sons of Ravello who gaze out across the view for eternity.

I got a great photo of Sally standing with an infinite canvas of sea and sky behind her. She placed her hand on her belly and smiled enigmatically. It was a Mona Lisa kind of smile, the type that invites you to speculate what it means.

When I look at that photo now I see an inkling of premonition in it. A premonition of the joys of motherhood ahead. And the terror of the unknown as well.

CHAPTER SIXTEEN

POSITANO, STILL

PATRON SAINT: PRINCESS DIANA

The day we went to Pompeii was the hottest day of the year. We didn't know that at the time of course. Our room in Positano didn't have a television or radio so we had no idea what was going on in the outside world. The weather had invariably been so gorgeous that we could tell what kind of day it was going to be before we opened the curtains. We'd look through the French doors that led to the balcony, note that the sky was indeed blue again and dress accordingly.

The day started ominously. The mountains to the south were covered in thick smoke. A bright yellow helicopter scooped water from the sea and dumped it on a point about halfway up the mountain. The fire looked like it was only a couple of hairpin bends away so I jumped on Marcello and told Sally I was going to see how close it was. I said I wanted to be sure we weren't in danger. But the truth was, I was missing riding Marcello. I rode up the road that wound around the hill wearing my straw hat instead of a helmet and felt immediately better.

It was only a small brush fire. A fireman on the road said they already had it under control.

Getting to Pompeii from Positano involved catching another SITA bus, this time north to Sorrento. From there the Circumvesuviana railway line would take us directly to Pompeii.

The Circumvesuviana train looked like an ancient ruin itself when we got on it. It was old and beat-up and covered in graffiti. It hugged the bay but passed ugly towns full of apartments with cracked pavements and a generally down-at-heel air. Within half an hour it had reached Pompeii Marina. A five-minute walk later, after running the gauntlet of crappy souvenir stalls, we had reached the ruins.

We entered the site through the Porta Marina Gate. There was a shop beside the ticket office. Sally bought two bottles of water to ward off dehydration. I bought two books to help us understand the ruins.

One was called *Pompeii – A Reasoned Archaeological Itinerary*. It promised to divulge the full scientific nature of Pompeii and revive the everyday life of the buried civilisation 'like a dream'. The other was a picture book called *Pompeii Past and Present*. It featured photos of the main ruins, with acetate overlay illustrations that filled in the missing bits and showed you what they looked like in their heyday.

I knew in my heart that I'd get the most use out of the picture book. When I look at ruins all I see is a pile of rocks. I'm not trained in ancient architecture or blessed with the ability to mentally reconstruct what once had been. That's why I loved the Doric temple in Segesta and the Temple of Concord in Agrigento. They were pretty much complete.

Pompeii is arguably the most famous ruined city in the world. Every schoolchild knows the story, or a rough outline of it at least. In 79 AD Mount Vesuvius erupted and buried the city in a rain of ash and cinders. It happened so suddenly and quickly that the city and its inhabitants were caught out.

When I learned about the destruction of Pompeii at school I imagined that the city had been buried in an instant. My teacher told us about archaeologists finding the bodies of people sleeping, and I imagined others caught mid-sentence, making a point with their hands. The reality was that the city was buried over two days. Because it was buried entirely under a mountain of ash and pumice, and not rediscovered until the mid-eighteenth century, it is largely preserved as it was at the time of the eruption. It still presents archaeologists with an exceptional opportunity to recover all kinds of items like furniture, food and other everyday items that would otherwise have been scattered or destroyed. The truth just wasn't as dramatic.

Pompeii was home to 20,000 people. That's about the same size as Armidale in Australia or Skegness in the UK. The streets were based on a loose grid pattern. They are still known by their original names today and the ruins of each house have a street number.

The heat and Sally's condition limited our visit to a few of the more impressive ruins. We visited the forum. Vesuvius was directly behind it. It was a large open space surrounded by the most important civil and religious buildings. It was once regarded as one of the most awe-inspiring plazas in the Roman Empire, but I didn't really get a sense of that until I flipped over the acetate panel on the corresponding page in *Pompeii Past and Present* and saw the impressive arcades that had lined either side.

I was similarly impressed by the picture of the Temple of Augusta. The squat square ruins gave no indication of the prancing horse that had adorned the top of the roof. And the plate for the House of the Faun did the job too. It had been the largest and finest house in Pompeii – over 3000 square metres – but you didn't really get any idea of the impressive wooden roof. Still, the ruin had some pretty cool mosaics of Dionysus as a boy riding a panther. While there was a bronze statue of Faun, both on the site and in the book, the original was in the Museum of Naples. Luckily I'd seen it when I was there.

The only ruin I didn't need my little book of reconstructions for was the Thermopolium, or tavern, on Via Della Fortuna. My years of drinking in pubs meant that I could imagine exactly what it had been like. It had marble-faced counters with round shallow circles in which food was slopped – an interesting innovation that sadly has not continued to the modern day – and a till where archaeologists found change. (The day's takings were 683 sesterces, apparently.) I liked the idea that the patrons continued drinking right to the end.

Next I wanted to see the brothel and the toilets. Sally rolled her eyes and told me I should just rent the DVD of Up Pompeii starring Frankie Howerd when I got back to London. I told her that in my experience toilets and brothels were the most interesting and instructive elements of any ancient Roman city. And I meant it.

When I visited Ephesus, the Roman ruins in Turkey, I liked the way I could sit on one of the ancient stone toilets and look directly up the main processional road, lined with columns, and out to sea. I was equally impressed by the sign carved in stone near the brothel that pointed the way in and showed a picture of a girl and the price you'd be expected to pay. It is regarded as one the world's oldest advertisements (fittingly, for the world's oldest profession). I was working in advertising at the time so I'd told myself it was research.

The only disappointing thing about Pompeii was that there weren't more 'crispy bodies', as Sally put it. She'd expected them to be dotted among the ruins – a guy sitting in the corner of a crumbling villa sipping on a cup of tea, perhaps, or a woman caught in the middle of doing the ironing. At the very least, she said, they should be press-ganged into a useful role in the ruins. Like standing on a corner and pointing the way to the *anfiteatro*, for example.

Sally was even more disappointed when I told her the bodies we *could* see weren't even real. Like all the organic material in Pompeii, they had decomposed over the centuries. What she saw was a cast made from plaster poured into the volcanic 'moulds' that had trapped them.

By early afternoon we were numbed from the oppressive heat and the sheer scale of Pompeii, and returned to the train station, eating a late lunch at a small pizzeria on the way. It was a family-run business, with tables outside under cover, and the pizzas were as good as the one I'd had in Pizzeria Sorbillo in Naples. We made the long trek back to Positano, arriving at our terrace just as the sun set. We sat on the balcony and watched the lights twinkle to life, resting feet that were still aching from all the walking we had done.

Our final day trip was to the island of Capri. A direct ferry to the island left from the dock opposite the church in Positano and within twenty minutes we were pulling up alongside the busy dock at Marina Grande. The town of Capri was perched high on the hill above it.

Travel writers throw all kinds of superlatives at Capri. It is in turns 'breathtaking' and 'charming' and a 'confirmed spot on the Mediterranean celebrity circuit'. That day I had no idea if they were right or not. I couldn't see Capri for the mass of people. Paris Hilton could have been within touching distance and I'd have been none the wiser.

Every tourist on the island was queuing for the funicular that carried people directly up the side of the mountain to the town. The queue snaked its way through the port past tacky souvenir shops and *gelataria* that sold ice cream directly to people in the queue. One Italian guy arrived and squeezed past the crowd to the front of the queue. Sally was immediately irritated. As an English person she considered queue jumping a capital crime and pushed me forward to confront him. He apologised and said that if we liked we could push in with him too.

The crowds were worse up in the town. People spilled directly from the funicular station onto Piazza Umberto. My guidebook said the piazza was stylish and compact but that day it had the ambience of a moshpit. Sally and I shuffled along with the crowds past shops we couldn't see before scrambling down a laneway to the bus stop. We abandoned the town without seeing the seventeenth-century Chiesa di Santo Stefano or Certosa di San Giacomo, the bare Carthusian monastery with a delicately painted chapel. We didn't get to the Gardens of Augustus either. We caught a bus back down to the harbour instead.

After the emptiness of Sardinia and Sicily and the laid-back charm of the Aeolian Islands, I found the whole experience traumatising. I wanted to get on the first boat back to Positano. Sally wanted to visit the Blue Grotto.

'I can't come to Capri and not see the Blue Grotto,' she announced determinedly.

The Blue Grotto was used by Tiberius in Roman times as a sea *nymphaeum*, a place to shag young boys when it got too hot outside in his garden. It was abandoned soon after and the locals avoided it, believing the cave was home to witches and monstrous creatures. It was discovered again in 1826 by the fisherman Angelo Ferraro. He showed it to a German writer called Augustus Kopisch. Soon the word got out about a wondrously illuminated cave and Capri was a must-see stop on the Grand Tour map.

I wanted to see the Blue Grotto too. But I was concerned whether the trip getting to it was safe for a heavily pregnant woman. Catching the tourist boat around to the mouth of the cave didn't worry me. It was the bit where Sally had to clamber over the side of the tourist boat into the smaller rowboat that I had reservations about. Clearly the Italian health and safety department didn't see any problems. They didn't even insist on passengers wearing life jackets.

My feelings surprised me. I'd travelled through Afghanistan, Somalia and warring Balkan states without thinking of my own safety for a split-second. But here I was obsessing about Sally and my unborn daughter. Sally sensibly suggested we go to the cave anyway and if she thought getting in the smaller boat was too dangerous she wouldn't do it.

I'd underestimated the reverence Italians hold for pregnant women. When we reached the mouth of the Blue Grotto, the coarse, weather-beaten 'captains' of the smaller boats went out of their way to help Sally onto a boat. The captain of our boat tightly held her hand, while the men in other boats ignored getting passengers for themselves for a moment and held his boat steady. They only rowed off when they were certain she was safely on board, waving and calling *complimenti* as they went.

The men rowing the boats get paid per person and usually insist on squeezing in as many people as possible. Our captain was happy to have just Sally and me on board. He said it was lucky to have a mother in his boat and rowed slowly over to the entrance, checking constantly that Sally was comfortable.

The rowboats jostled at the tiny entrance, waiting for their chance to go inside. Entering the cave demands precision and daring. At the right moment, when the swell drops for a second and the small entrance is momentarily bigger, the captain grabs a chain attached to the side of the cave and hauls the boat through. It is a tight fit and both captain and passengers have to lean back to get through. Sally's pregnant belly made it through with a few centimetres of clearance to spare. When we got to the other side and sat up we were greeted by a pool glowing the most astounding shade of blue.

'Wow!' I said. 'That's blue.' It wasn't the most eloquent thing I've ever said, but the Blue Grotto has that effect. It's flabbergasting. But in a good way.

The incredible colour and freaky glow are caused by the concurrence of two natural phenomena. The sun beams in through a large underwater entrance below that effectively filters out any red tones. Then the limestone bottom of the cave reflects the light directly up. It truly was one of the most astounding things I've ever seen.

Suddenly the crowds, the heat, were all worth it.

Generally the boatmen drag tourists in and out in a matter of minutes, but our captain rowed to the back of the cave so we could stay a bit longer. He took our photo. He sang us a song. He pointed out the faint outlines of paintings from the time of Tiberius. And as we left the cave he sang another song, this time directly to our daughter in Sally's belly. It was an Italian lullaby, he said.

The night of my birthday was also Sally's last night in Positano. We started in a groovy bar down by the sea. The DJ played chill-out music and we drank Camparis. (Sally had discovered a non-alcoholic version.) Then we wandered arm in arm up a pathway covered in flowering wisteria towards the Hotel Le Sirenuse, where a table awaited us in their spectacular terrace restaurant, La Sponda. It is difficult to get a reservation, but Sally had had the forethought to book it before she left London.

As we walked past the Hotel Palazzo Murat, a crowd of elegantly dressed people blocked our way. They had gathered to listen to a local author Silvana Giacobini talk about her new book, *Diana – Il Romanzo Verità*.

I'd seen posters around Positano advertising the event. They featured an edition of *Hello* magazine with Diana on the cover and the headline: 'The explosive new book that will change the way you think about Princess Diana.' A picture of Silvana's book was superimposed at a jaunty angle with the inference that *Hello* magazine were talking about her book. A closer look at the cover revealed they were talking about the Andrew Morton book they were serialising inside. Cheeky.

Our reservation at La Sponda was for 8 p.m. It was only 7.15 so I asked Sally if we could stay and watch. The poster had promised that the book was *'una grande storia d'amore'*, a grand story of love, and detailed the untold story of Diana's romance with Dodi Fayed. Sally rolled her eyes and said OK.

A hassled man with foppish hair was selling copies of the book from a table so I joined the queue to buy one. They were €6 each. When I gave the guy a €10 note he asked if I had a €1 coin so he could give me a €5 note as change. I said no and he looked at me suspiciously.

'Are you sure?' he asked. When I said I was sure he turned to Sally and asked her if she had change. She shook her head and he looked at us in disbelief.

'Neither of you have change?'

He tried to broker a complicated loan deal between me and the man behind me. From what I could gather it involved the man giving me a €1 coin and me taking his bank account details so I could deposit €1 into it. The man sensibly refused to get involved with such a risky scheme. The guy on the table said that he was sorry, but he wouldn't be able to sell me a book after all.

There was a tin brimming with change sitting on the table next to the pile of books. Sally pointed to it and told the guy he had a planet of change.

'I know,' he replied. 'But I may need it for later.'

I think he realised how ludicrous he had been and sold me a book anyway, reluctantly handing me four €1 coins as change. He winced noticeably as he did it.

I'd like to say that this was the only change-related incident I'd suffered in Positano but it was just one of many. I'd already upset the guy at the local *lavanderia* (laundromat). When I went to pick up a bag of washing he wanted me to give him the exact change too. When I said I didn't have it he told me to check my pockets, insisting I turn them out for him to see. He asked Sally to check her purse too and wanted her to empty it out onto the counter.

In the end I told him I wasn't a *bankomat* and as a shopkeeper it was his duty to keep sufficient change. There might well have been a few expletives added to the mix, but that was the gist of it. He told me that as a shopkeeper it was his prerogative to serve who he wanted and that I wasn't to darken his door again. From that point on I tried only to purchase items I could pay for with the exact change.

Silvana stepped up to a lectern in the foyer of the hotel to polite applause from the audience. She had a mane of blonde hair, chunky jewellery, big sunglasses and a tan that was just a little too dark. It was all designed to distract you from the wrinkles on her face, of course, but she did look glamorous. Like a lot of older Italian women do.

Silvana explained that her book was about the last days of Diana when she finally found true love with her soulmate Dodi Fayed. How she knew this she never said. I have since learned that she is a journalist and gossip columnist by trade. She presented her theory on Diana and Dodi with such conviction that it was hard not to believe her.

Each chapter started with a poem and it was these that Silvana performed. In a deep husky voice she recited odes to the crumpled metal of 'the eternal Mercedes' and described how Trevor Rees-Jones's airbag 'swelled like a message of terror'.

Each poem was delivered in that dramatic way Italian women have. She finished her presentation with a poem that started with an unfortunate couplet about the smell of dead women. But she recovered sufficiently by the end to conjure Diana's final moments.

'There is no time to think. There is no time for fear,' she whispered dramatically. She paused, breathed deeply and delivered the last line with fiery eyes and a clear voice. 'There *is* no time!'

Her shoulders slumped and she bowed her head. The applause from the crowd was rapturous.

'Not quite the tone I was expecting,' said Sally.

The Sirenuse Hotel sits directly above the church and the beach and enjoys the most stunning views in Positano. It was opened by the Marquis Paolo Sersale in 1951 when he turned his family's summer home into a hotel. It is painted rustic red, with details picked out in startling white, and has the bearing of a 1950s aristocrat with a taste for fine wine, fast women and pencil-thin moustaches. The hotel has a vintage Riva Aquarama wooden speedboat to pick up guests from Naples or Capri. That tells you all you need to know about the place.

Of course, this quiet elegance and European charm don't come cheap. Even in the low season double rooms overlooking the ocean start at €850 a night.

The La Sponda restaurant is on the third floor of the hotel, on a grand terrace overlooking the ocean. Bougainvillea covers the arches. Potted lemon trees are arranged artfully between the diners. We were ushered to our table just back from the white columned balustrade and all thoughts of car wrecks and airbags of terror were immediately banished. It was, quite frankly, beautiful.

Our waiter told us we were only 'eighty steps above the sea'. It certainly felt like we could reach out and touch it.

'This is perfect,' sighed Sally.

Two men in black suits silently walked through the restaurant lighting candles. Our waiter said there were 400 in total. They twinkled and blinked in elegant wrought-iron holders suspended from the walls. It was simple but beautiful. I think I must have been a bit emotional from my birthday and impending fatherhood because it brought a lump to my throat.

The dinner menu at La Sponda was developed under the guidance of Alfonso Iaccarino. He was the first chef in the south of Italy to be awarded three Michelin stars and our waiter said that the menu was designed to showcase the classic flavours of the region. The dishes were based on traditional Neapolitan recipes reworked in creative ways and featured whatever had been bought fresh from the local fish markets that morning.

I had *linguine le Sirenuse*, with lobster, scampi, and crayfish. Sally had linguine with artichoke hearts cooked *en papillote* (in parchment). She couldn't eat seafood because of her condition. Even the slightest case of listeria would have dire consequences. I probably should have known that too but I'd been reading Vespa manuals, not baby ones. The food was as elegant and sophisticated as our surroundings.

Another waiter brought a pastry cart around. Sally took my hand across the table and said she was glad she had come to Positano. I said I was glad she came too.

John Steinbeck wrote that Positano doesn't seem quite real while you are there but 'becomes beckoningly real after you have gone'. That night, on the terrace of La Sponda, overlooking the sea underneath the twinkling candles, I knew what he meant. I was determined to hold on to that moment and treasure it as long as I could.

It would be a long time until Sally and I had a holiday – or an evening out – like this again.

CHAPTER SEVENTEEN

SAN GIOVANNI ROTONDO

PATRON SAINT: PADRE PIO

In 1952 Pope Pius XII called for the church to embrace automation to ensure 'greater and greater speed to the glory of God'. Italian priests heeded his call and by 1956 *Time* magazine said that 30,850 of them were riding Vespas. The same article noted that the church's religious proficiency increased by 3000 per cent in the areas where priests tended their flock by motor scooter.

At the same time the chairman of the company that made Vespas, Enrico Piaggio, confessed to the *American Mercury* that he had a 'profound religious faith that guides and inspires me'. With the extra cash brought in by the free-wheeling Fathers, I wasn't surprised.

Not all the religious orders were enamoured with the idea of using scooters to perform their godly duties. Some refused on the grounds that scooters were the work of the devil. The *Time* article said that this led to 'the decline of the more introverted Benedictines and foot-slogging Franciscans in favour of the

VROOM BY THE SEA

fast-moving Jesuits, whose high-octane practicality thrives on the motor-scooter age'.

Alone with Marcello again, I was on my way to San Giovanni Rotondo, a small town in the heart of the wild Gargano promontory, the spur above the heel of the Italian boot. It is the burial place of one of Catholicism's newest Saints – Padre Pio. Born Francesco Forgione, the Padre received the stigmata, the five wounds corresponding with those suffered by Christ on the cross, making him the first stigmatised priest in the history of the Catholic Church. He also 'appeared' before cardinals in Rome while asleep in his cell in San Giovanni Rotondo. That's called bilocation, in case you're wondering, and it's a handy little skill that a lot of saints seem to have.

Padre Pio is one of the most popular saints in Italy. I'd spotted him in nearly every town I'd passed through. He typically appeared either in the form of a bronze statue in a park – like in Corleone – or in a portrait, smiling down at me from the wall of a small *alimentari* in Positano as I bought slices of parma ham.

The good Padre was a Jesuit but I have no proof that he heeded Pope Pius XII's call and rode a Vespa. He was sixty-five at the time and his stigmata were giving him so much grief that his hands were constantly in bandages. If he had ridden a Vespa I'm sure Piaggio would have got a photo of him on one, probably with his robes flowing behind him. But Vespa fan or not, on my previous trip around Italy he had become the patron saint of my Vespa Sophia.

Padre Pio hadn't started the journey as Sophia's protector. Sophia's wellbeing, both physical and spiritual, was entrusted to Mary, the Mother of God. I'd bought a fridge magnet bearing her benign countenance from Saint Mary's Cathedral in Sydney before I left. When I set out from Milan I placed it reverentially beside Sophia's speedometer.

The early part of my journey with Sophia was plagued with an assortment of mechanical problems. The atheists among you may see that as proof that my superstitious emblem wasn't working. I must admit that in my darkest moments, stranded beside a lonely road, covered in oil, I did have the odd crisis of faith. I told myself that the generosity I encountered from Italians because of these problems was proof that Mary was working in more mysterious ways, something that divine figures the world over are inclined to do.

It wasn't until I reached Livorno that I discovered the real reason. Marco and Filippo told me that I had chosen an old saint. Mary was worn out from centuries of requests and prayers. I needed a new saint, someone new to the team, fresh off the bench with energy to burn. At that time there wasn't anyone fresher than Padre Pio. He'd only been canonised two weeks before. I swapped the Mary fridge magnet for a freshly minted one featuring the Padre and I never had another mechanical problem with Sophia.

After I finished the trip I took the Padre Pio fridge magnet off Sophia and kept it as a lucky charm. It was currently on our fridge in London, among postcards, bills and shopping lists. I took great comfort that the visage of the Padre, a little faded from the sun, was looking down upon Sally and our unborn child.

My trip to San Giovanni Rotondo was a pilgrimage of thanks. It was close to 200 kilometres out of my way – a long ride through the dry plains of Puglia. But I felt that it was the least I could do for the trouble-free days of scootering, first on Sophia and now on Marcello.

San Giovanni Rotondo nestles under Monte Calvo, the highest peak on the Gargano promontory. The first sign that I had reached the 'holy land' was a display village for a mobile home company called Prefabbricati Padre Pio. It sat on the rocky outskirts of town and featured a life-sized Padre Pio atop a tower. His arms were outstretched in greeting but it looked more like he was about to dive off into a tub of water 30 metres below.

San Giovanni Rotondo itself was a forest of construction cranes. Seven million pilgrims visit the town each year, making it the most visited pilgrimage site in the world after Lourdes. If China is using 44 per cent of the world's supply of cement to fuel its building boom, I reckon at least half of the remaining 66 per cent is going directly here. San Giovanni Rotondo was a mini-Shanghai of multistorey hotels, car parks and apartment blocks.

It wasn't difficult to find somewhere to stay. I got a room in a new hotel next to a drive-thru McDonald's just on the edge of the 'pilgrim zone', the area on the edge of town where the old church (the Santa Maria delle Grazie), the new church (Chiesa di San Pio) and a million souvenir stalls were located.

The foyer of the hotel was littered with Padre Pio paraphernalia and the check-in counter doubled as a souvenir stall. There was a notice in the lift that listed the times that mass was held in both the old and new churches and a picture of Padre Pio carrying a lamb. Indeed, everywhere you turned there was a portrait of the Padre gazing down upon you. Sometimes he wore a smile, sometimes a frown, but he always sported a brown robe and a grey, grizzly beard.

The only place free of the Padre in my room was the wall behind my bed. A mini crucifix hung there instead. When I lay down and looked up though, I noticed that there was a little sticker featuring Padre Pio tacked onto the bottom of Our Saviour's feet.

The hotel manager told me parking was impossible in the pilgrim zone. Spaces were limited – even for Vespas – and the parking police were zealots. He suggested I caught the tourist train instead. It stopped right out front and would deposit me at the Santa Maria delle Grazie, the old church where I could prostrate myself before Padre Pio's belongings in his old room.

The tourist train wasn't really a train. It was a tractor made to look like a train that pulled three carriages full of pilgrims.

It was the sort of thing you see in Disney World, not the Catholic world's No. 2 pilgrimage destination. Still, my fellow passengers seemed cheerful enough. It did a loop from the bottom of the town, past the hotels, and up to the main square. After disgorging its passengers outside the Santa Maria delle Grazie and the massive, austere Casa Sollievo della Sofferenza (House for the Relief of Suffering, or hospital to you and me), it went back around again.

The 'engine' of the tourist train looked like a kiddie version of the locomotives that steamed across America in the days of the Wild West. Indeed, it bore the nameplate 'Muson River 1894'. I scribbled down the name to do a Google search later. I thought perhaps it was modelled on a real train that had played a significant role in the taming of the American frontier. The sad reality was that the Dotto Road Train Company of South Korea had made the name up in an attempt to give their little train a bit of Wild West credibility. I was tempted to email them that any credibility lent by the name was extinguished by the flashing orange safety light and the limiter to stop it going faster than 20 kilometres per hour.

A pathway to the left of the old church led up a hill that overlooked the whole town. It was La Via Crucis and I was surprised to find it topped by a statue of Mary cradling the baby Jesus, not Padre Pio. Mary would have been left in no doubt who was the favoured saint now though. She looked down upon the massive new church built in the Padre's name and a forest of construction cranes.

I returned to Santa Maria delle Grazie behind a happy-clappy group of young pilgrims that flowed down the stone staircase following a man with a beard playing a guitar. At the bottom, a flock of nuns, some in black, others in white, gathered to have their photo taken in front of a bronze statue of Padre Pio.

Santa Maria delle Grazie is austere and simple, a lot like the Padre himself, some would say. But when it was opened in 1959 he wasn't impressed. The story goes he exclaimed, 'What have you made? A matchbox?' He already knew that a large building would be needed to hold the multitudes of the 'faithful that would answer his call'.

The entrance to the church was a small arched door to the side of the original chapel. A scrum of people were waiting in line in the oppressive heat, fanning themselves with pages of scriptures. The chapel used to house Padre Pio's tomb but that was in the process of being moved to the new church. The faithful came now to see *la cella*, the bare room where the Padre had spent most of his adult life.

When I finally entered the chapel I was handed a form by a young friar wearing the same brown robes Padre Pio wore. I asked what it was for and he said I was to write down my intentions. I told him I planned to have a quick look at the room Padre Pio had lived and died in and then make my way around to the new church, which from all accounts was a much more impressive building.

The young friar patiently explained that an intention was a prayer for someone. Every night at 8.30 he and the other Frati Cappuccini gathered at the tomb of Padre Pio and recited the rosary for the people that day's pilgrims had asked to be remembered. I scribbled down Sally's name, and Daisy for my unborn daughter (it was the only name that had received any sort of support in Positano). I handed it to the young friar and rejoined the queue shuffling towards Padre Pio's cell.

Ten minutes later I was in a tiny bare room looking at a bed, a basin and a bedside table. Beside the bed the slippers worn by Padre Pio to the last hour of his death were placed on a stand.

Padre Pio's other personal belongings were displayed in a glass cabinet in the middle of the room. There was a pair of fingerless gloves, some white socks with bloodstains on them, a piece of bandage that had been used on his chest wound, a casket containing blood clots from the stigmata, books on spiritual subjects and the handkerchief with which Padre Pio blessed the pilgrims from his window. There was also a can of fly spray he'd used. I imagine the company that made it have borrowed his endorsement for their ads – 'As used by Padre Pio!'

The room was guarded by another young friar in brown robes and after only a minute or two he told me to move along. I followed the other pilgrims down a bare corridor that deposited us, blinking from the bright sun, in the vast concrete square in front of the brand spanking new Chiesa di San Pio, the church of Saint Pio.

The new church was designed by world-famous architect Renzo Piano. Born in Genoa, Piano designed the Pompidou Centre in Paris and the international airport in Osaka, and he designed the masterplan for the reconstruction of Berlin's Potsdamer Platz. He won the Pritzker Architecture Prize, the world's most prestigious architecture award, in 1998.

Renzo Piano is best known in Australia for building Aurora Place, an award-winning office tower and residential block on Macquarie Street in Sydney. The curved and twisted shape of the east façade was designed to correspond spatially with the Opera House and to represent the marine environment of the harbour. If you look at it from the Botanical Gardens, it achieves that aim admirably.

I'm afraid the same can't be said of the Church of Saint Pio. It looks like a dissected insect, pinned down on a huge expanse of white, glaring concrete. That vast square is filled with bits and pieces, including a rack of bells, some concrete doves that looked more like seagulls, and a fountain that makes the Princess Diana memorial fountain in London look stylish and functional. The result is an eclectic pastiche of ideas rather than a satisfying whole.

It wasn't any more edifying closer up. The sandstone arches looked like the knobbly legs of a praying mantis and stained-glass biblical scenes were done in the fashion of an advertising storyboard that was knocked up using marker pens a few minutes before the client arrived.

It struck me as the kind of building a televangelist in the deep south of America would build. That feeling was only confirmed when a young girl in jeans and a T-shirt handed me a brochure for *Tele Radio Padre Pio*, a subscription service broadcasting the teachings of the Padre.

I didn't catch the Muson River train back to my hotel. I wandered back through the souvenir stalls instead. The enterprising stallholders had managed to rework the normal tourist tat so that somehow everything was connected to Padre Pio. There were Padre Pio fridge magnets and teaspoons, of course. But there were more innovative re-imaginings too. My favourite was a little plastic camera on which you watched a slideshow of the life and times of the Padre through the viewfinder. You clicked the shutter button to cycle through pictures that included the Padre blessing children through to gruesome close-ups of his stigmata wounds. It was the first thing I bought.

There were also Padre Pio statues of all shapes and sizes. Most were sensibly small enough for a pilgrim to put in their hand luggage. But there were also life-size statues close to six feet tall going for €2500 apiece. They were too big to display inside the tiny shops, and instead gathered outside in packs, arms outstretched like a gaggle of eager politicians fighting to kiss a single baby.

It wasn't all Padre Pio snowdomes and holy salad bowls. There were also more serious shops that sold liturgical goods and scholarly books about the Padre. I bought a few for my library. Two bore self-explanatory titles – *Padre Pio: The Early Years* and *Padre Pio: The Great Sufferer*. Then there was *Have a Good Day*, a handy pocket-sized book that had a thought from Padre Pio for every day of the year. For my birthday the Padre admitted that he couldn't 'tolerate criticism and speaking ill of our neighbour'. Sally's birthday message was that 'the battlefield between God and Satan is the human soul'.

My most cherished purchase was a book called *The Devil in the Life of Padre Pio*. I'd misread the title as *The Devil in Padre Pio* and expected it to be an affectionate tale of the pranks the Padre used to pull on novitiate monks – short-sheeting the beds in their cells, putting farting powder in their soup, that sort of thing. It was only €5 so I purchased it immediately.

The Devil in the Life of Padre Pio turned out to be a theological treatise on the existence of the devil. In it Padre Pio attempted to counter the secularised mentality that has relegated Satan to a figure of mythology or folklore.

I was startled to learn that from the age of five the Padre was assailed by 'diabolical apparitions' that were 'extremely obscene, inhumane and, above all, bestial'. Mostly, they took the form of young nude women dancing lasciviously. I immediately felt a connection with the Padre. During my teens I'd been assailed by those apparitions as well. At the time I'd put it down to sexual frustration. I can't tell you how relieved I was to discover it was all the work of the devil.

With my respects paid to the good Padre, I decided to spend the rest of the afternoon riding through the wild hills of the Gargano promontory. I headed for Monte Sant'Angelo, an ancient hilltop town perched 800 metres above the Gulf of Manfredonia.

In the fifth century the archangel Michael is supposed to have made four separate appearances in Monte Sant'Angelo. It quickly became the premier pilgrimage site in the world. It was the San Giovanni Rotondo of its day and the Santuario di San Michele Arcangelo, the church built on the spot where the archangel Michael was seen, was the equivalent of Renzo Piano's monstrous Chiesa di San Pio.

In 999 AD the Holy Roman Emperor Otto III called by to pray that the world didn't end in the year 1000. When prophecies of doom and destruction went the way of our very own millennium bug, the reputation of the place was enhanced even more.

When I rode into the town that afternoon, it was comatose. The cobbled streets were empty and the pizzerias closed. There were a few souvenir stalls, but they sold the same Padre Pio tat that was on offer back in San Giovanni Rotondo.

I parked Marcello in the courtyard in front of the Santuario di San Michele Arcangelo. In San Giovanni Rotondo he would have been clamped and towed. Here no one bothered to stop me. I entered the church and clambered down an impressive stone staircase to a chapel set in a grotto deep underground without seeing another soul.

I was pleased to see that the chapel in the grotto was more old-school and the influence of Renzo Piano's dead hand was nowhere to be seen. No one gave out brochures to Tele Radio Archangel Michael. There was a simple altar and a panel of icons.

And it was silent. It felt infinitely more holy than either of the churches dedicated to Padre Pio in San Giovanni Rotondo.

I took the long way back to San Giovanni Rotondo, riding around the back of Monte Sant'Angelo and through a jumble of buildings on top of a ridge that looked directly over the sea. I stopped at a pretty viewpoint and watched the sun set beyond the horizon. It was the closest I'd felt to God all day.

That night I was too tired to eat out so I popped next door to McDonald's. I'd hoped that the Happy Meals came with a Padre Pio toy but they didn't. The pilgrim children had to make do with a more secular Mattel Hot Wheels car if they were a boy or a My Scene doll for the girls. I returned to the hotel feeling a little guilty about squandering an opportunity to eat another wonderful meal. Sometimes, even in Italy, a Big Mac can really hit the spot. I returned to the hotel and found a couple shagging in the lift.

OK, they weren't really shagging. But the woman had her left leg hitched up on the handrail and the man's hand had disappeared from view. What was worse was that I knew they hadn't entered the hotel as a couple.

Let me explain. When I left the hotel to get my Big Mac I had heard unholy laughter coming from the hotel bar. Being a curious chap I poked my head around the door to see what was going on. An attractive French woman was sitting at the bar drinking with an Italian man who told her he was from Milan. They had just shared a joke and he reached across to brush the hair from her face. He let his hand linger a little on her cheek and she blushed, giggling like a schoolgirl. She excused herself and went to the bathroom.

The Italian man watched her leave. When she was out of sight, he nudged the barman and leered that he reckoned he was in there, or Italian words to that effect.

It was nothing you wouldn't see in a hotel bar any night of the week in any country in the world. But I was shocked. The guy was trying to pull while he was on a pilgrimage to a saint who'd spent his entire life fighting this kind of behaviour. In Palermo, Sergio had told me that Italians make quite a big show of being religious but then instantly forget about it. Not that the French woman was blameless either. She was on a pilgrimage too.

Now the Italian guy was performing a tonsillectomy on the French woman with his tongue in the lift taking me to my room, under the watchful eye of a portrait of the Padre himself. I wondered if they were losing the brownie points they'd got from doing the pilgrimage in the first place. I'd seen the guy at the museum at Padre Pio's old cell. He'd looked at the slippers like they were holy relics. He'd thrust a €50 note into the donation box next to the exit, pausing to give a prayer of thanks before he left. Now he was virtually shagging a woman he'd only just met in the lift next to me.

I was tempted to tap the couple on the shoulder and alert them to the work of moral theologian Father Antonio Rungia, who hailed from south of Naples. He had authored a useful pamphlet entitled 'A User's Guide to Chastity' in which he proposed a version of the Australian skin-cancer campaign 'Slip, Slop, Slap' to prevent teenagers succumbing to the temptations of the flesh. These two weren't teenagers obviously, but they were succumbing. Badly.

Father Rungia proposed that where Australians slip on a shirt to cover themselves against the harmful rays of the sun, teenage girls should slip on clothing that revealed nothing to roving eyes. Instead of slopping on sunscreen he wanted those having impure thoughts to slop themselves with ice-cold water. If that didn't work, he advised young people not to slap on a hat, but rather to slap themselves instead.

Father Rungia also warned against 'gatherings that encouraged sexual advances'. I wouldn't have thought a pilgrimage to Padre Pio's home town was such a place but it obviously was. And he suggested being wary of friends with questionable morals, 'especially in summer'. The signs were all there and the alarm bells were ringing, baby.

I held my tongue. 'To lack charity is like sinning against nature' had been the Padre's message for that very day.

I decided that the couple probably thought that the Padre was blessing them for their devout pilgrimage. The Italian guy had a large, hooked nose so he possibly even regarded it as some kind of miracle.

I checked out the next morning. As I left I bought my last Padre Pio souvenir from a vending machine on the wall in the corridor outside my room. It was a tiny figurine of the man himself, maybe 4 centimetres tall. It cost €2 and came in a small box with the letter P on the front. The P was in a shield like the S of Superman, as if the Padre was a superhero himself.

I was tempted to leave it outside the room where the shagging pilgrims had spent the night. I imagined them freaking out when they opened the door and saw that Padre Pio had been watching them.

Instead I made my way down to Marcello in the car park, opened his glove box and tossed the Padre in with the litre of oil, spark plugs and a dozen or so other saints.

Note: Shortly after I visited San Giovanni Rotondo, the Catholic Enquiry Office (CEO) in London declared Saint Pio the patron saint of stress relief and the January blues. A spokeswoman for the CEO said that the decision was based on their belief that Padre Pio's famous spiritual advice, 'Pray, Hope and Don't Worry!' would help drive out despair from the minds of people.

CHAPTER EIGHTEEN

ROME

PATRON SAINT: FEDERICO FELLINI

In Italy you don't pay a set amount for using a toll road. The cost is calculated according to the number of kilometres you drive along it. You take a ticket dispensed by a machine at the barrier you pass through when you enter the autostrada. And then you hand it to an attendant at the barrier at the exit you leave the autostrada from. The fee is then calculated.

It's a simple, fair and efficient system. You pay for what you use rather than subsidise other drivers making much longer journeys. It only becomes complicated when you foolishly put the ticket in your top pocket on the outskirts of Foggia and lose it somewhere along the route to Benevento.

I only realised that I had lost the ticket when I reached up to get it as I exited the autostrada just north of Benevento. I didn't have time to construct a suitable excuse in Italian. Luckily the old guy manning the booth spoke passable English. I explained that I had put the ticket in my pocket and that somewhere along the autostrada it had blown out. I expected him to roll his eyes and treat me like a moron but, surprisingly, he was very understanding.

'A Vespa like this is *molto velocemente* (very fast),' he said. Then he suggested that next time I put the ticket in the glove box instead.

That still left the issue of a missing ticket to deal with though. The booth attendant said that if it was up to him he would simply let me pass. But Austostrade per l'Italia, the company responsible for over 2850 kilometres of toll roads in the country, had just installed CCTV cameras to record every transaction. If he waved me through they'd simply compute the most kilometres I could have travelled on that stretch of the autostrada and dock it from his pay.

Losing your autostrada ticket automatically incurs a €60 fine. As a foreigner I should have been made to pay it on the spot. The old guy gave me a stub giving me seven days to pay instead and suggested I visited the head office of Austostrade per l'Italia in Rome.

'They have the power to cancel your fine,' he said. 'They will only charge you the fee.'

The offices of Austostrade per l'Italia were in the southern suburbs of Rome, just off Via Tuscolana, the main road that I would be following into the heart of the Eternal City. It was also just around the corner from Cinecittà, the famous Italian film studio where Marcello Mastroianni did most of his best work, including *La Dolce Vita*.

I parked my Marcello outside the iconic front gates and took a photo. The studios were designed by the great Italian architect Gino Peressutti and are regarded as one of the best examples of modernist architecture in Europe. They were opened by Benito Mussolini in 1937 and the art deco-style lettering used to display the word 'Cinecittà' above the gate reflects the mood of the time. Marcello looked right at home.

Cinecittà Studios has a long and illustrious history. Over 3000 films have been made there, 83 of which have received Academy Award nominations. Of those, 48 have won Oscars. It is where Charlton Heston won a chariot race, Peter Ustinov fiddled while Rome burned, and Richard Burton played Antony to Liz Taylor's Cleopatra. Their tempestuous real-life relationship started here too.

In the 1950s it became known as Hollywood on the Tiber. It was where all the blockbusters of the day were made. *Roman Holiday*, *Ben Hur*, *Cleopatra*, and later the Pink Panther movies and Sergio Leone's spaghetti westerns were all shot here. Fellini shot all his films at Cinecittà. The studios themselves were a character in his 1987 pseudo-autobiographical film *Intervista*. He once famously said that 'every journey starts and ends at the studios of Cinecittà – it's my ideal world, the cosmic space before the Big Bang'.

Today Cinecittà Studios is the largest film and television production facility in continental Europe. It stills holds an allure for the biggest names in the industry. Martin Scorsese filmed

The Gangs of New York there in 2002. He said he found 'the sense of the place and the history and the spirit of it inspiring and humbling'. Terry Gilliam called Cinecittà the 'seductress of the great, famous and mad'. I've got to say, that morning, in front of the famous gates, I could feel a little of that magic too.

That magic must have rubbed off on me because when I visited the offices of Autostrade per l'Italia shortly afterwards, the little matter of my lost ticket was resolved within moments. The young girl on the counter pulled up a map of the Italian autostrade system on her computer, got me to point out where I had entered the motorway and where I had got off, clicked a button on the screen that said *calcolare* and told me that I owed Autostrade per l'Italia the grand sum of €3.30.

Soon I was riding past the ruins of the vast complex built by Emperor Domitian in Palatine, heading straight for the Colosseum along a road lined with ancient trees. I was back in the Rome I knew. Sally and I had spent a long weekend here at the end of my first Vespa trip around Italy.

I stayed in the same hotel we'd stayed in that weekend. It was a quaint, modest establishment on the block behind the main train station, Stazione Termini. I got a quiet room out the back. The shuttered windows opened onto an internal courtyard where washing lines criss-crossed all the way up the building, filtering out the bright afternoon sun.

There is nothing more exciting or invigorating in life than riding a Vespa through the streets of Rome. A quick scooter through Naples comes close. The vicarious thrill of knowing that your life could be over any second gives it an added charge. But Rome has the scenery. Given a choice of riding around the roundabout outside the Centrale station in Naples or the Colosseum in Rome, the Colosseum wins every time.

On my first visit to Rome on Sophia I devised a 'route' that I particularly liked. It took me past the Vittorio Emanuele II

Monument (the one that looks like a giant wedding cake), up the Via dei Fori Imperiali beside the ancient Roman Forum, before executing a slingshot manoeuvre around the Colosseum and doing it all over again. Thousands of years of history and cobblestoned vibration therapy all bundled up into a few two-stroke-powered minutes.

That route was even more exhilarating on Marcello. With a twist of the throttle I could weave dramatically through the traffic and lean into the roundabout around the Wedding Cake for added velocity. Marcello seemed to enjoy it too, letting out a throaty roar. The guys dressed up as Roman centurions looked up as I passed them and gave Marcello an approving nod.

I parked Marcello in front of the Colosseum and asked a passing tourist to take a photo of me sitting on my Vespa there. It was close to the spot where the photographer Slim Aarons took a photo of Louis Armstrong sitting on a Vespa in 1949. Satchmo was playing his trumpet, of course. Aarons remembers him sitting on the steps inside the Colosseum writing a song and then playing it as he sat on the Vespa. The photographer never said whether it was the ancient building or the sexy new Vespa that inspired the tune. I'd like to think it was the Vespa.

My favourite time to ride in Rome is early evening. The edge has been taken off the heat of the day, but it is still warm. And as you pass the trees among the ruins the cicadas are so loud that you even hear them over the sound of a two-stroke engine.

It is also when the people of Rome come out to enjoy their city. That night as I buzzed around Piazza della Repubblica I came upon a large group of Latin American houseworkers gathering outside the Basilica di Santa Maria degli Angeli. They sat along the fence, talking, laughing, gossiping, embracing and drinking Heineken out of long-necked bottles. The manager of my hotel told me later they gathered there every Thursday night.

The workers brought their children with them too. They ran among the boom boxes playing salsa tunes, hollering and waving at Marcello when I rode past.

I finished the evening in Rome at the Trevi Fountain. Sally loved the movie *Three Coins in the Fountain* and had wanted to see the famous fountain that featured in it. The movie's tag was 'You've never lived until you've loved in Rome!' and it followed the trials and tribulations of three American girls who threw coins into the fountain and made a wish that they would meet the man of their dreams.

The tradition is that if you throw a coin into the fountain, over your shoulder and facing away, you'll return to Rome. Toss a second coin and you'll fall in love with an Italian. A third will ensure that you marry them.

When I visited the fountain with Sally she wouldn't let me watch how many coins she threw in. Nor would she tell me what she wished for. Two years later we were married and having a baby so I'll let you draw your own conclusions.

The seventeenth-century fountain is also the setting for one of the most famous scenes in cinema history, in *La Dolce Vita*, when Anita Ekberg jumps in and starts frolicking in the water. The sight of the voluptuous Swede prompted Marcello Mastroianni's character to proclaim: 'You are the first woman on the first day of creation. You are mother, sister, lover, friend, angel, devil, earth, home!'

A few months before my visit, a forty-year-old woman from Milan known only as 'Roberta' had performed an X-rated re-enactment of the scene by skinny-dipping in the fountain. The temperature was unusually high and she wanted to cool down. Police led her away to rapturous applause from hundreds of onlookers, most of them toting camcorders and mobile phones. The police charged her with indecent exposure. She said, 'The water belongs to everyone and it was hot. What is wrong with taking a dip?' Shaky footage from a tourist's camcorder led the news bulletins on Italian television that night.

That night there wasn't a woman from Milan called Roberta in the fountain, just an old woman fetching coins out with a stick. Thankfully, she was fully dressed. I texted Sally to tell her I was back at the fountain. She texted back that our baby had been kicking like a kangaroo and not to throw any more coins in.

The next day I visited the Bocca del Verità, the Mouth of Truth, a man-like face carved from pavonazzetto marble, placed against a wall in the portico of the church of Santa Maria in Cosmedin, just down the hill from the Colosseum. The sculpture is of a pagan god and is thought to be part of an ancient Roman fountain, or perhaps a manhole cover. It was moved to the church in the seventeenth century.

Since medieval times the sculpture has garnered fame as a lie detector. Legend has it that if you tell a lie with your hand in the mouth of the sculpture (a convenient hand-sized slot, by the way), it will be bitten off.

Gregory Peck and Audrey Hepburn famously visit the Mouth of Truth in *Roman Holiday*. The scene is a pivotal one in the movie. Neither Hepburn's nor Peck's character has been truthful with the other. She hasn't told him she's a princess. He hasn't told her he's a journalist.

In the movie Gregory Peck challenges Audrey Hepburn to place her hand inside the mouth. She does it reluctantly, but with no ill effects. When Gregory Peck does the same he yells and pulls his arm out to reveal his hand is missing. Audrey Hepburn shrieks in horror. He's hidden his hand up his sleeve, and ends the practical joke by popping his hand out into a handshake position and saying 'Hello!' Cue much relieved laughter all around.

Apparently the scene was a real practical joke pulled by Gregory Peck on Audrey Hepburn while the cameras were rolling. Her shrieks were real. The director William Wyler liked it so much he incorporated the scene into the finished film.

I parked Marcello on the footpath outside and joined the long queue to have my truthfulness tested. When I reached the sculpture I got the Japanese tourist in front of me to take a photo of me with my hand in the mouth, and another immediately after showing my fingers intact – to verify my standing as a true and honest man.

With that done I visited an internet café in Museo del Corso to email the photos to Sally. The café closed at 7 p.m. It was 6 p.m. when I entered. I paid for an hour and made my way to the terminal suggested by the manager. At 6.15 the same guy came over and told me to get off the computer. He was closing. I pointed to the sign behind the counter saying the café closed at 7 and he shrugged his shoulders.

'I have to close the connection and set the alarm,' he said. I told him that in any other country that would be done after they closed. He looked at me as if I was mad.

'Then I'd have to stay after 7,' he said incredulously. I wanted to tell him to change the sign to say that the café closed at 6.15, but I knew I'd be wasting my breath.

One of the few emails I'd been able to check was from Gianluca Grande from the Vespa Club Roma. He had emailed me for the first time a few months before, after reading *Vroom with a View*. He told me that if I was ever in Rome again I should contact him. I was in Rome again. I'd contacted him. And the next morning I was meeting him for coffee. I *was* starting to make a habit of emailing Vespa Club presidents.

We arranged to meet in a café down near the Pantheon. He'd be the one riding a black Vespa PX with a sticker of a yellow bull on the side. He'd got the sticker in Spain on the way to the Euro Vespa rally held in Lisbon. It helped distinguish his battered black Vespa from the thousands of others buzzing around Rome.

Gianluca was a muscly young guy in his twenties with a friendly smile. We had coffee and pastries and he asked me about my adventures so far. I told him that Marcello hadn't missed a beat. He said he wasn't surprised.

'The Rally is a strong Vespa,' he said. 'I would buy one if I could afford it.'

At 10 a.m., Gianluca announced that he had to go. He said he would have liked to have shown me around Rome but at 1 p.m. he was heading off with a buddy from the Vespa club to a night rally in Pisa.

'It is the only rally in Italy held in the dark,' he said with excitement. The route sounded amazing too – a long, circuitous loop through the high, rugged mountains of the Alta Versilia.

My mind started ticking over. I'd been planning to leave Rome and start heading north the next day. My intention was to follow the coast, just like Gianluca and his friend planned to, but maybe break the journey at Grosseto. What if I went to the rally instead?

The more I thought about it, the more it made sense. The night rally started and finished in the fields around the San Piero a Grado church. The church was in Marina di Pisa, a mere 15 kilometres from Livorno where I planned to finish my grand adventure anyway. And a crazy, no-holds-barred night-time ride through some of the wildest mountains in Italy would certainly bring the old, less responsible era of my life to an end. It would mean giving Grosseto a miss but I could live with that. I'd only wanted to see a quirky, allegorical statue of Leopoldo II protecting Mother Maremma by crushing the serpent of malaria anyway.

The rally, on the other hand, sounded amazing. I asked Gianluca if I could tag along and he said 'Sure!'

I rushed back to my hotel at the back of the train station and quickly packed my bags.

CHAPTER NINETEEN

PISA

PATRON SAINT: BOBBY SOLO

The second annual Tappa Notturna (Night Rally) organised by the Vespa Club of Pisa started at 7 p.m. Gianluca turned up at my hotel in Rome at 1 p.m. We had six hours to travel 375 kilometres. When I texted Sally to tell her what I was doing she said I was mad. I felt incredibly excited.

I followed Gianluca through the back streets of Rome. We were heading for a petrol station on the northern outskirts of the city to meet Pieter, the treasurer of the Vespa Club Roma and our companion for the trip. We took a short cut around the back of Saint Peter's where Gianluca insisted we stop momentarily so he could take a photo of me and Marcello with the Swiss Guards. It amused him that the orange in their gaudy tunics matched Marcello perfectly.

By 1.30 we had reached the petrol station. Pieter was already waiting for us and had passed the time attaching plastic windmills to the rack on the front of his blue PX125. The plan was that they would spin as he rode along, giving his Vespa a jaunty, festive spirit. Pieter looked like Roberto Benigni and it struck me that attaching children's toys to the front of a Vespa is something he'd do too.

We took the autostrada north towards Civitavecchia to make up time. We tore along it as a triangle of Vespas with Gianluca at its apex. The afternoon sun glinted off the sea and the windmills whirred furiously on Pieter's Vespa. Pieter and Gianluca took turns in front, leaning forward over their bikes for extra speed when it was their turn to lead. I felt like a teenager again, a member of a reckless gang. This was exactly the sort of thing Renato Tassinari had in mind when he organised the mass gathering of 'Vespisti' at the Milan Fair back in 1949.

At Civitavecchia the autostrada ended and we rode along a narrower state highway that hugged a coastline dotted with massive seaside camping grounds. The high-speed riding along the autostrada had worked something loose in Marcello's speedometer, causing it to make an unholy whirring noise. The needle that indicated the speed started flicking back and forth too. I signalled to Gianluca that I needed to stop. We pulled over and he asked me what was wrong. I told him that my speedometer had been possessed by the devil.

'I need a young priest and an old priest!' I joked.

Gianluca didn't get that I was alluding to the movie *The Exorcist*. That could well have been because I was really alluding to another allusion in *Austin Powers* when Dr Evil's rotating chair takes on a life of its own. Gianluca ratted around in his toolbox for a spanner instead and disconnected Marcello's speedo cable at the wheel, taping it up with black electrical tape and onto the front shock so it didn't get damaged.

We passed through Grosseto just after 3.30 p.m. and stopped for petrol 28 kilometres later at Gavorrano. After we had filled our Vespas with petrol and added the appropriate amount of oil, I wheeled Marcello across the forecourt and parked him next to a pack of dirty black Harleys. They were parked in the

shade of the awning and I wanted to leave Marcello to enjoy the cool of the shade too while I paid for the petrol. Gianluca looked horrified.

'They are the Liars from Rome,' he hissed. 'They are the worst of the Italian bikers.'

On cue the bikers rolled out of the restaurant in dirty leather vests and put on helmets similar to the Hun helmets German soldiers wore in the First World War. The biker parked nearest Marcello, a large chap with crumbs in his beard from a motor services snack, looked Marcello up and down and then, after ascertaining that he belonged to me, held me in a long, steady stare. I thought he was going to push Marcello over with his boot. Instead he said, '*Bella moto*,' and kick-started his Harley. Like his namesake Marcello Mastroianni, my Marcello had a *machismo* appreciated by all Italian men.

Inside there was a queue of half a dozen people paying for petrol. Pieter pointed at a fat bloke wearing black jeans, a black T-shirt and a very bad wig.

'I can't believe it,' he said excitedly. 'It's Bobby Solo!'

Bobby Solo was an Italian teen singing sensation from the sixties in the mould of Cliff Richard. His song 'Una Lacrima Sul Viso' (One Tear on the Face) sold 6 million copies and is still guaranteed to get the oldies swaying on the dance floor at weddings. He starred in a movie of the same name and his career was revived in 1978 when a disco version of 'Una Lacrima Sul Viso' was released. It knocked the band Cugini di Campagna off the charts.

I had taken an interest in Cugini di Campagna on my last trip through Italy. Their name translates as 'Our Cousins from the Country', which amused me immensely, as did their ability to sing in very high voices. They were an Italian version of the Bee Gees. What appealed to me most, however, was that Italians use the phrase *cugini di campagna* to describe people who are a little slower and dimmer than the rest. An abbreviation of the term, *cugi*, is shorthand for anything that is tacky or in bad taste, like the word 'dag' in Australia.

I asked Gianluca if he thought Bobby Solo knew the guys from Cugini di Campagna and he said yes.

'I think they are his friends,' he said, impressed that I knew of the band.

Gianluca said that Bobby Solo was considered the Italian Elvis. Like his inspiration, Bobby had put on the pounds. Bizarrely, he also wore make-up. It was thick foundation like the 'pancake' make-up people wear on TV to stop their faces from shining. I mentioned this to Pieter and he said enigmatically that Bobby wasn't as young as he used to be.

Bobby Solo had married an American woman and made most of his money these days playing to Italians in America. He noticed Gianluca in the line and asked him if he worked out. When Gianluca said he did, Bobby Solo asked him for a detailed description of his workout routine.

Gianluca and Pieter asked Bobby Solo for his autograph. As he signed a serviette each for them – it was the only paper close to hand – I asked him about the guys from Cugini di Campagna. His face darkened.

'I have not spoken to them for a while,' he muttered. It was a topic he wasn't keen to discuss further.

With our tanks filled and an encounter with a sixties Italian pop sensation successfully completed, we buzzed north, passing Follonica, San Vincenzo and Cecina in quick succession. Soon we were closing in fast on the outskirts of Livorno. This was my hood now, and after we passed through the tunnel that cut through Montenero I manoeuvred to the front of Gianluca and Pieter and showed them the way to Marina di Pisa.

Marina di Pisa held a very special place in my affections. In the fields around San Piero a Grado, the very fields in fact from which the night rally would commence, I had attended my very first pine nut festival. Indeed, the Sagra del Pinolo of Marina di Pisa is still the only pine nut festival I have attended. Anywhere in the world.

I went with Marco and Filippo. We arrived pretty much as I was now, on the backs of Vespas and Lambrettas like a cool beatnik group in *The Many Loves of Dobie Gillis*. A band played. Children danced. Pine nuts were served with spaghetti, added to a noxious-tasting drink, and used to fire the barques that grilled chunks of steak.

It was at the Sagra del Pinolo that Marco and Filippo had alerted me to Mary, Mother of God's fading powers and put me on to the fresher Padre Pio.

I'd also learned that in Livorno the voluptuous curved cowls at the back of Vespas are called '*puppa*', slang for breasts. It was, by any estimation, a night of instruction about the way things worked in Italy.

Most of the other riders had arrived for the rally already and were parked in front of the San Piero a Grado church. It is one of the oldest churches in Italy, built on the spot where Saint Peter landed after coming from Antioch in

44 AD. Coincidentally a new bell for the church was being inaugurated on the same day, so the Vespa riders sat on their scooters and listened to the speeches given by local dignitaries. When the mayor rang the bell for the first time they all beeped their horns. It sounded like a bunch of ducks quacking. It was one of the funniest things I've ever seen or heard.

I made my way with Gianluca to the registration desk. Registration for the rally had closed a week before but Gianluca seemed confident I would still be able to sign up. If not, I could always just follow the other riders in an 'unofficial' capacity.

This being Italy, the organisers had expected people not to bother registering in advance and I was able to register with a minimum of fuss. The registrar asked which club I belonged to and Gianluca quickly chipped in that I was with the Vespa Club Roma. He handed me a club T-shirt he had hidden behind his back and told me to put it on.

'Tonight you ride with us,' he said. I was touched.

As a registered rider on the second annual Pisa Night Rally I was given a special pack that included an official cloth badge and vouchers for a photo taken at the starting ramp, a snack at a *panini* shop halfway through the ride and a meal at the awards ceremony in a chalet on top of Monte Pisanino at Gorfigliano. I also received a numbered orange safety vest. I was number 131. Most of the vests were small and tight-fitting but because I had registered at the last moment I got one of the bigger ones with shoulders so wide it looked like something Joan Collins might have worn in *Dynasty*. It was the exact same shade of orange as Marcello so I at least looked coordinated.

I spotted Marco and Filippo's friend Roccia wandering through the crowd so I went and said hello. Roccia runs an English clothing shop in Pisa called Made in England that sells shirts made by Lonsdale and Ben Sherman. He's also a bigwig in the Pisa Scooter club, the club that organised the rally. I'd met him and his girlfriend, Rossana, at the pine nut festival and he greeted me like an old friend.

'I'm settling down too,' he said when I told him I was about to become a father. 'Rossana and I got married last year at the Elba Rally!'

Marco had told me about the wedding. They'd roasted a pig on the beach and after they had eaten it they stuck the head over the headlight of Roccia's Vespa. When he turned the headlight on it shone through the eye sockets.

It all got a bit Lord of the Flies after that. A huge fire was lit. A vast amount of wine was consumed. Then wedding guests took turns riding the Pig Vespa up and down the beach. One of them crashed into a log washed up onto the darkest part of the beach and the Vespa – and the pig's head – was left lying there until dawn.

I still had my bag strapped to the rear luggage rack of Marcello so I asked Roccia if there was anywhere I could keep it while I did the rally. From all accounts the route he and his club mates had chosen was pretty demanding. I didn't want to worry about the bag with all my worldly possessions in it falling off somewhere high in the mountains. He introduced me to a guy with a campervan who took my bag and gave me a spare key so I could get it out of his mobile home whenever I wanted. I thanked him and told him that he was very kind.

'You are a friend of Roccia's,' he said.

The first annual Pisa Night Rally had put the Pisa Scooter Club on the very top of the Italian Vespa scootering calendar. It had been a simple affair, a straightforward ride up to Abetone, a ski town high in the mountains above Lucca, and back again. But no one had thought of riding at night before, under a full moon, and a legend was born.

This ride was an altogether more audacious affair. We would be riding through the Alta Versilia, the mountainous region that rose steeply from the coast. The route wound through treacherous mountain passes, some of which weren't even on a map. And the forecast was for thunderstorms.

The rally was attended by Vespa clubs from all over Italy. Their Vespas proudly wore sashes bearing the club name across the front like beauty queens.

Right on 7 p.m. the call went out that the rally was about to start. I joined the scrum of Vespas jostling at the back of the church, and waited for my turn to ride up onto the starting stand and have my complimentary photo taken. I was then ushered out onto the road in front of the church and waited with the 130-odd other Vespa riders for the signal to begin.

A guy on a yellow Rally 180 rode to the front of the jostling Vespas, held up a portable horn and blew it. Then he rode out onto the road and accelerated away.

'Follow that guy,' yelled Gianluca as he buzzed past me. The second annual Pisa Night Rally had begun.

There's nothing quite like the sensation of finding yourself in the middle of a swarm of Vespas. A hive mentality takes over and, without thinking, you are ducking and weaving and tearing along at a speed you'd normally consider reckless. It's one of life's great sort-of-natural highs and I heartily recommend it. Even if it means knocking a couple of years off your life expectancy from breathing in way too many blue two-stroke fumes.

Marshals employed by the Pisa Vespa Club stood along the way in yellow reflective vests, motioning the scooters onto the proper route. Gianluca was weaving among the bikes, steering with one hand and taking photos on his mobile phone with the other. He was taking the photos for the Roma Vespa Club website. The scary thing was that he wasn't the only one doing it.

Our first stop was just past Viareggio, at a pretty church surrounded by fields of sunflowers. We were here to watch the sunset, apparently, which goes to show that even the gnarliest of Vespa riders are romantics at heart. Gianluca found me and took me to meet the president of Vespa Club Italia.

'He wrote *Vespa Technica*,' he said in reverential tones.

Vespa Technica is a four-volume technical guide to every Vespa built. It is the tome enthusiasts turn to when they want to know what colour to paint their Vespa to keep it original or whether the 1964 GS special edition was really the first Vespa to feature a glove box like their mate down the pub said.

The president was a quiet and dignified man. He had owlish features and looked like someone who would write a technical manual. Thankfully he spoke English. My Italian wasn't at presidential standards. I told him I was from Australia and he was impressed. I think he thought I'd come especially for the night rally.

I told the president that I had stayed in Casa Solotti, the B&B on Mount Ortobene that he'd also stayed in. I said that Mario Zizi, the guy who ran the place, had mentioned him specifically.

'Ahh, the historian!' he said enigmatically. 'How is he?'

I told him that Mario was fine although the restoration project on his 1964 GS had ground to a halt. He was having problems getting some of the authentic parts from the list the president had sent him. It was a surreal conversation. I was standing in front of a church surrounded by fields of sunflowers in Tuscany talking about a mutual acquaintance who lived in the wild mountains of Sardinia. My new best mate from Rome was standing right next to me listening in. It struck me that I was getting quite a network of Vespa friends around Italy.

The guy on the yellow Rally 180 sounded the horn and we were on our way again. We left the coast and headed straight up into the mountains. I was glad I was on Marcello. Even after the long trip from Rome he was powering up the steep inclines with insolent ease. Sophia would have coughed and spluttered and refused to go any further with a petulant sigh. I noticed five other Rallys: three red ones, a drab green one from the 'lead years', and an orange one like mine. They appeared to be relishing the mountain roads as much as Marcello.

I rode into a tiny village in the low foothills of the mountains and noticed that my fellow scooter riders had stopped outside a small café. A man with a megaphone directed us to form a line. This was where the green voucher we'd got in our special rally packs would secure us a ham and cheese *panini* and a can of Coke. The owner had been expecting us. He'd prepared the sandwiches and was handing them out at the doorway. Each was wrapped in a serviette. The cans of Coca Cola were handed out straight from the carton.

Huge black clouds were hanging low in the mountains and shortly after we left the café the heavens opened.

I know I'm probably going to be certified for saying this but I actually enjoy riding a Vespa in the rain. There is something liberating about having rain splashing in your face at a gentle 40 kilometres per hour.

The surface became greasy so everyone slowed right down and crawled up the snaking road. Once we got higher in the mountains the road was lined by trees that formed a canopy over the tarmac. The canopy kept out the worst of the rain but new dangers emerged. The road here was covered in leaf litter whipped from the trees by the wind and the rain that did come through made them extremely slippery.

The organisers had chosen a scenic route along roads that were little used. When I looked at a map after the ride I noticed that some of them were marked by faint, broken lines. At one point we roared through a thin tunnel that appeared to have been hacked through the mountain with pickaxes. It looked like something out of *Lord of the Rings*.

Just on the other side of the tunnel half the road had washed away and a man in a vest stood with a lamp to direct us around it.

'Watch out for the puddles,' yelled Gianluca as we passed. The puddles were big enough for elephants to bathe in.

There was a meeting point just ahead so I stopped and looked for Pieter and Gianluca. I noticed for the first time that we were being tailed by two ambulances, following up the rear of the long line of motor scooters with their sirens off but their emergency lights flashing.

'They are necessary for insurance,' explained Gianluca. I was impressed by the level of planning but more than a little worried that they were regarded as a necessity.

The rally recommenced and we set off again, climbing higher and higher into the mountains. I rode around one corner and found a tree lying across the road. Just beyond that Roccia's wife, Rossana, had come off her Vespa and hurt her knee. Roccia was crouched beside her. I stopped and asked if she was hurt.

'She seems OK,' Roccia pronounced. 'We will wait here for the ambulance in case it is more serious.'

The awards ceremony and dinner was supposed to be held at 10 p.m., but at midnight we were still riding up the mountain beside the Serchio River.

At Camporgiano, the kind of tiny mountain village that closes down for the night just after sunset, the only petrol station I'd seen so far was open and serving riders on the rally. The petrol station was little more than a shed really and had a single pump. To the credit of my fellow riders, everyone queued in a most un-Italian manner – that is, calmly and orderly – and we were soon all on our way. Again the organisers had everything planned, right down to the fact that a voucher for €5 worth of petrol from this particular place was included in the €20 registration fee.

The furthest point on the rally was a chalet at Gorfigliano that sat atop Monte Pisanino at 485 metres. It was here that the awards ceremony would be held and we'd enjoy an evening meal. I finally reached the chalet with all the other riders at

1.30 a.m. According to the official schedule we should have been back in Pisa di Marina by then.

The chalet was tucked down a dirt road and looked like a hunting lodge. A guy with a megaphone directed us into a huge hall decorated with stuffed stag heads and towards long trestle tables, set up in rows, where we would be served our meals. Harried waiters darted between lines of scooter riders with steam rising off them, depositing plates of ham, pasta and bread as quickly as possible so they could get home to bed.

Logistically, we were only halfway through the ride. We still had to go all the way back to Pisa di Marina. But everyone was recounting spills and thrills and near misses with trees and cliff faces with such gusto you'd be forgiven for thinking that it was all over. Wet clothes hung over the backs of chairs to dry. It was noisy, chaotic, raucous. And the flagons of red wine plonked down along each trestle were knocked back with alarming speed. Looking out across the room felt strangely life-affirming.

After the plates were cleared, the awards ceremony was held. I'm pleased to say that the Vespa Club Roma won the cup for the most kilometres travelled to reach the rally. The organisers take the number of kilometres from the club's headquarters to the starting point of the rally and then multiply it by the number of members who had come along.

'It was your kilometres that won it for us,' grinned Pieter.

One of my favourite photos from the trip is of me holding the cup: wet, steamy and tired, and staggering under the weight of it.

At 4 a.m. the hardcore scooterists were ready to head back to Marina di Pisa. Pieter and Gianluca were too tired to continue after the long trip from Rome and had organised to take a room at the chalet.

I was running on adrenaline and wanted to continue. I hooked up with some guys from the Vespa Club in Lucca and headed off. They took a more direct route. The rain had slackened off and it was a much easier ride. I stopped for a pre-dawn photo opportunity at the Devil Bridge. An hour later I was back at Marina di Pisa. I grabbed my bag from the campervan, left the key on top of the rear right tyre as instructed, and headed for Cevoli and Filippo's villa.

I arrived at Filippo's at dawn, just as the birds started tweeting, a streak of orange behind Lari Castle. The villa was still. I knew

that I was waking them up at an ungracious hour but I was too exhausted to care. I just hoped that my gifts from a local café of donuts and espresso would lessen the blow.

I'd been on the back of a Vespa for 48 hours straight and I needed somewhere to lie down.

CHAPTER TWENTY

LIVORNO, AGAIN

PATRON SAINT: OUR MARY OF MONTENERO, AGAIN

I washed Marcello for the last time on the lawn covered in daisies outside Filippo's villa. I pulled off the luggage racks and emptied the glove box of everything, including the saints. I sponged him down with warm soapy water and noted the scars from our 2500-kilometre journey. The rear luggage rack had rubbed away the paint above the tail light. The cowls were flecked with tiny chips from stones on lonely mountain roads. And at the bottom of the speedometer, there was the scratch left by the Butcher of Naples when he fitted a new cable. I flinched involuntarily when I saw it. It looked like a scar from a knife fight deep in Marcello's past.

When I stayed with Mario Zizi in his B&B on Monte Ortobene in the wild heart of Sardinia he told me that he believed Vespas had human emotions. Over the course of my journey with Marcello I became convinced that he may well have a point. Marcello behaved exactly as you'd expect of a Vespa wearing white go-fast stripes and the colour of too much fake tan. He strutted along the beaches, tore up mountain roads with vigour, and showed off to young children and pretty girls. Men wanted to be him. Women wanted to be with him.

However, Marcello had begun to show his 'human' frailties too. He wasn't a young motor scooter anymore. He was pushing 24, which by my reckoning made him about 48 in Vespa years. (My formula for ascertaining a scooter's age in Vespa years was simple. I counted the years since the bike was manufactured and doubled it.)

Now that the journey was at an end he was beginning to let his guard down. The accelerator cable stuck occasionally. The switch that turned on the rear light when I braked had broken off. And the Rally 200 badge under the rear luggage rack was bent out of shape. When he wasn't being directly challenged by brash new Vespa GTs and LXs down by the beach, Marcello stopped putting on the macho front and accepted that maybe, just maybe, he wasn't as young as he used to be.

I was reminded of Bobby Solo and his dyed hair.

The difference with Marcello was that with a bit of elbow grease and polish I could make him look almost as good as new again.

Filippo and Valeriya had taken my early morning arrival in good spirits. The coffee and donuts had helped. We sat and ate them at a table outside. The early morning streamed through the olive trees, birds tweeted and at 8 a.m. the bells of the church in the village rang out, calling the locals to mass. It was lovely.

Filippo had called me at various points along my journey to check how I was going. He had already heard most of my stories but wanted to hear them again. He was interested to know what the Aeolian Islands were like. He wanted to take Valeriya for a holiday there. And he never tired of hearing the story about my encounter with the *carabinieri* in Sardinia, especially the bit when I asked to take their photo.

'I told you that it was the most legal Vespa in Italy!' he said with a laugh.

I dragged out my bag. I fished around looking for a copy of the photo and found the shepherd's knife I had bought Filippo in Nuoro. He spotted my copy of *La Smorfia* and asked excitedly if he could look at it.

'*La Smorfia*!' he guffawed. 'I can't believe you bought a copy of *La Smorfia*!'

Valeriya had been dreaming about her teeth falling out. Filippo looked through the book for the appropriate lotto number.

'Are your teeth falling out in the dream or have they already fallen out?' he asked.

'Falling out,' she replied. That was number 68. There'd been a number for both.

I found the ceramic Vespa Joe had given me in Caltagirone. Marco had a collection of Vespa toys and memorabilia in his workshop so I had decided I would give it to him as a token of thanks. I asked how Marco and Lucilla were and Filippo told me they had gone to Capraia, a tiny island 64 kilometres off the coast of Livorno.

'They want you to go and visit them,' he said.

I wouldn't be able to take Marcello. Private motor vehicles were banned on Capraia. Filippo said that he would take me down to the ferry and look after Marcello for me. It would be the first time Marcello and I had been apart since I bought him. He'd probably appreciate the break.

I hadn't considered visiting Capraia. To be truthful I had never even heard of it. I spent the ferry journey across reading my guidebook to learn as much as I could about the island. In the hour and a bit it took to make the crossing I discovered that Capraia had 27 kilometres of coastline, covered an area of 1930 hectares and had 8 kilometres of roads that were served by a small municipal bus that met every ferry. It was part of the

Tuscan Maritime Park and had a small winery and an anchovy factory.

Courtesy of Google I have since learned that the name Capraia comes from *capra*, which means wild goat in Latin, and that the island was a penal colony until 1986. (You can still see the prison atop the highest mountain there.) Horatio Nelson occupied the island briefly in 1796, when he was trying to get a foothold on Corsica, only 30 kilometres to the north.

Marco and Lucilla were renting a holiday apartment overlooking the marina at Porto Vecchio, the sleepy harbour that services the island. A handful of people met the passengers getting off the ferry. Lucilla was waiting for me and looked tanned and relaxed.

'The fossil is having diving lessons,' she said. 'He will be back soon.'

The fossil was Marco of course. He was forty-five years old to Lucilla's more youthful thirty-four.

The apartment was only a couple of hundred metres from the port. It was set in one of the terracotta coloured buildings nestled into the mountain that rose sharply behind the port. We reached it via an old stone staircase, past clumps of giant jojoba plants that grew wild here.

I threw my bag on my bed, a bunk that had been squeezed into the tiny entrance hall, and we returned to the harbour and a bar/*gelataria* overlooking the water.

'Marco always looks here for me first,' explained Lucilla as we ordered our ice creams. Twenty minutes later he flopped in still wearing his wetsuit and flippers.

'*Ciao!*' he said with a grin.

That night Marco cooked a simple seafood pasta which we ate at a table outside. It was quiet and peaceful and the only sounds came from the swallows darting around the cliff face and the boats clunking together in the harbour below.

After we'd finished eating Lucilla insisted I pulled out my copy of *La Smorfia*. Filippo had texted her that I had a copy and she had texted back insisting I brought it with me.

'I have been dreaming of a wild pig swimming underwater with oxygen tanks on its back,' she said with a laugh. 'Let's see what the number is for that.'

Lucilla flicked through the book quickly and deftly like she'd done it before. First she looked up wild boar, then oxygen tanks, then underwater. She found numbers for each individually but nothing for them together.

'It is too crazy even for Neapolitans,' she said with some pride.

Marco suggested that she should write to the publishers and dictated the form the letter should take.

'Dear Sirs,' he said. 'I recently purchased your book *La Smorfia* and was disappointed to find that there wasn't a number for a wild boar swimming underwater with oxygen tanks on its back. Perhaps you can correct this oversight in the next edition.'

It was a perfect evening. We drank wine, searched *La Smorfia* for the most bizarre combinations we could find, or sat listening to the faint sound of a radio playing in an apartment down the lane. The night was balmy, but cooled by a gentle breeze. And above us, a carpet of stars, shining brightly, undimmed by civilisation.

Lucilla has been holidaying on Capraia since she was seven. The locals know her. They have watched her grow up. When we hired a boat to explore the rocky coastline the next day, the old lady running the boatshed let us use the boat for free. All we had to pay for was the fuel.

We chugged around the point that protected the harbour. I was immediately struck with a sensation that I was a million miles from civilisation. Sheer volcanic cliffs rose steeply from the sea, creviced with tiny bays where we could drop anchor and swim from the side of the boat. I'd seen an ad on TV at

Filippo's villa for a new Dolce & Gabbana fragrance called Light Blue where a chiselled, tanned couple moor a boat off a dramatic rocky coast. But here, on Capraia, it was infinitely more beautiful.

It struck me that now, at the end of my journey, I had discovered the ultimate Italian seaside experience. We were alone on clear seas, a world away from beaches lined with cabins and crammed with deck-chairs, umbrellas and people. It reminded me of the old movie *Boy on a Dolphin*, in which a young Sophia Loren dived in waters like these off a boat like this, searching for an ancient statue. It was set in Greece, but there was something distinctly Italian about the way Sophia pouted petulantly in her wet peasant blouse.

The air was invigoratingly fresh out here too. When I sat on the pebbly beach at Pollara on Salina in the Aeolian Islands, I'd been overwhelmed by the smell of wet tobacco. There were hundreds of cigarette butts lodged between the pebbles. The ocean around Capraia was delightfully litter-free.

On a previous visit Marco and Lucilla had found an old Roman wreck lying in the sand. They'd told the authorities and it was declared a wreck of historical significance.

'Its location is kept a secret to guard it from looters,' said Lucilla. Sadly, neither of them could remember exactly where it was.

We returned to the harbour tired, a little sunburned, but refreshed and relaxed.

At dusk we made our way up to the old town on the hill. It felt still and ancient and sat atop a rocky cliff that dropped 466 metres to the sea below. From the viewpoint at the back of the town I spotted the Looney Tunes livery of a Moby liner heading to Sardinia. It suddenly seemed an age since I was on a similar ship, starting my last big adventure before fatherhood. I got a funny feeling in the pit of my stomach that it wasn't just the trip that was finally over, but a certain part of my life

as well. It wasn't a feeling of impending doom or dread. Just a natural mourning of something loved that was passing.

We ate that night at Bar Centrali, a rustic shack on the edge of the old town with beat-up chairs and rickety tables decorated with plastic flowers. It wasn't slick at all. In fact, it reminded me of a cantina in Mexico. But the food was cheap and good and the laidback atmosphere was totally in keeping with this wonderful island.

The three of us walked back down the hill to the harbour. The air was filled with the scent of lentisk, asphodels, rosemary and elicriso, and Lucilla pointed out a tiny yellow orchid. It was the *orchis provincialis capraria*, which is endemic to the island.

Marco and Lucilla walked arm in arm ahead of me. It made me think of Sally, and I texted her to see how she was going. She said it was cold and raining and that she wished she was back in Positano at Le Sirenuse eating linguine with artichoke hearts again.

Down at the harbour a bunch of pre-teen kids were sitting on the concrete break wall. It was quite high and required a running jump to get up onto it. Marco and I got up first time. Lucilla needed a helping hand. Lucilla noted that things hadn't changed since she'd sat here as a kid.

'I had my first kiss on this breakwater,' she said, slapping the concrete. Marco made a face of mock disapproval.

It was only early but I already felt like going to sleep. It seemed like I had spent a good deal of my time on Capraia sleeping. Lucilla said that was OK, she and Marco had spent their first few days on Capraia sleeping too.

'There is a drug in the breeze,' she explained. 'It cannot be helped.'

Lucilla added that I should get all the sleep I could. 'Soon you will not be able to sleep,' she said. 'Your *bambino* won't let you.'

I thanked Lucilla sarcastically for reminding me I was going to be a father. My days as an orange-Vespa-riding man were coming to a close.

I returned to Livorno the day before I was due to fly back to London. Filippo was waiting at the ferry dock with Marcello and my helmet so I could ride him one last time. Valeriya had followed in their car, and he asked if I wanted to have one last drink at Station Galleria, a small bar tucked away in Castiglioncello, a seaside town south of Livorno.

I'd visited Station Galleria on my first trip. It was full of elegant people drinking cocktails and I regarded it as the epitome of the cool Italia I'd envied in the old black and white movies I'd watched as a teenager. It was exactly the sort of place Marcello Mastroianni would drink in and hence the ideal place to finish this journey, to underline it three times and end it with an exclamation point.

The ride down the coast was also one of my favourite in Italy. It winds its way along a dramatic road that clings to rocky cliffs over a pounding sea. Marcello liked it too. His aches and pains, creaks and crunches were forgotten as we wound our way past the pines and the oleanders, enjoying the cool evening breeze and the sound of the waves crashing on the rocks below.

Soon I was pulling up outside Station Galleria. It was exactly as I remembered it. The flamboyant owner greeted Filippo and Valeriya like old friends and gave me a cocktail on the house for mentioning his bar favourably in *Vroom with a View*. When he found out I had just finished another Vespa adventure around Italy, he insisted I sit at the bar and tell him all about it.

My abiding memory of my first night at Station Galleria was the elegant brunette I'd spotted drinking there. She sat on a cushion up the back, drinking peach schnapps and cognac and languorously smoking a cigarette like a screen siren from the 1960s. But this night a different girl was on the cushion. She looked wrong, all fake tan and bling. I pointed her out to Filippo and asked him if he remembered the girl who had sat there on my first visit.

'Danielle,' he said with a smile. 'She's sitting at the other end of the bar.'

Danielle was sitting on a stool because she couldn't sit on the cushions anymore. She wasn't drinking peach schnapps and cognac, or smoking a cigarette, languorously or otherwise. She was pregnant. And her baby was due a week before mine.

In Italy such coincidences are regarded as a miracle of the highest order and space was made for me to sit with Danielle and her partner, Roberto. When they found out I had been riding a Vespa instead of attending to my pregnant wife, they gave me useful hints and tips about the best feeding formulas and sleep techniques. Roberto got me up to speed on the things I'd missed by not going to Lamaze classes.

'The secret is to breathe through the contractions,' he said. I nodded as if I knew what he meant.

As I talked with Daniella and her boyfriend about bottle sterilisers and sleepsuits, I realised that I was finally ready to accept fatherhood. And not just accept it, but embrace it with the same *gusto* with which Italians had embraced me and my Vespa. My trip had come to an end and so had a particular stage of my life. A new and exciting one was about to begin.

It wouldn't involve buying a Vespa on a whim and riding around Italy, but I could live with that. Well, at least until my daughter was old enough for me to buy her one too.

Have you enjoyed this book? If so, why not write a review on your favourite website?

Thanks very much for buying this Summersdale book.

www.summersdale.com